"Your book is great! I believe there are a lot of older people who would like to get into computing and are afraid to because they believe that it would be too difficult to learn. I never touched a computer until I was 60. I bought 15 books about computing which did help me get started, but your book would have been all I needed. Thanks."

—Joe Spriggs

"At 73 I thought the Internet was too much for me. But with the help of Mr. Modem's book it was a snap."

—Wally Hoffman, New Berlin, WI

"Thank you for introducing me to computers and the Internet. I am now supporting my household trading stocks on the 'Net. I am forever indebted to you."

—Susie

"I will be 69 tomorrow. They say you can't teach old dogs new tricks, but I am learning. Your book has helped me tremendously, and I am very grateful."

—Jack

"My husband was attending a conference and my plan was to sit by the pool and drink little umbrella drinks. I started reading your book and the next thing I knew, I cracked open the old laptop and was in my hotel room connecting to the Internet. Darn you, Mr. Modem!"

—Deb

Mr. Modem's Internet Guide for Seniors

Mr. Modem's™ Internet Guide for Seniors

Richard A. Sherman

SYBEX®

San Francisco • Paris • Düsseldorf • Soest • London

Associate Publisher: Amy Romanoff
Contracts and Licensing Manager: Kristine O'Callaghan
Acquisitions & Developmental Editor: Sherry Bonelli
Editor: Bronwyn Shone Erickson
Technical Editor: Rima Regas
Book Designers: Maureen Forys, Kate Kaminski
Illustrators: Michael Obrenovich, Daniel Ziegler
Electronic Publishing Specialist: Maureen Forys, Happenstance Type-O-Rama
Project Team Leader: Shannon Murphy
Proofreader: Bonnie Hart
Indexer: Ted Laux
Cover Designer: Daniel Ziegler
Cover Illustrator: Daniel Ziegler
Cover Photographer: Frank Zampino
Permissions: Kate Kitchen
Screen Captures: Beth Gorman-Hackstadt
Manuscript Formatting: Bonnie Bills

Screen reproductions produced with Collage Complete.

Collage Complete is a trademark of Inner Media Inc.

SYBEX is a registered trademark of SYBEX Inc.

Netscape Communications, the Netscape Communications logo, Netscape, and Netscape Navigator are trademarks of Netscape Communications Corporation.

Netscape Communications Corporation has not authorized, sponsored, endorsed, or approved this publication and is not responsible for its content. Netscape and the Netscape Communications Corporate Logos are trademarks and trade names of Netscape Communications Corporation. All other product names and/or logos are trademarks of their respective owners.

TRADEMARKS: SYBEX has attempted throughout this book to distinguish proprietary trademarks from descriptive terms by following the capitalization style used by the manufacturer.

The author and publisher have made their best efforts to prepare this book, and the content is based upon final release software whenever possible. Portions of the manuscript may be based upon pre-release versions supplied by software manufacturer(s). The author and the publisher make no representation or warranties of any kind with regard to the completeness or accuracy of the contents herein and accept no liability of any kind including but not limited to performance, merchantability, fitness for any particular purpose, or any losses or damages of any kind caused or alleged to be caused directly or indirectly from this book.

Photographs and illustrations used in this book have been downloaded from publicly accessible file archives and are used in this book for news reportage purposes only to demonstrate the variety of graphics resources available via electronic access. Text and images available over the Internet may be subject to copyright and other rights owned by third parties. Online availability of text and images does not imply that they may be reused without the permission of rights holders, although the Copyright Act does permit certain unauthorized reuse as fair use under 17 U.S.C. Section 107.

Mr. Modem™ and Ask Mr. Modem™ are trademarks of Get-the-Net, Inc.

Library of Congress Card Number: 99-63317
ISBN: 0-7821-2580-8

Manufactured in the United States of America

10 9 8 7 6 5 4 3 2 1

This book is dedicated to every person over 50 who harbors a curiosity about the Internet, and to every son or daughter who just hasn't had the time to show their parents how to use it.

—RAS

Acknowledgments

It all began for me early on a Saturday morning in April of 1983. Feeling uncharacteristically adventuresome due to the unstructured, unencumbered, no-obligation, no "honey-do" weekend that lay ahead of me, I wandered into an electronics store and saw It for the first time. No hard drive, just a dual 5.25-inch floppy-disk-drive Zenith computer with a nauseatingly yellow-hued monitor undoubtedly emitting more radiation than Three Mile Island on its worst day. But the symptoms were unmistakable. It was love at first byte.

It transformed my life, if not my molecular structure, and resulted in the educational, recreational, professional, and social experience of a lifetime. When I crossed the digital threshold for the first time in 1988, supported by the love of a good modem, little did I realize the profound impact electronic communication would have upon me, first on local bulletin board services, then Prodigy, CompuServe, and ultimately the Internet.

I have been truly blessed to have met tens of thousands of my senior peers online over the years, and not a day goes by when I do not think how many warm, wonderful individuals I would have never known had I not wandered into that electronics store so many years ago.

Special thanks and acknowledgments are due to many extraordinary people who have contributed to this book, whether through their moral support, spiritual encouragement, or by suggesting that I close the bag of Cheese Doodles, get off the couch and get back to work:

My parents, without whose love and guidance I would probably still be collecting string.

Emerging cybernaut Trisha and our two furry, feline cover girls, Itty and Bitty. (E-mail the girls at `itty-bitty@home.com`. They love e-mail almost as much as they love their crunchies.)

The incomparable Paul Harvey to whom I remain eternally grateful for his graciously eloquent support.

Cyber confidante Stan Demory, publicist extraordinaire Kate Kitchen, literary agent Djana Pearson Morris, and the members of Computers West computer club in Sun City West, Arizona.

The warm and wonderful professionals at Sybex who worked tirelessly to bring this project to fruition, including Amy Romanoff, Associate Publisher, Sherry Bonelli, Acquisitions and Developmental Editor, Bronwyn Shone Erickson, Editor, Shannon Murphy, Maureen Forys, Ann Telthorst, Margaret Rowlands, Amy Dhillon, Laura Arendal, and Bonnie Hart.

Richard A. Sherman, "Mr. Modem"
Phoenix, Arizona

Contents at a Glance

Table of Contents

Chapter 8   WebTV   161

Chapter 9   The Battle of the Browsers   173

Appendices

Introduction

Technology is fun! If your reaction to that statement is, "How can computers, bits, bytes, modems, and lots of other things I don't understand be fun?" then this is the book for you!

The Internet need not be a dark and foreboding place. Cozying up to the Internet and developing functional skills is actually much easier than learning how to operate many home appliances. I can surf the Internet with the best of them, but the last time I attempted using a juicer at home, I got my tie caught in it. And using the microwave oven? Forget about it. As far as I'm concerned, there are two settings: "Nuke it!" and "Off." Trust me, if you can use your microwave, you can download.

I'm very enthusiastic about the Internet. That, coupled with the fact that sooner or later we're all going to be using it anyway, led me to share what I've learned over the years to help you become comfortable with this communications marvel in the simplest, least-traumatic way possible. That's why I wrote this book.

Is This Book for You?

First, let me ask, do you consider yourself a reasonably intelligent person? If you can answer "yes" to the preceding in-depth PRC (Potential Reader Candidacy) survey, then indeed, this is the book for you.

Learning about the Internet is really simple if you're a reasonably intelligent person—if you're neither a dummy nor an idiot, neither a buffoon nor even a baboon. (Not that I've got anything against baboons, you understand. In fact, some of my best friends are…well, let's not go there.) If you're a reasonably intelligent person with a desire to learn about the Internet and other technological annoyances in an easygoing, non-intimidating, non-technical manner—and actually have fun in the process—this is *definitely* the book for you!

Why Is This Book Different?

I'm glad you asked! This book is different because I, Mr. Modem, your soon-to-be-beloved author, am different. In this book I'm not going to spend a lot of time discussing the philosophy of why things are done in a certain manner or the Zen of the Internet. It's been done countless times before, and typically greeted with the yawn heard 'round the world.

During the past several years, I have conducted hundreds of seminars throughout the country. I have also answered tens of thousands of questions, both online and through my "Ask Mr. Modem!" newspaper column. If I learned one thing, it is this: What most people want to know is what key to press to make something happen or what button to click to make something else happen. As an everyday Internet user myself, that's all I really want to know, too. I understand that you have a life beyond your computer and beyond the Internet. And enjoying that life is what's most important. Contrary to popular opinion, spending days and weeks trying to master your computer, software, or the Internet isn't a lifestyle.

I want you to have fun. I want you to enjoy the process of learning about the Internet, and most importantly, I want you to know that you have a friend at the other end of the modem. If you have a question, send me an e-mail. I want to hear from you. If you love this book, if it transforms your life, if it puts spring in your step and romance in your heart, I want to hear from you. If it gives you a headache and causes a nosebleed, please keep it to yourself. Nobody likes a whiner.

So why is this book different? Because I am not a nameless, faceless author of just another computer book. I enjoy people, so my focus is less on the technology and more on the people struggling to use it. My objective is to help people use available technology to help establish and reestablish lines of communication with friends and family near and far. And computer technology—more specifically, the Internet—is the easiest, most convenient, certainly most cost-effective way of accomplishing this objective. The Internet has the ability to bring people together, and as members of this global community, we are the ultimate beneficiaries.

Whew! Pretty profound stuff from a guy known as "Mr. Modem."

I'm not going to ask you to plow through pages of mind-numbing text—other than this introduction—in order to ferret out the information you need to put the Internet to work for you. I am, however, going to share with you lots of things I've discovered as an Internet user for many, many years, as well as share countless insights I've gleaned from others along the Information Super—well, you know. I'll explain to you what the Internet is, how it differs from the World Wide Web, and I'll explain in POE (Plain, Old English) what all the cryptic words and acronyms mean, as well as how to get started in this wild and wacky world of online communications. In fact, I'll actually cover most, if not all, of the items listed in the Table of Contents. What a novel idea!

How to Use This Book

If you've arrived at this point, I'd say you're already doing a very good job using this book, so I'm not sure you need any help from me in this department. I wrote this book with the idea that it be very flexible in order to accommodate your specific needs. You are welcome to read this book starting with page one and stopping when you reach the end of the book or begin weeping with joy, whichever comes first; or you can refer to the table of contents or index, locate a specific task or function you need assistance with, and read about that particular item. You decide what's best for you.

I've also included a comprehensive, geekspeak-free glossary, called "Mr. Modem's Internet Terms of Endearment." The glossary is included so you can begin peppering your conversations with technical-sounding words to give the appearance that you know what you're talking about—just like I do! I've also included lots of tips, tricks and frequently asked questions I've received from readers of my column over the years.

The bottom line is that you're the boss when it comes to navigating the pages of this book, just as you're the boss when it comes to navigating the pages of the World Wide Web. Whatever works best for you is the best way to proceed. Even though you are not required to begin at page one, I hope you'll glean some measure of comfort in knowing that each chapter progresses in a logical manner and gently eases into the next one. So sit back, relax, pour yourself a refreshing beverage, and enjoy your escorted journey into the world of the Internet.

This book is not a hardware or software manual and any similarity to manuals living, dead, or still in their original shrink-wrap is purely coincidental.

How This Book Is Organized

Mr. Modem's Internet Guide for Seniors begins with a general overview of the Internet, then segues into a musical history of the Internet. And you asked why this book is different? Puleeeze!

Following a typical Internet installation, which we'll explore in excruciating detail, we'll move on to e-mail, browsers, search engines, and an extravaganza of interesting, informative, bizarre, and arguably useful

Web sites. Along the way we'll explore newsgroups, Internet chat, WebTV, e-commerce—which is the fancy-shmancy name for online shopping—and tips for effective online communication. For the big finish, I'll share with you a peek into the future of the Internet, explore the often-confusing world of online abbreviations and its own unique shorthand, present a comprehensive glossary of Internet terminology, set my hair on fire, and call it a day.

Chapter 1, "What Is the Internet?", provides a big-picture perspective of the ethereal presence known as the Internet. I'll define the Internet and the World Wide Web, then explain some of their basic components.

Chapter 2, "A Musical History of the Internet," is the embodiment of all that's right with the world. For the first time ever, a tasteful blend of the sounds of the Internet era, melded with its historical development. Grown men have been known to sob uncontrollably while reading this chapter, so please proceed at your own peril, hankie-at-the-ready.

Chapter 3, "Getting Started," explains—uh, well, it explains how to get started. I'll also recommend some minimum configurations if you're computer shopping. I'll demystify modems, help you locate an Internet service provider, explain how data gets from Point A to Point B, and explain how to establish an account so you can access the Internet any time the CyberSpirit moves you.

Chapter 4, "A Typical Internet Installation," is a step-by-step tour through modem setup, configuration, and dial-up networking. Though somewhat technical appearing at first glimpse, you'll find obsessively detailed instructions, destined to warm the hearts of psychiatrists everywhere. Personally, I never met a compulsive I couldn't obsess over.

Chapter 5, "The ABCs of d'E-Mail," Get it? A, B, C, D'E-mail? Okay, in this chapter I'll discuss transmitting documents via the Internet, the joys of file compression, working with attachments—not vacuum cleaner type attachments, but files that you can send to others. Also included are tips for the e-mail software shopper, and a quick test drive of several current e-mail software programs.

Chapter 6, "Internet Chat," offers a look into the increasingly popular world of online chat. Learn how to converse with friends, family, and people you wouldn't want to be seen with in public, all courtesy of the Internet.

Chapter 7, "Newsgroups," focuses on online discussion groups. This chapter contains information about participating in newsgroups, how to find them, how to subscribe, as well as appropriate newsgroup behavior.

Chapter 8, "WebTV," tells you all about the exciting technology that allows you to send e-mail and surf the Internet without a computer. "Look, Ma! No hard drive!"

Chapter 9, "Battle of the Browsers," explores Netscape and Microsoft's Internet Explorer Web browser software. Both are excellent, both are continually introducing new features, and both are driving us crazy. Join the fun!

Chapter 10, "Internet Search Engines," provides information about many of the most popular search programs. Learn from the results of Mr. Modem's patented "tuna melt" testing protocol.

Chapter 11, "Mr. Modem's Web Sites for Seniors," shares more than one hundred Web sites, each with a brief description, proving definitively that Mr. Modem truly has no life.

Chapter 12, "E-Commerce: Shopping Online," takes a look at the world of online shopping. Billions of dollars are spent online every year. Is it legitimate? Is it safe? Will you be able to find a parking spot? I provide answers to these and other probing, insightful questions.

Chapter 13, "How to Communicate Effectively Online," explores the responsibility that attaches to online communication, and provides helpful tips to recognize, avoid, and cope with the cybersickos you'll encounter along the way.

Chapter 14, "The Best Is Yet to Come," offers a peek into the future of the Internet and the profound impact it will continue to have upon our lives and the lives of future generations. This is the coveted "The World According to Mr. Modem" chapter.

Appendix A, "Desperately Seeking Cruisin' (Or 50 Questions to Ask Before Selecting an Internet Service Provider)," is the place to learn the ABCs of ISPs and the right questions to ask in order to make an informed decision when comparison shopping for Internet access.

Appendix B, "FUIA: Frequently Used Internet Acronyms," helps you to decipher cryptic 'Netspeak so you can talk the Internet talk, walk the Internet walk and annoy all your friends—just like Mr. Modem does! This appendix will help you FIAO (Figure It All Out).

Appendix C, "An Extravaganza of Emoticons," presents a plethora of primitive symbols that thousands of years from now archeologists will ponder over and speculate about. So strap on your cervical collar, tilt your head to the left, and have fun! < :)

Appendix D, "Mr. Modem's All-Time Favorite Signature Tag Lines," offers a glimpse into the creative wit and wisdom of e-mail signature lines. If reading these tag lines touches even just one reader and makes a difference in just one life, then this book shall not have been written in vain.

Appendix E, "The Best of Ask Mr. Modem!" contains lots of answers to Internet users' most frequently asked questions from my syndicated "Ask Mr. Modem" column.

The Glossary, "Mr. Modem's Internet Terms of Endearment," decodes the encoded, unscrambles the encrypted, and demystifies the mysterious words so pervasive within the Internet culture. Learn the buzzwords and impress (or alienate) your friends.

The Web Site, located on the Web at `http://www.mrmodem.net`, offers another dimension of this book. There you will find bonus chapters, additional information, late-breaking technology news, hundreds of my favorite and highly recommended Web sites, as well as my speaking, book-signing, radio and TV appearance schedule. And you thought you were just buying another book? Heck, no! Think of this as the book that never ends! For more information about *Mr. Modem's Internet Guide for Seniors* and other great computer books, check out `http://www.sybex.com`.

Conventions Used in This Book

Bold font is used for words you type in as well as buttons, menus, tabs, and just about anything that you can click. Nothing drives me crazier than continually losing my place as I move my bifocaled eyes between the pages of a book and my computer screen as I attempt to follow instructions. So in addition to the larger font used throughout this book, we've made it a point to use **bold font** in the instructional sections to make this book even more senior-friendly.

Throughout this book, I utilize the ➤ symbol as an arrow or a visual instruction, indicating the next step or next selection. For example, **File ➤ Open** indicates that you should click the **File** menu. When you do that, the **File** menu items are displayed, and among them you will see **Open**. Click **Open**. Likewise, **Edit ➤ Preferences** means to click the **Edit** menu, then click the menu item **Preferences**.

Tip: You'll see a lot of these—quicker and smarter ways to accomplish a task.

Note: You'll see these types of notes, too. They usually represent alternate ways to accomplish a task or some additional information that needs to be highlighted.

Warning: In a few places, you'll see a warning like this one. When you see a warning, pay attention to it!

There are also some great Internet statistics sprinkled throughout the pages of this book.

You'll also see "Sidebar" boxes like this

These boxed sections provide added explanation of special topics that are noted briefly in the surrounding discussion, but that you may want to explore separately.

Preface

Perhaps no other technological advancement has had such far-reaching impact—professionally, politically, personally, and socially—as the ability to "go online." In recent years, such phrases as "I'll send you an e-mail," "Check out my home page," and "I hate this computer!" have been uttered by millions of citizens of cyberspace, now known as *Netizens*. Terms once disdainfully referred to as *geekspeak* have found their way into our society's vocabulary. For better or worse, the Internet has become as omnipresent and ubiquitous as pretentious authors using big words stolen from *Reader's Digest*'s "It Pays to Improve Your Word Power."

Whether you're sending e-mail from home or while traveling, downloading software updates, or transmitting photographs of your children or grandchildren to a friend or family member anywhere in the world, the ability to communicate electronically is now an integral part of our global boomers and seniors communities today.

Communicating online is also a natural extension of all the communication skills we have learned throughout our lives. Most of us don't have time to engage in telephone tag or to wade through layers of voice-mail menus only to be placed on hold. (Not that listening to 17 minutes of The Captain and Tennille's *Muskrat Love* as interpreted by the Tuskeegee Philharmonic is so terrible, but don't we all have better things to do with our time? Of course we do.) Using e-mail and the Internet to obtain technical support, pay bills online, shop for groceries, renew automobile and voter registrations, are all a reality in certain areas of the country already. And we haven't even scratched the surface!

Communicating online is the most consistently productive form of communication available to us, and as ever increasing numbers of people are accessible online, it will only get better. Members of every segment of society and from every demographic group are flocking to the

Internet in record numbers, and none more so than members of our 50+ generation.

Consider the following:

- More than 13 million U.S. adults over the age of 50 have Internet access, and this number is growing rapidly, according to a recent study conducted by SeniorNet and Charles Schwab Inc.

- The thousands of questions I receive each year from readers of my "Ask Mr. Modem!" column reveal that seniors have an above-average interest in Web sites that deal with politics, government, investing, news, travel, religion, medicine, and culture.

- "Older adults today are turning to the Internet as a natural component of their active lifestyles," said Mary Furlong, chief executive officer of Third Age Media, which co-sponsored the Excite survey.

For the latest in current statistics about seniors on the Internet, visit Nua Internet Surveys at `http://www.nua.ie/surveys/` and select **Seniors** under the **Demographics** heading. For general Internet statistics and information, visit The Internet Society at `http://www.isoc.org`. If you're fed up with statistics and couldn't care less about them, just keep reading and for heaven's sake, don't be so grumpy!

While writing this book I visited with thousands of my 50+ contemporaries at seminars, book signings, and in online discussion. Not surprisingly, the overwhelming majority of us utilize Internet e-mail to establish or enhance communication with our children or extended family members worldwide. Isolationism is a thing of the past for online seniors. Forget about "Gray Power," we're now entering the era of "Modem Power!"

In the early 1960s when I was a tie-dyed, bell-bottomed, lava lamp-basking, groovy hipster; the mantra of the day was "Turn on, tune in, and drop out." Today, as a Polo-clad, khaki-wearing, wide-bottomed, aging hipster, it's "Turn on, boot up, log in." Still groovy after all these years. Who would have thought?

Okay, you've heard enough about me, and now I would like to hear from you.

I am currently in the process of assembling a collection of heart-warming, life-altering, first-person accounts focusing on how the Internet and online communications have affected the members of our online seniors community. To the hundreds of you who have already shared your stories, I sincerely thank you. To new readers, I extend this invitation: If the Internet has had a positive effect upon your life, if it's connected you with distant family members, loves old or new, served as a resource for life-saving medical information, or provided you emotional support in a time of need—whatever your experience, I would like to hear from you. Please e-mail me at MrModem@home.com or visit me at http://www.mrmodem.net and share your unique story.

So fire up your computer, jump start your modem, and let's head out together on what's been referred to as the Information Superhighway, the Mother of All Networks, and the end of leisure time as you knew it.

No matter what you call it, one thing is a certainty: Life will never be the same.

What Is the Internet?

The Internet is often described as a computer network and indeed, it is. But beyond the ability to connect computers on a worldwide basis, the Internet is a communications phenomenon, a vast informational resource and best of all, a grand adventure for you, for me, and for everybody who chooses to participate. In this chapter, we'll take our first big-picture look at the Internet, the World Wide Web, and their basic components.

The best way to begin when trying to describe the Internet is to describe what it isn't. It isn't a building, it isn't a place or a destination, it isn't anything tangible that you can hold in your hands, nor can you back out of your garage and run over it. Rather, it is a group of connected computers—a network created to transport data from one computer to many other computers. Conceptually, the Internet is nothing more than a computer network similar to one found in any small office anywhere in the world today.

What is difficult to conceptualize about the Internet is its size. It might be helpful to think of the Internet in the same way we think about the telephone system.

If you're in Sacramento and want to call someone in Atlanta, the electronic signal travels through a number of phone lines and switching computers owned and maintained by many different telephone companies (courtesy of deregulation). What makes it work, assuming you have a pocket full of quarters or can remember to dial the prefix 10-10-WHO-IS-MY-CARRIER, is that all the companies follow the same standards or adhere to the same rules, called *protocols*. Each piece of equipment along the route can handle and accommodate the same electronic signal as it passes from one connection to the next.

When the telephone connection is established, your voice is transmitted by a system of computers, telephone lines, satellites and/or other electronic devices. Once the connection is made, either you're in luck and somebody miraculously picks up the phone on the first ring or (as is more common these days) the answering machine kicks in and you've wasted a long-distance call. Or a three-year-old picks up the phone, makes a few gurgling noises, then drops the receiver on the floor.

Just like the traditional phone system we all know and love, the Internet is also a network of telephone lines, other computers and switching devices; but instead of transmitting voices, the Internet transmits electronic computer data in digital format. It all sounds so high-tech, doesn't it?

One of the most popular forms of computer data being transmitted today is electronic mail. Individual parts of a single electronic mail (e-mail) message might travel through many computers and phone lines as it weaves its way to its final destination. Because there are so many different computers involved, it's often said that nobody owns the Internet. (I don't know who said that, but it's true.) So the Internet is a big cooperative effort with many people and companies owning small parts of it, each maintaining and controlling their specific piece.

There are 1.46 million new Internet users each month,
365,000 every week,
52,000 every day,
2.166 every hour,
36 every minute,
1 every 1.67 seconds.

Source: eMarketer, http://www.emarketer.com/

Remember protocols? Well, the reason the Internet even works at all is because millions of connected computers all speak to each other in the same language, just like the telephone system. Internally, different computers might use different operating systems such as DOS, Windows, Unix or Linux, and may utilize those operating systems on a variety of platforms— sometimes referred to as environments. But externally, they can all translate what is called *TCP/IP (Transmission Control Protocol/Internet Protocol)*. TCP/IP is a communications standard that permits every computer connected to the Internet to exchange data with every other computer.

All communication requires a communications standard or some commonality between participants. For example, in order to read this book, it must be written in a language that you can read and understand. That requires me to follow certain language-related protocols when writing that I know are universally accepted by all readers. In English, we read from

3

ght, starting at the top of a page and we use certain forms of punc-
uch as periods, commas, semicolons, exclamation marks, and
marks. As long as we all follow the same rules or adhere to the
same communication standards or protocols, we can communicate.

Prior to being transmitted, data is chopped up into tiny pieces, called
packets. I refer to this process as the Popeil DataMatic Syndrome because it
slices and dices the data into these packets, assigns an address to each, and
then blasts them out into cyberspace, heading for a specific destination.
Think of it this way: you have four friends flying from Los Angeles to New
York's JFK airport, each on a separate flight. One person is routed through
Dallas, one person is routed through Chicago, one is routed through
Atlanta, and one is routed through St. Louis. But all four individuals arrive
at JFK at approximately the same time and meet each other in New York.

The reason these data packets travel via multiple routes is not because
they're sightseeing, but rather because each data packet is seeking the
most direct path to its final destination. Even though this all happens in
milliseconds, it's not at all unlike what we do as we drive on our city
streets. For example, if we turn down a street and see that it's congested
with traffic or road construction, we'll turn around and take an alternate
route to our destination.

Data packets whizzing throughout
cyberspace also encounter traffic jams
or obstacles that may impede their
progress. When a roadblock is
encountered, the data packets automatically reroute themselves and they
do this hundreds of thousands of times
while traveling to a final destination.

So, in a very simplistic way—
which is the only way Mr. Modem can
grasp complex concepts—that's how
data is transmitted over the Internet via TCP/IP.

So what is the Internet? In a 'Netshell, the Internet is a worldwide network of computers connected through a system of modems, satellites, digital cable and telephone wires. It's the Mother of all Networks, sometimes referred to as the network of networks, and most accurately described as the end of leisure time as you knew it. At least that's my definition and I'm sticking to it.

What Is the World Wide Web?

The *World Wide Web (WWW),* which is a specific area or subsection of the Internet, is a visual and aural buffet of sound, video, photographs, animation and text and is arguably the most educational, entertaining and possibly productive area on the Internet today. It's also great fun! By snooze-inducing definition, the World Wide Web is a linked collection of informational resources on the Internet, but more significantly, it is responsible for the incredible interest in and exponential growth of the Internet. What's more, navigating the Web is very easy, and that is a large part of its appeal. You just position your cursor and click your mouse. With apologies to Lauren Bacall, "You know how to click your mouse, don't you? Just put your finger and mouse together and click."

Lucky for us, the name *Web* really doesn't require much explanation as it is already a great metaphor for what the World Wide Web is. The World Wide Web resembles a giant spider's web that contains within it a vast amount of information. When you request a particular piece of information—a Web page, for example—an order for that information is sent by your computer when you click your mouse on what is referred to as a *hyperlink.*

It is this ability to ferret out information by mouse-clicking your way to digital Nirvana that makes the Web so compelling, so time-consuming and so darn much fun! Once you click on a link you will be presented with a Web page containing requested information. Contained within the page presented will be other links to other Web pages containing related information, and each of those pages will contain links to even more related information. Think of the process as an informational mystery that you're trying to solve. Links are clues to the information you're seeking. Each time you click on a link, you're ordering up a fresh batch of clues as you continue to drill your way down to that one delicious morsel of information that you've been seeking.

That's why it's important when you're at home to scream, "Order in!" every time you move to a new Web page. Your family will thank you.

After you click your mouse and fire off a request for a particular Web page or piece of information, your request then scurries across the Internet's worldwide neighborhood until it gets to the particular data requested. It knows where it's going because your order or request for information contains the address of the particular information you are seeking. That address is called a *URL* (verbalized as "U-R-L" or "Earl"), short for Uniform Resource Locator or Universal Resource Locator. Nobody really knows for sure, so you'll see it defined both ways. I prefer Uniform Resource Locator, but then again, I always did have a thing for uniforms. They don't call me the Duke of URL for nothing, you know.

When the requested data is located, it is sent back across the Internet to your computer and the results are displayed on your monitor. Voila!

The *World Wide Web* should not be confused with the *Internet*, though the two terms are often incorrectly used synonymously. While the Internet is the collection of interconnected computer networks that evolved from the ARPANet of the late 1960s, the Web (or WWW) is the electronic, graphical, and textual information that can be accessed via the Internet. But who really cares? After all, what's a couple of terms among friends?

Think Links!

Any <u>underlined</u> text you see on a Web page is referred to as *hyptertext*. The term *hypertext* was coined in the 1960s by Ted Nelson, who defined it as "non-sequential writing." I recall Ozzie, Harriet, David and Ricky, but Ted must have been away at CompuCamp during the 1960s. Regardless of Ted's whereabouts, he suggested that hypertext applied not only to locating and reading information, but also to creating it. Nelson waxed expansive about this concept in his books and his vision of a global hypertext system called *Xanadu*, though I don't think he had Olivia Hyphen-Newton in mind at the time.

Hypertext documents contain *hyperlinks* to other documents located throughout the Internet (see Figure 1.1). Hyperlinks, in addition to connecting related documents located hither and yon on the Internet, may also connect related information within the same document or on a single page. Think of hyperlinks as your window to a world of information contained on other Web pages. It is irrelevant if the information is located inches away on the same page you're reading, tens of thousands of miles away on a Web page in a foreign country, or perhaps some day even in a galaxy far, far away. (Insert theme from "Twilight Zone" here.)

By the way, over-stimulated Web surfers are sometimes referred to as *hyperdinks*.

You will need Web browser software to navigate the Web, but obtaining browser software is easy, convenient, and, depending on the software, free (see Chapter 9, "The Battle of the Browsers").

<u>Hypertext</u> is the backbone of the World Wide Web and is so simple to use, *I* even figured it out. (Boggles the mind, I know.) Here's how hypertext works: If you were viewing this page on the Web, you would be able to click on the underlined word *hypertext* at the beginning of this

paragraph. That simple action would magically transport you to one or more related pages which might be located anywhere on the Internet. In this case, it could take you to a definition of *hypertext*, a history of its development, or an explanation of how to create your own hypertext documents.

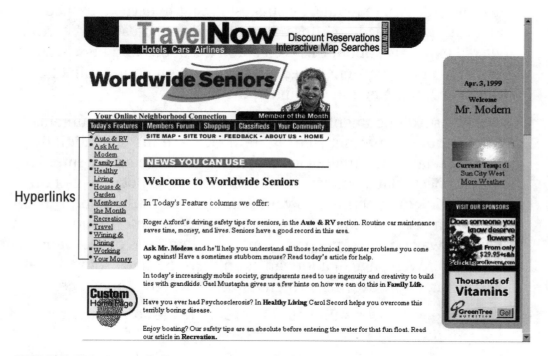

FIGURE 1.1: Hyperlinks appear as underlined text.

These related documents will in turn contain hypertext links to other documents. Continuing to select these hyperlinks will take you on a self-conducted, graphical, or textual journey through the World Wide Web. Clicking on the Back button or viewing the history file of your browser software will permit you to retrace your steps. (See Chapter 9, "The Battle of the Browsers.") The moral of this story is that while you're surfing the Web, you're actually leaving a trail of environmentally friendly cyber breadcrumbs, so you will never be lost.

The Big Picture

To completely understand what the Web is, you need to first understand its place in Internet history. Well, you don't *really* need to, but work with me here, will you, please?

During the very early stages of its development in the late 1960s and early 1970s, when bell-bottoms ruled the land and tie-dye was king, the Internet was made up of only a very few computer-connected universities and government agencies. It wasn't until the early 1980s that students and teachers at educational institutions began to appreciate the value of being connected to the Internet and started using it for academic purposes, as well as to help spread the word about toga parties, fraternity pledge rushes, and keggers.

The primary means of online communication during these early years were e-mail and online bulletin boards which made it convenient for individuals to *post* (electronically publish) the results of their own research and other academic efforts.

This was the state of the Internet when Dr. Tim Berners-Lee of the European Laboratory for Particle Physics (CERN) created a program in an effort to preserve and enhance some of his work. The program he developed, entitled *Inquire*, provided the ability to cross-reference his research papers by using a single hyperlink. The hyperlink provided access to an accompanying document that related to a statement, conclusion, or claim contained in his main thesis, thus bringing life, sizzle, and some sorely needed pizzazz to the arcane world of footnotes.

A Cause for ConCERN?

Astute readers may be disoriented, dazed, and confused by the acronym CERN, used for the European Laboratory for Particle Physics. One would assume ELPP would be the appropriate acronym. Be confused no more! The acronym CERN originated with the laboratory's previous name, the European Center for Nuclear Research. Okay, okay, so that would be ECNR. That explanation clears up absolutely nothing until we take a look at the original French name, *Conseil Europeen pour la Recherche Nucleaire*. Impressive, ain't it? Okay, back to our hyper-exciting look at hypertext!

Dr. Tim and his employer decided that expanding his original idea would be a pretty neat thing to do. The result of that expansion would be lots of hyperlinked documents stored on a centralized storage device for ease of access by anybody with the appropriate authority. Thus was born what later would become the World Wide Web.

The first Web site, a text-only presentation aimed at educating and, no doubt, impressing other physicists (Heaven knows that's not an easy thing to do), made its debut in 1991. At first used exclusively by educators at prestigious universities, top-secret government agencies, and 13-year-old hackers, the Web grew slowly and remained the best-kept secret on the Internet for the next two years.

In 1993, with the release of the Mosaic Web browser, the first navigational software program to utilize a *Graphical User Interface* or *GUI* (pronounced "gooey"), the Web stepped into the spotlight for what some thought would be its 15 minutes of fame. What was once a virtual Bore-O-Rama of text-only documents became a festival of multimedia—a kaleidoscope of sound, video, photographs, animation and text. Private Web usage exploded in the home, and the business community slowly began to realize the commercial potential of the Web. Miraculously, no injuries were reported as a result of the explosion.

To give you some sense of the phenomenal growth of the Internet in its early days, Web traffic increased 341,634 percent in 1993 alone, and that's not a tpyo. Since that time, its growth has steadily increased every year. It is no wonder that the Web has transformed the world in less than 10 years. This rapid growth has been in large measure a direct result of the Web's vast resources and its ease of use. And as our generation continues to embrace the Internet in ever-increasing numbers, we will likewise continue to be an integral part of that societal transformation.

Imagine keeping in touch with family and friends around the globe, exchanging words, photographs or even hearing the sound of a loved one's voice! Think of the convenience of researching investments or planning that dream vacation by "visiting" hotels online, shopping for the best airfare, making your seating selection, and purchasing your airline tickets all from the comfort and convenience of your computer keyboard. Whether it's listening to new music releases, screening video clips or receiving late-breaking news personalized for your particular interests, it's all happening on the Internet, and it's all available to you today.

What's Next?

In the next chapter, we'll waltz through a musical history of the Internet.

A Musical History of the Internet

Now, be honest, aren't you glad you bought this book? Where else could you possibly find a musical history of the Internet, complete with modulating modems, binary beauties, and hyperlinked hunks? In this chapter, we'll take a melodious look at the evolution of the Internet, tying significant events to popular songs of the day. Can you remember where you were when e-mail made its debut? Groovy!

Passed down from modem to modem through the years, a retelling of the history of the Internet generally begins with the U.S. Department of Defense in the late 1960s. The DOD began a project that aimed to establish a redundant communications network within the United States. The seeds of what has blossomed into the Internet were first planted, however, in the fabulous '50s with the establishment of the Advanced Research Projects Agency (called ARPA)—the sound of which, when articulated, will be very comforting to seal enthusiasts worldwide. Go ahead, say it out loud!

In 1957, in the chilly days of the Cold War, the Department of Defense founded ARPA to give American science and technology a boost in response to the Soviet Union's launching of Sputnik, the first artificial satellite. The big fear at the time was that the Soviets were rapidly gaining technological ground on the United States and something had to be done about it.

The next important milestone came in 1962. While most of us were responding to our Cold War concerns by twisting the night away, other, less serious individuals were frittering away their time in think tanks. A think tank was a very popular cerebral device where great minds gathered  to discuss serious problems of the era. Personally, I always wondered how many people could cram into a think tank. Perhaps that's why I was never invited to participate in one.

In 1962, Paul Baran of the highly respected RAND Corporation think tank, proposed an information-moving system called a packet-switching communications network with "no central authority," which would ensure continued communications during or subsequent to a nuclear war or extreme disaster. Oh, those fun-loving rascals did have a way with words, didn't they?

So the genesis of the Internet actually goes back more than 40 years, to an era of postwar innocence, relative prosperity and pretty darned good times. In 1957, Eisenhower was president, Elvis was king, and I received my first training modem. What follows is a timeline which focuses on the development of that fabled, cabled, network we have come to know and love as the Internet, along with a few historical points of interest, some musical mileposts, and an occasional scenic overlook along the way.

1889   Herman Hollerith patents a calculating machine that utilizes punch cards. Hollerith Calculating Machine Company (HCMC) is later absorbed by another upstart company that in 1924 adopts the big-shot sounding name International Business Machines Corporation (IBM). Musically, the Chicago Auditorium opens with Adelina Patti singing *Home, Sweet Home* to an audience that includes President Benjamin Harrison. Rumor has it he loved the song, but hated the laser light show.

1945   Rear Admiral Grace Hopper records a moth stuck between two relays on the Harvard Mark II computer. Thus, the term *bug* was introduced to the wild and wacky world of computers. Nominated for an Academy Award, Johnny Mercer's *Accentuate the Positive* placed a positive spin on computer bugs.

1947   Bell Laboratories invents the transistor. John W. Tukey names the fundamental unit of information the *binary digit*, which becomes *bit*, for short. Making its musical debut is the politically incorrect, today-there-would-be-a-lawsuit *Too Fat Polka* by Ross MacLean and Arthur Richardson.

1951   The microprocessor is invented. *It's Beginning to Look a Lot Like Christmas*, by Meredith Willson, brightens the holiday season.

1956   Arguably the first rock n'roll record, *Rock Around the Clock* by Bill Haley & the Comets, is released. Real hep kittens and cool cats purchase transistor radios by the millions, annoying an entire generation of parents in the process.

1968   RAND presents its decentralized network communications concept to ARPA. Top musical hits of the year include *Love is Blue, Grazing in the Grass*, and *Hey Jude,* by Paul Mauriat, Hugh Masekela and The Beatles, respectively.

1969   ARPANet is commissioned by the Department of Defense to research the feasibility of networking. ARPANet establishes the first node at the University of California, Los Angeles. First moon landing. Haight-Ashbury. Jefferson Airplane. Most-frequently heard refrain at Woodstock: *"Sex, drugs, and the ARPANet!"*

1970   John Draper uses the toy whistle from a box of Cap'n Crunch cereal to duplicate the 2600 frequency of a Wide Area Telecommunications System (WATS) line by blowing it into a telephone receiver. This historic event was one of the earliest examples of the technology gods suggesting that somebody get a life. This illegal activity is called phone *phreaking,* a precursor to what we today refer to as *hacking.* It was a year of long song titles, as B.J. Thomas's *Raindrops Keep Fallin' on My Head,* Simon and Garfunkel's *Bridge Over Troubled Water,* and The Beatles' *The Long and Winding Road* topped the charts.

1971   Intel Corporation produces the first 8008 microprocessor chip. *Maggie May,* by Rod Stewart and Cher's *Gypsies, Tramps, and Thieves,* all had a *Family Affair* (courtesy of Sly & The Family Stone) this year.

Fascinating Bonus Tidbit

The term *surfing the Internet* derives from the last name of a programmer with the ARPANet project and co-developer of the TCP/IP protocol, Vinton Cerf. In the late 1960s, a group in San Diego got into the networking business and called themselves the California Educational Research Foundation network, or cerf.net. They requested Mr. Cerf's permission, obtained it and shortly thereafter "Cerfing the Net" T-shirts appeared in California.

1972   ARPANet is demonstrated at the first International Conference on Computer Communications in Washington, D.C. E-mail is invented. Within an hour the first annoying "You can make $100,000 while sitting in your kitchen, wearing your old bathrobe," mass e-mailing—called *spamming*—is transmitted. Our musical tastes included Don McLean's *American Pie*, America's *A Horse with No Name*, and Bill Withers' *Lean on Me*.

1973   ARPANet establishes the first international connections to England and Norway. Musical taste apparently took the year off in 1973, as number-one records inexplicably included Tony Orlando and Dawn's *Tie a Yellow Ribbon*, Cher's *Half-Breed*, and Eddie Kendricks's *Keep On Truckin'*.

1974   Micro Instrumentation Telemetry Systems releases the Altair 8800, a $400 personal computer kit, and the era of the personal computer begins. A fully-assembled Altair 8800 will fit comfortably beneath a bell-bottomed trouser leg of the fashionable 1974 Altair 8800 user. *The Way We Were* by Marvin Hamlisch and Paul McCartney's *Band on the Run* kept us groovin' in 1974.

1975   The term *flame* is first used at Worcester Polytechnic Institute. A flame is a hostile e-message. One who sends a flame is said to be a *flamer*. One who receives a flame is said to be *flamed* (or *digitally scorched*, by those who don't know any better). Scorched individuals took a welcome respite and soul searched to the strains of *Philadelphia Freedom*, *When Will I Be Loved?*, and the disco classic, *The Hustle*. We truly had no shame in this era when polyester reigned supreme, though the U.S. Supreme Court ruled that death by disco was indeed cruel and unusual punishment.

1977   ARPANet launches a test in which a programmed packetized radio signal is transmitted over 94,000 miles and correctly reassembled at the other end. Signal, shmignal. So why can't these geniuses write understandable instructions for programming a VCR? A packetized signal is one in which the *signal* (data) is broken down into tiny pieces, each piece assigned an address, sent out, then hopefully reassembled at the receiving end. Disco is mercifully dying as the soothing sounds of Barbra Streisand's *Evergreen*, Barry Manilow's *Looks Like We Made It*, and Debby Boone's *You Light Up My Life* nudge us toward the 1980s.

1978   The first BBS (Bulletin Board System) was created by Ward Christensen and Randy Suess. White polyester suits were a hot topic of conversation online as the Bee Gees' *Stayin' Alive* rattled medallions around the country.

1979   Duke University and the University of North Carolina establish USENET (*USErNET*work), the first of the Internet-based forums where users post and read messages. Sex is a hot topic, both online and offline, as Rod Stewart inquired, *Do You Think I'm Sexy?* and Donna Summer scored with *Hot Stuff* and *Bad Girls* at the top of the musical charts.

1980   Tim Berners-Lee, a consultant for CERN—the European Laboratory for Particle Physics or *Conseil Europeen pour la Recherche Nucleaire*, as I like to call it, writes a program named, but somewhat awkwardly translated, "Inquire Within Upon Everything." The program allows links or connections between documents and becomes the basis for the World Wide Web. *Funkytown*, by Lipps, Inc. (Lip Sync— get it?), Diana Ross's *Upside Down*, and Billy Joel's *It's Still Rock and Roll To Me* are the leaders of the musical pack.

1981   The City University of New York and Yale University establish BITNET (Because It's Time NETwork) to provide e-mail service between the two universities. Musical mileposts include Kim Carnes's whip-cracking *Bette Davis Eyes*, Diana Ross and Lionel Richie's *Endless Love*, and Christopher Cross's *Arthur's Theme*.

1982   ARPA enacts the Transmission Control Protocol (TCP) and Internet Protocol (IP) and the Department of Defense declares TCP/IP as its standard. The number of Internet host computers reaches 235. The term *cyberspace* is coined by science fiction writer William Gibson in his novel *Neuromancer*. Olivia Newton-John got *Physical* with us as Joan Jett's *I Love Rock n' Roll* and Paul McCartney and Stevie Wonder's *Ebony and Ivory* permeated the airwaves.

1984   The National Science Foundation (NSF) introduces the Domain Name System (DNS), a naming convention identifying seven major organizational components of the Internet: .com, .edu, .org, .net, .int, .mil, and .gov. Number one hits of the year include Cyndi Lauper's *Time After Time*, Prince's (thank heaven's he hadn't changed his name yet) *When Doves Cry*, and Ray Parker's "who-you-gonna-call" *Ghostbusters*.

1985   NSF develops NSFnet and connects five supercomputing centers. An unexpected result is an explosive increase in computer connectivity between universities. The number of Internet hosts reaches 5,000. Musical mileposts: Lionel Richie's *Say You, Say Me*, and Huey Lewis & The News's *The Power of Love*.

1986   Vidal Sassoon creates HAIRNet to control unruly hair-related rumors and provide support to community service agencies seeking to assist victims of follicular homicide. Whitney Houston's *Greatest Love of All* and Paul Simon's *Graceland* had us wiggin' out in 1986.

1987   The number of BITNET hosts exceeds 1,000. The number of Internet hosts reaches 20,000. The number of talk show hosts surpasses 500,000—or maybe it just seemed that way. Linda Ronstadt and James Ingram's *Somewhere Out There* and Michael Jackson's *Bad* were very good in 1987.

1988   Robert Morris, a graduate student in computer science at Cornell University, injects his Internet worm into the Internet (you should pardon the expression). The virus moves through the Internet faster than a speeding pullet before Morris chickens out and pulls the plug, but not before more than 6,000 invaded Internet hosts lost data or had their hard drives corrupted. Security becomes a hot topic throughout Geekdom. Big hits in Musicville include Expose's *Seasons Change*, Rick Astley's *Never Gonna Give You Up*, and Gloria Estefan's *Anything For You*.

1989   The number of Internet hosts exceeds 100,000. Tim Berners-Lee makes his proposal for a World Wide Web network to CERN. CERN accepts. Lucky break for us. Milli Vanilli lip-synced their way into our hearts with *Girl You Know It's True*. Shortly after, their career crashed faster than a Sears hard drive in a Montgomery Ward computer.

1990   The U.S. Department of Defense incorporates ARPANet into NSFnet. CERN works on developing the initial World Wide Web platform. Internet hosts reach 250,000. Internet enthusiasts listen to Paula Abdul's *Opposites Attract*, Janet Jackson's *Escapade*, and Mariah Carey's *Vision of Love*.

1991   The University of Minnesota, "Home of the Fighting Gophers," introduces Gopher—a UNIX-based system that provides access to information and services on the Internet. The number of Internet hosts almost doubles in a 10-month period from 375,000 to 615,000. Guns N' Roses' *Use Your Illusion* was playing somewhere, but I never heard it.

1992   CERN makes the World Wide Web available to the public. The National Center for Supercomputing Applications releases the first version of Marc Andreesen's Web browser called Mosaic. WWW traffic measures a scant .01 percent of all Internet traffic. During the year, Web traffic increases over 300,000 percent as the Web is "discovered." The number of Internet hosts reaches one million. Garth Brooks' *"Fences"* and Michael Jackson's *"Dangerous"* albums are also discovered by millions of fans.

1993   NSF creates InterNIC (InterNetwork Information Center) to provide specific Internet services including domain name server (DNS) registration. The White House goes online. Vice president Al Gore coins the phrase "Information Superhighway." The number of Internet hosts reaches two million. When we weren't trying to figure out how to get on the Internet, we were listening to *If You Asked Me To* by Celine Dion, *Mi Tierra* by Gloria Estefan, and Billy Joel's *River of Dreams*.

1994   Marc Andreesen and Jim Clark form Mosaic Communications Corporation (MCC), later to become Netscape Communications. In October, MCC releases the first version of Netscape Navigator on the Internet. Mass-marketing companies begin using the Internet for e-mail advertising. The number of Internet hosts reaches 3.5 million. The Arizona law firm of Canter & Siegel "spammed" the Internet with e-mail advertising green card lottery services. *Streets of Philadelphia* by Bruce Springsteen and Sheryl Crow's *All I Wanna Do* waft across the airwaves.

1995   In August, Netscape announces its initial public offering of five million shares of common stock. Microsoft releases its Internet Explorer Web browser in conjunction with the Windows 95 operating system. The number of Internet hosts reaches six million. Alanis Morisette's *You Oughta Know* and *Let Her Cry* by Hootie and the Blowfish keep us entertained while we're waiting for Web pages to ooze onto our monitors.

1996   In February, the U.S. Congress passes the Telecommunications Act of 1996 in an attempt to regulate the Internet. By December, there are more than nine million Internet hosts in more than 240 countries. An estimated 44 million people are using the Internet and more than 60 million individual Web pages are available for our surfing pleasure. Twenty billion dollars worth of goods and services are purchased via the Internet, the majority of orders emanating from my household. *You're Makin' Me High* by Toni Braxton and *All Eyez on Me* by Tupac Shakur top the musical charts.

1997   The Supreme Court rules the Telecommunications Act of 1996 unconstitutional. The number of Internet hosts reaches 19.5 million. This year in music, Puff Daddy dominated the charts with three number-one singles, none of which I know or have ever heard.

1998   The formerly red hot Internet becomes white hot as America Online purchases Netscape and the U.S. Department of Justice files suit against Microsoft. Internet stocks result in unprecedented stock market growth. America Online hosts the first ever interspecies Internet chat with Koko the gorilla, while Celine Dion keeps us grounded with *My Heart Will Go On* from the movie *Titanic*.

The percentage of Americans over age 55 who are online has nearly doubled in the last year alone.

Source: Ziff-Davis Internet Trak

1999   No matter whether your musical intention is to waltz, twist, boogaloo or hip-hop into the future, by year's end, an estimated 90- to 100-million mouse clickers will be using the Internet. Please keep reading so I can make sure you're one of them.

What's Next?

Every adventure must begin with a first step. The next chapter, "Getting Started," is that first step towards the Internet. Enjoy the journey!

Getting Started

Millions of people worldwide are asking the same question: "I want to be on the Internet, but I'm not sure where to start." Mr. Modem feels your pain. In this chapter, you'll receive suggestions for purchasing a new computer and learn what you need to access the Internet. I'll teach you a little bit about bytes and help you find an Internet service provider (ISP).

Since the World Wide Web is a visual buffet full of graphical images, animation, sound, video and incredibly vast informational resources, to fully experience what all the excitement is about, you will need a computer capable of handling all the technology the Web is capable of delivering. You'll also need a modem, software, and a point of access provided by an ISP.

Buying a New Computer

So when is the best time to purchase a new computer? Any time is the best time if it's the right time for you. Don't delay purchasing a new computer, waiting to buy until all the new technology has been invented. Whatever you purchase today *will* be obsolete in a matter of time and the price will inevitably plummet—that's simply the nature of the computing beast. But if what you purchase today will serve your purposes for the foreseeable future, how much better does it really get than that?

My friends have become accustomed to timing their computer purchases to coincide with any purchases I make. They have come to know and appreciate the fact that whenever I purchase any computer technology, they can rest assured the price of that item will plunge within a week of my purchase. It's the story of my life, what can I say?

The computer you purchase today will function for years. But because computer technology is evolving at a blistering pace, newer technologies will replace older technologies, so at some point you may want to upgrade your new computer. Perhaps in two or three years, budget permitting, you may want to purchase another new computer so you can have the latest and greatest technology available.

We'll take a look at the software required to escort you onto the Internet in Chapter 4 when we explore a typical Internet installation and set up.

Hardware Recommendations: Computers and Dream Machines

If you're computer shopping, the general rule of thumb is to purchase the fastest computer with the most memory that you can comfortably afford. Here's my recommended MINIMUM configuration for a brand new desktop computer, with a money-is-no-object recommendation appearing in parenthesis to the right. The minimum configuration should cost approximately $1,000 to $1,200. Mr. Modem's budget-bustin' dream machine configuration, however, costs approximately $3,000.

Processor: 333Mhz Pentium (Pentium III, 500Mhz with 512KB cache)

Memory: 64MB of SDRAM (128MB of SDRAM)

Hard Drive: 4.0 gigabyte (GB) (17.2GB)

1.44MB floppy disk drive

Video: 4MB of SDRAM (16MB 3D AGP graphics accelerator)

Monitor: 17-inch with 0.28 or 0.26 dot pitch (21-inch with 0.26 dot pitch)

Modem: 56Kbps V.90 (cable Internet access, if available in your area)

Mouse: Microsoft's IntelliMouse

Multimedia: 32x CD-ROM (40x CD-ROM and/or DVD III-ROM; recordable/rewriteable CD-ROM)

One Universal Serial Bus (USB) port (Two USB ports)

Operating System: Windows 98 (should be pre-installed and you should receive the Windows 98 installation CD-ROM—insist on it)

The iMac Option

In an effort to provide information so exhaustively complete that you'll be ready for a nap just reading it, I cannot—I dare not—talk about accessing the Internet without discussing the fabulous iMac computer by Apple.

The iMac is a Macintosh computer that was designed with one thought in mind: To get you on the Internet as quickly, economically and as easily as possible. And that's what the *I* in iMac stands for: Internet.

Sparing no expense in researching this section, I drove to my local iMac dealer and groveled my way into his heart as I pleaded for an opportunity to try out an iMac for free. When the store manager's laughter subsided, I was escorted to a dimly-lit back room, strip-searched—wait. No, I'm sorry. That was a bad speaking engagement I had last summer. Sometimes I get confused.

The manager graciously agreed to let me tinker with a lime green iMac. Other than inexplicable cravings for Jello, it took me about 40 minutes from the time I opened the box until I was actually on the Internet navigating to `http://www.sybex.com`. I always like to navigate to `http://www.sybex.com` and look for "Mr. Modem." It's a spiritual, quasi-existential experience: *I am on the Web, therefore I am.* But then again, I don't get out much.

Aesthetically, the iMac is about as appealing as a computer can be. It looks like fun and it is fun! Its distinctive appearance looks like a cross between R2D2 and a gumball machine. Available in strawberry, lime, tangerine, grape or blueberry colors, the iMac is delicious in its simplicity. Setup and installation consists of five steps:

1. Plug in the power cord.
2. Plug in the modem cord.
3. Attach the keyboard and the mouse.

4. Press the power button.

5. Scream "Surf's up!" to let family and neighbors know you're ready to ride the wild Web surf.

When you first fire up the iMac, a short instructional video appears that entertainingly explains how to use the Web and send e-mail.

Connecting to the Internet is a breeze. If you already have an Internet service provider your personal Setup Assistant will escort you through the process. If you need a provider, you can connect to Earthlink for $19.95/month. The first month is a freebie and the $25 setup charge is waived for iMac signer-uppers. America Online is also available along with browser buddies Netscape and Microsoft's Internet Explorer.

The iMac includes a 15-inch color monitor. At first I was disappointed with the blurriness of the screen image and text, and complained to the manager about it. Nothing like wearing out one's welcome. The manager sneered and said everything looked normal to him. It was only then that I discovered that I had kitty saliva on my glasses. How embarrassing! Once I cleaned my specs it was a whole new ballgame. By this point, the manager was looking at his watch. "Only a few more minutes!" I whined.

The retail price for the lime green iMac I had the pleasure of test surfing was just $1,299 plus tax. So if you're in the market for a low-priced computer and would rather be out on the golf course or enjoying a refreshing beverage instead of tinkering with a Windows-based personal computer, consider the iMac.

I think one of the most compelling features about the iMac is that you can't help but look at it and smile. It's cute, it's non-threatening, it's warm, friendly and completely approachable. Just like Mr. Modem.

For more information on connecting to the Internet with either Windows or a Mac, check out *Internet Complete* (Sybex, 1998).

Extras, Add-Ons, and Options

A few extra goodies are worth considering to enhance your computing experience:

- First, an internal Iomega 100MB Zip drive, which will enable you to store huge amounts of data that you'll never use again or remember where you stored it. Very cool. You're not really computing until you can confidently tell your friends, "I know I've got that on my computer, but I'm not sure where."

- Secondly, what's life without a scanner? Scanners are great fun. I'm currently using a Hewlett Packard ScanJet 6200C. Use your scanner to convert photographs to computer files that you can then e-mail to distant friends and family members. With a little practice, you'll be annoying people worldwide with your digital snapshots.

Mr. Modem Caveat: When scanner shopping, you'll encounter nifty three-in-one or six-in-one devices that may include a scanner, fax, printer, copier, hedge clipper, vegetable slicer and grout scrubber. While these all-in-one devices can be very handy, just be aware that if any one of these components malfunctions, you'll have to send the entire unit in for repair.

- Lastly, but not leastly, what self-respecting computerphile (not to be confused with a computer file) would be caught comatose without a digital camera? A digital camera doesn't use film. Photos are recorded on a memory chip or floppy disk. I prefer the floppy disk cameras because you can remove the disk from your camera, insert it in your computer's floppy drive and copy the files. One 1.44MB floppy disk will hold approximately 20 photos, depending upon the resolution. Higher-resolution pictures consume more disk space.

There is a plethora of peripherals and countless add-ons, extras, gadgets, and other digital doodads available to computer enthusiasts today. My best advice is to use a little common sense when purchasing a new computer. Think of it as you would if you were purchasing options for a new car. Sure, some things would be nice to have, but will you really use them all?

I Want My WebTV

Okay, so you've now read about purchasing a computer and various gadgets to go along with it. Fine and dandy. What about those of you who would like to join the online lifestyle, but really don't want to purchase a computer? Mr. Modem cares about you, too.

It wasn't very long ago, however, that I'd be forced to break it to you gently by telling you, in my uniquely inarticulate way, "It ain't gonna happen." But now, through the courtesy of WebTV, yesterday's impossibility is today's reality. With WebTV you can surf the World Wide Web using your television instead of a computer. For more on WebTV, see Chapter 8.

Modems

First, a definition: A modem is a gizmo which I believe comes from the French word *guizmeaux*. The literal translation is "Beware of writers who use fancy-sounding French words." A *modem* is a device that allows your computer to "talk" to other computers, whether they're located next door or around the world from each other. When we say that one computer is talking to another computer, it's really just exchanging data.

The data your computer produces is stored in digital units called *bits* and *bytes*. There are eight bits to one byte, and one byte equals…Wait. Shhhh! What's that sound I hear? Ah, yes, it's the unmistakable sound of eyes glazing over. Okay, let's move on.

In order for this data to slither out of your computer and onto the Internet (or vice versa), it needs to be converted from one format to another, from digital to analog. Think of it as translating the data from one language to another. And that's what a modem does. It modulates or translates the outgoing digital signals, turning them into analog, then demodulates or retranslates the incoming analog signals back into digital ones. Neato, huh?

Now, put the first two letters of the word MOdulate together with the first three letters of the word DEModulate, and what does it spell? It spells MODEM. Yes, indeedy, the word *modem* is actually an acronym and stands for MOdulate/DEModulate. Thank you, thankyouverymuch. That concludes the worthless information section of this chapter.

Purchasing a Modem

Modems are rated by their speed, measured in bits-per-second or bps, just like your car's speed is measured in miles-per-hour or mph. Because speed does not kill on the Information Superhighway, you'll want your new modem to be as fast as possible.

The fastest modems on the market for home users promise speeds of up to 56,000 bits-per-second, abbreviated as 56Kbps or just 56K. Of course, talk is cheap and they only *promise* speeds up to 56K. You won't actually achieve that speed yourself, of course, so try not to be too disappointed.

With telephone line noise, signal quality and your grandkiddos picking up the extension to use the telephone while you're online, the best you can expect to receive is 40 to 45K. But that's plenty fast enough to enjoy a rollicking good time in the Internet surf.

We'll discuss modems and data transmission (can't you just feel the excitement?) in greater detail in the section "Data Transmission 101," later in this chapter, but if you're shopping for a new modem, you'll want a 56K modem that supports the V.90 protocol.

One other thing to be aware of: All telephone lines are not created equal. It's possible, though not likely, that the telephone line between your home and your ISP may not support a 56K connection, so be sure to check with your telephone company as well as inquire of your ISP.

Your ISP will probably disavow all responsibility concerning telephone lines and refer you to your telephone company. Your telephone company will thank you for your call, tell you that your call is very important to them, and then place you on hold for a minimum of 37 minutes before disconnecting you. When you are able to access your telephone company's technical support department, they will probably disavow all responsibility and refer you back to your ISP.

In some areas, "bad" or old telephone cable in your area can present a problem when accessing the Internet or transmitting data. If you have neighbors who are online, ask them if they have experienced any difficulties accessing the Internet and if so, if they called the telephone company; or ask how they resolved the problem.

The V.90 protocol is supported by every Internet service provider, which was not the case with the old X2 and 56Kflex protocols. One distinct advantage to this standardization will be readily apparent if you're not happy with your current service and decide to move to a new ISP. You can now do that without having to worry about whether or not your new ISP will support your modem type.

What if you already have a pre-V.90 56K modem? Since there isn't any particular speed advantage to the V.90 over the X2 or 56Kflex, there's no need to upgrade to the V.90 version at this time. But if you upgrade from your current 56K and your ISP doesn't support it, it can actually reduce your connection speed. When in doubt, contact your ISP to see if your provider supports this new modem, and how long it will continue to support the type of modem you currently have.

There are a number of ways to determine the speed of your connection. While connected, place your cursor over the little icon on your Windows 95/98 task bar that shows you have a connection (it looks like two little computers connected together). This will display the speed of your connection by showing the number of bytes received, the number of bytes sent and at what overall transmission speed in bits-per-second. For a more comprehensive analysis, visit `http://www.toast.net` and click Performance Test.

So is it worth getting a 56K modem? Of course it is! Remember, the Internet is a grand adventure! Sure, something may not work perfectly right now, but technological improvements and enhancements arrive in rapid succession on the Internet, so if something is not working well for you at the moment, check back in an hour.

Modems and Cordless Telephones

It's an all-too-familiar scenario: Your modem dials-up to the Internet, you wait to hear the sound of your modem squealing with delight, and you get a busy signal. You give it another try. And another. Thirty minutes later, you're wondering why you ever bothered to venture onto the Internet in the first place. And much later, you're muttering and jabbing pins into your Mr. Modem voodoo doll.

It's very tempting at that point to blame your Internet service provider for substandard service, but that may not be the problem. If you're having trouble getting online and you share your residence with a cordless telephone, that may be the culprit. Yes, a cordless phone can hamper your ability to connect with the Internet. Hard to believe, but it can.

These powerful phones can continue to broadcast at 900 megahertz even when the cordless phone base is unplugged from the telephone line, resulting in busy signals when your modem is attempting to connect to the Internet. If unplugging the base of your cordless phone doesn't do the trick, try removing the batteries and unplugging the AC adapter. You might also try logging on from another phone jack.

If all else fails, try burying your cordless phone in the backyard and calling your local phone company for additional suggestions.

Ready, Willing, and Cable

Super high-speed access to the Internet is affordable, convenient, and becoming available in many areas of the country thanks to cable modems. I had one installed, and other than having to wear a cervical collar to prevent painful datalash from the speed at which Web pages snap onto the monitor, it's a very painless process.

Why would you want cable? Three words: Speed, speed, and more speed. Well, okay that's actually five words. If you're online now using a 28.8, 33.6, or 56K modem, that's theoretically 28,800, 33,600, or 56,000 bits per second and represents the speed at which data is transported into and out of your computer, e.g., downstream, upstream or download and upload.

Cable modem speeds vary, but in the downstream direction (surfing the Web, for example) speeds average between 2 and 10Mbps—million bits per second. In the upstream direction (sending files, for example), speeds average between 128K (128,000 bits per second) and 2Mbps. "Blazingly fast" about sums it up. Even at a "sluggish" 2Mbps, Web pages appear almost as rapidly as the images that fill your television screen when you switch channels. Downloading files from the Internet now takes seconds instead of minutes or even hours.

If you are interested in exploring high-speed access to the Internet, first check for availability of the service in your area by calling your local TV cable company. (Yes, this is the same cable that brings Nickelodeon into your home providing hundreds of mirth-filled hours of *Green Acres* reruns. Oh, that Mr. Haney!) Be sure to ask your cable provider how many subscribers to their Internet service will ultimately share a local node or point of access. This is important because too many people connecting at the same time can adversely affect access speeds. In my area, 1,000 subscribers per node is the maximum the cable provider will permit and that works out very well.

Cox Communications is one such company offering @Home cable access in many areas of the country. You can check service availability in your neighborhood by calling 1-800-234-4600 or by sending an e-mail to signup@cox.com.

For cable modems, recommended minimum computer requirements include a 486 DX2 with 66Mhz clock speed, 60MB available hard disk space, 16MB RAM, and Windows for Workgroups 3.11 or Windows 95/98. Those are the minimum requirements, which really are on the conservative side. If you're using a 486/66, I'd suggest investing in a new Pentium II or III computer first, then consider cable access to the Internet. It's no fun driving a Yugo on the Autobahn.

Once you determine service availability, your high-speed access specialist will ask you a few questions about your computer to be sure you have the minimum configuration requirements. Assuming you're "acceptable," an installation appointment will be scheduled and you'll be given some pre-installation instructions: i.e., nothing to eat after 10:00 P.M. and no fluids after midnight the evening before the procedure.

You will be instructed to back up your important files prior to the installation. You will also be advised that the folks doing the work will not be responsible for any data loss, power loss, hair loss—you name it, they're not responsible. If the cable modem bursts into flame and burns your house to the ground, they are not responsible. There are lots of caveat, hold-harmless, and indemnification clauses in the subscriber agreement that you probably won't read either. It's a document only a lawyer could love and much too scary for the rest of us.

On my C.I. Day, (Cable Installation Day), two friendly, courteous technicians (Jerry and James) appeared at my door. Jerry was the computer technician and James was the cable guy. I had existing cable service to my home office, so it wasn't necessary to install a new cable line. Instead, they placed a splitter device on the existing cable and attached a filter to the cable to prevent data bleed. I get queasy just thinking about it.

While James performed his cable work, Jerry set his perspiring 64-ounce Slurpy down on my mahogany desktop forming a lovely "Olympic rings" motif at no extra charge, and proceeded to deftly open up my computer as if it were a can of sardines. He then installed a

10Base-T Ethernet card. I don't know what a 10Base-T Ethernet card is either, but I sure do feel knowledgeable using technical sounding terms whenever I can.

Quick detour from the installation: The most popular kind of local-area network (LAN) is called an Ethernet, pronounced *EE-ther-net*. Most Ethernet networks use an architecture called 10BaseT, which stands for 10 million bits per second using "baseband" communications over Twisted Pair wire. 10BaseT networks require a network adapter card in each computer, special cables, and—does anybody really care about this? I didn't think so. Let's continue with the installation.

If you already have an Ethernet card in your computer, bully for you; if you're not sure, the installers will tell you. If you need one, the installers will have one in the truck. Trust me. They have everything in the truck.

With the Ethernet card installed and the cable splitter in place, one end of the split cable was hooked back up to the television and the other end inserted into the spiffy new cable modem sitting on my desk next to the monitor. The back of the cable modem has three orifices—or is it orifii? There's one for the cable, one for the power supply, and one that looks like a regular telephone jack on steroids. That one is provided for the cable that runs from the modem into the 10Base-T Ethernet card in the computer.

That completed the hook-up. The installer did it all. My sole responsibility was to stay out of the way, and I handled that responsibility quite nicely, if I do say so myself.

The cable modem is $10 \times 2 \times 7$ inches in size, has a series of reptilian fins on it that exist for cooling purposes and can double as a series of small shelves upon which to place your biscotti. The modem rests on its two-inch side, so it takes up a very small amount of desktop real estate. More importantly, it looks very, very high-tech.

The modem has four lights, tastefully arranged in two rows of two. Jerry explained that the top-left light signifies that the modem is powered on; the top-right light, which should be continually illuminated and not flickering, indicates a solid connection to the network (Internet); the bottom-left light indicates something, I can't remember, and the bottom-right light indicates traffic, whatever that means. Once I saw that the upper-right light was illuminated, I never heard another word. Who cares what the other lights represent? If I ever need to know, I'll call tech support.

Once everything was connected, the computer technician installed some software while the cable guy attached an oscilloscope to the cable and then insincerely, but enthusiastically exclaimed, "Wow! Look at that throughput! I've never seen a better connection than this. Yo, Jerry! Check it out, dude! You're going to have unbelievably fast access, Mr. Modem." The magic of the moment was only briefly interrupted when I screamed, "Praise the Cable!" and fell sobbing to my knees—not a pretty sight.

The installers departed and I sat down at the keyboard, eyeball-to-eyeball with the new @Home icon displayed on my Windows 98 desktop. The excitement was palpable. Clicking the new icon presented an opportunity to take a 10-minute tour of a wealth of resources provided by the cable company. It also afforded an opportunity to scream "hot diggity download!" in the privacy of my own home.

So what does all this excitement cost? It's surprisingly cost-effective when contrasted with typical $20/month, dial-up modem access provided by an Internet service provider. The installation cost $150, and the monthly charge for unlimited access is $44.95, which includes a $15/month charge for the cable modem rental. Unlike dial-up access to the Internet that ties up a telephone line, cable access is dedicated for full-time, 24-hours-a-day, 7-days-a-week access. You can also purchase the cable modem for approximately $400, but with the pace at which technology keeps changing, I wouldn't recommend buying a cable modem. Then again, I do own more than 300 8-track tapes, including "Abba's Greatest Hits," so what do I know? Helpful technical support is available 24-hours a day and is included in the cost of the service.

Contact your local television cable provider for additional information and to determine if access is available in your area.

Alternative High-Speed Access

When it comes to accessing the Internet, the one thing we're not lacking is options. The good news is that if there's a will to access, there's a way to access. We've already touched on 56K dial-up modems, WebTV, and high-speed cable access. The even better news is that cable isn't the only high-speed access alternative.

ISDN

ISDN stands for Integrated Services Digital Network, which is a method for sending voice, video and data over telephone lines. In essense, ISDN increases the capacity of your telephone line by converting the data transmission process from analog to digital.

ISDN service provides access speeds as high as 128K, which is twice the speed of the fastest 56K analog modem. ISDN lines can carry simultaneous connections, meaning you can be talking on the phone at the same time you're checking e-mail or visiting Web sites.

A friendly rivalry exists between enthusiasts of alternate high-speed access technologies. DSL and cable access subscribers like to say that ISDN stands for "It Still Does Nothing," but that's really not the case. ISDN has been a bit slow to evolve, but that's rapidly changing.

For more information, check with your local telephone company to determine if ISDN service is available in your area. There's also an ISDN hotline for additional information that's sponsored by a consortium of Baby Bell telephone companies. Call 800-992-4736 or visit `http://www.bellcore.com/isdn` for more information.

DSL

As exciting as cable and ISDN access to the Internet are, they are not the only high-speed access games in town! A DSL (Digital Subscriber Line) uses modem technology that transforms ordinary phone lines (called twisted copper pair lines) into high-speed digital lines for super-fast Internet access.

There are a multitude of flavors of DSL, though ASDL (Asymmetric Digital Subscriber Line) and XDSL are the two most commonly referenced members of the DSL family. DSLs run the gamut from ADSL through VDSL or more DSLs than you can shake an acronym at.

A Digital Subscriber Line uses digital coding or programming to squeeze up to 99% more capacity out of a telephone line without affecting regular voice and related telephone services. This means that you can be talking on the phone and sending a fax while surfing the World Wide Web. All you need is a pair of cymbals fastened between your knees and even the best of the one-man bands would have nothing on you!

DSL access can provide speeds up to 2Mbps or million bits per second. Cable access, by comparison, ranges from 2 to 10Mbps, while ISDN lags behind at a sluggish (relatively speaking) 128K. All these alternative high-speed methods of accessing the Internet share one common attribute: they're all very fast when contrasted with a 56K modem.

Pricing for DSL service is very competitive with cable access, and the service is available in many major markets. Contact your local phone company to determine availability and pricing in your area.

Data Transmission 101

Understanding the relationship between data transmission and modem speeds can be confusing. Speeds are quantified in either bits per second (bps) or thousand bits per second (Kbps, meaning kilobits per second). Sometimes modem speed is incorrectly characterized as the baud rate of a modem. If you have previously referred to the baud rate of a modem, don't be ashamed. You're in very good company. Technically, baud is the number of times per second that the carrier signal shifts value—whatever that means. For example, a 1,200bps modem actually runs at 300 baud, but it moves four bits per baud—and that ain't good. ($4 \times 300 = 1,200$ bits per second.)

So, what's a bit? A bit equals four henways. What's a henway? Oh, about three or four pounds. (Insert rim-shot here). And you thought baudeville was dead? Shame on you!

Okay, back to bitness. A bit is the smallest piece of data recognized by a computer, with the possible exception of Cheese Doodle crumbs that occasionally fall into the keyboard. There are eight bits to one byte, and a byte is a letter or a character. The word character is nine bytes because it contains nine letters. Such brilliance! (Memo to self: Increase the price of this book. It's just too darned informative.) One page of text, double-spaced, is approximately 1,820 bytes or 1.8 kilobytes, also referred to as 1.8KB.

Since there are eight bits to a byte, multiply the number of bytes by eight to determine the number of bits; i.e., one page of text is approximately 14,560 bits. So if a modem is capable of transmitting 28,800 bits per second, by comparison that's almost two pages per second.

Here's an easy way to keep the relationship between data transmission speeds straight—if there's any reason in the world to keep it straight. Think of data flowing in and out of your modem at 28,800bps as water flowing from a faucet about as fast as you'd fill up a water glass.

Using a 56K or 56,000bps modem would be analogous to water flowing from a garden hose that you might use to water your flowers.

ISDN access is higher-speed access, with data transmitting at 128K. This would be the equivalent, using our cloying water-through-the-hose analogy, of the water flow from two garden hoses.

A more recent form of Internet access is via satellite. A small satellite dish will receive (download) data from the Internet at 400K which would be like the flow of water through seven garden hoses. Satellite access is one-way access, however. Data transmitted from your computer to the Internet (uploading) would still be governed by the speed of your modem.

Cable access, which was mentioned earlier in this chapter, moves information at a data-dusting 2 to 10Mbps or million bits per second. Roll up your cuffs for this one, because it's the equivalent of water flowing through 53 to 78 garden hoses. A virtual deluge of data!

In a survey of 7,000 Internet users aged 50+, Excite! search engine discovered 83% log on every day and spend more than ten hours a week online.

Source: Excite!, http://www.excite.com

High-speed access to the Internet will greatly enhance your Internet experience and is the Holy Grail for surfers worldwide. The rule of thumb is, "the faster, the better." If you're using an older computer with a 28.8K modem, you can upgrade your modem to 56K for less than $100. It's well worth considering.

If you belong to a homeowners' association, inquire at your next meeting if members would be interested in joining together to bring high-speed Internet access into your community. You'll never know who is surfing the Internet if you don't ask. Today, many homeowners' associations are utilizing e-mail and their own Web sites for disseminating news and information to residents. It's convenient, cost-effective, environmentally responsible, and is rapidly evolving into the Welcome Wagon of the millenium.

Locating an Internet Service Provider

For most of us, obtaining access to the Internet through an Internet service provider (ISP) is the most cost-effective and efficient way to join the online lifestyle.

Locating an ISP within your community or on a national level isn't difficult. Check your local newspaper's business section and chances are you will find a plethora of providers trolling for your Internet access dollars. You can also check the Yellow Pages or visit a bookstore and purchase a copy of just about any Internet magazine, which will include listings for national level Internet access providers, as well.

Other suggestions for locating an ISP would include asking for a recommendation at several local software stores, asking friends, or calling an Internet consultant for a recommendation. Most Internauts are more than happy to share this information. If you belong to a computer club, social group, high-tech religious cult or similar organization, be sure to check with other members. In increasing numbers, residential communities are being constructed already prewired for high-speed cable or other access to the Internet. Could there be more of an incentive to move in? I think not.

Readers of my "Ask Mr. Modem!" column frequently ask about the difference between an ISP and a service such as AOL (America Online). It's actually a very good question and fortunately, one that I can answer or this paragraph wouldn't make a great deal of sense.

While an ISP provides access to a spectacular selection of informational resources on the Internet, the focus of an online service such as America Online or CompuServe is more narrow. It provides information, or *content*, within its own perimeter. An ISP, on the other hand, exists primarily to provide access to the global Internet. Think of an ISP as a gatekeeper or toll collector at the on ramp to the Internet. Once you're connected, you're effectively pulling out into the high-speed lane.

Due to the enormous popularity of the Internet, information services such as AOL and others have been compelled to provide access to the Internet itself, as well as to their own content. Within that context, the service then becomes a *gateway* to the Internet. Think of AOL and other online services as taking a bus tour on the information superhighway. You're on the highway, but looking through the bus windows as your tour guide points out sights of interest. An Internet service provider doesn't typically provide content other than perhaps a cheesy home page that you probably won't want to look at each time you log on.

If you already have access to the Internet via America Online or you know somebody who has access to the Internet, you can easily locate a local ISP by utilizing any of the following Web-based resources:

The List   This Web site allows you to locate a provider that offers the access speed and related services to meet your needs and budget (see Figure 3.1). More than 6,500 ISPs are searchable by area code, country code, United States only, or exclusively Canada.

```
http://thelist.internet.com
```

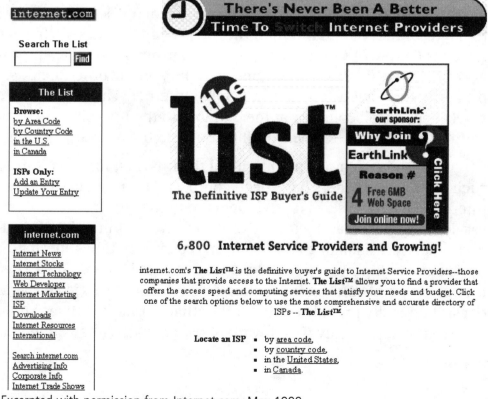

Excerpted with permission from Internet.com, May 1999.

FIGURE 3.1: Use The List to locate an Internet service provider.

isps.com   Sponsored by Earthlink Network, this site provides searchable access to more than 4,000 ISPs. You can search by price, area code, name, as well as national ISPs and toll-free ISPs.

```
http://www.isps.com
```

The Ultimate Web ISP List   Use this site's "Simple Search" for a quick search of all matching ISPs within any area code. Use the "Power Search" to include variables such as modem or connection speed, then refine your search by selecting additional criteria.

```
http://webisplist.internetlist.com
```

There are other ways to obtain access to the Internet as well. For example, if you have an affiliation with a college or university, chances are that institution provides Internet access to its students and faculty. Many corporations and businesses also provide access.

Most communities offer access via *freenets* or community-sponsored access available to residents of a given city or state, typically through the local library. A call to your state or municipal Chamber of Commerce will assist you in this regard.

So what does an Internet service provider actually do? An ISP maintains a full-time, high-speed connection to the Internet that is "subdivided" to provide you, me and other individuals with an inexpensive connection.

There are several things to look for when selecting an ISP: location, stability, customer service, performance and price—or LSCPP, verbalized as *liskp* for mnemonic enthusiasts.

Location

It can actually be more expensive to dial an ISP within your state than to dial one out of state if you cannot locate an ISP in your local calling area. Many larger ISPs do offer 800 access numbers but typically charge for connect time on a per-minute basis which tends to average around $6 per hour. While that might seem expensive at first, it is usually more cost-efficient than almost any long distance direct-dial price if you are required to dial outside of your local calling area. Whenever possible, select an ISP that is only a local phone call away.

Stability

It's always best if you can open an account with an ISP that has an established track record. The entire ISP industry is only a very few years old, so be wary of any ISP that claims to have been "Serving the Internet Community since 1952." Stability is particularly important because once you are on the Internet you will be sharing your e-mail address as you begin corresponding with friends and family. Your e-mail address will become as important to you—and as widely distributed—as your telephone or fax number. If at some point in the future you have to change your e-mail address because your ISP takes a nose dive (term of art); at best, it can be inconvenient, at worst it can ruin your life and kill your houseplants.

There are "lifetime" e-mail addresses available, though I'm not sure if they're referring to my lifetime, the company's lifetime, or the lifetime of the typical fruit fly. If it's my lifetime they're referring to, I'm not sure I like the sound of that. Perhaps they know something that I don't.

Technical Support

If you're new to the Internet, customer service or technical support is particularly important. The Internet is a wild and woolly grand adventure, and that means that you are blazing new cybertrails in the process of learning what it's all about. While that's poetic as all get out and sounds very adventuresome, what it actually means is that the technology of the Internet isn't at the plug-and-play level. Close, but not quite. Many would-be Internetters will have to install a modem, install software, and configure the software to work with a particular ISP, so it might be comforting to know you can call your friendly ISP's tech support people for a helping hand, if necessary.

The good news is that purchasing a new computer today will be as close to Internet ready or plug-and-play as anything. So if you're teetering on the brink and can't decide whether to upgrade your trusty 486 to make it Internet capable or purchase a new computer, my advice is to go for what's behind curtain number two, Monty, and buy a new computer.

Most ISPs are acutely aware of the hurdles new users face while dipping a toe in the Internet pond for the first time. They are also aware that it's not always a walk in the park for newbies. Because of this heightened awareness, many ISPs offer wonderful technical support and ease of installation with very detailed instructions. Some ISPs will even make house calls (don't tell the AMA) and for a small fee ($50 to $75), will install and configure everything for you and get you up and surfing. While this service is not absolutely necessary, if you don't enjoy tinkering with your computer or cursing loudly in the privacy of your own home, you might want to explore the availability of on-site installation service. Look at it this way: Even if it costs you $75, it's still cheaper than Prozac.

Performance

The average ISP continues to grow at a rate of more than 50 percent per year. As in any business, that type of extraordinary growth can have an adverse effect on performance. It doesn't appear to be a function of large ISP versus small ISP—sometimes referred to as ISP-envy, nor a manifestation of performance anxiety, it's more a function of the ability of the

ISP to manage its own growth. Inability to log on, repeated busy signals, heartburn, indigestion, and gastrointestinal distress are just a few of the most common indications of a lack of performance on the part of an ISP.

One question that is an absolute must to ask any prospective Internet service provider, and one that directly affects performance is, "What is your user-to-modem ratio?" Anything less than 12:1 is acceptable. The higher the ratio; i.e. 15:1 or 20:1, the more likely that you will experience a busy signal when you attempt to log on. A user-to-modem ratio of 10:1 is ideal. We can dream, can't we? (See Appendix A, "50 Questions to Ask an ISP.")

Pricing

Though it varies throughout the country, the average price range appears to be $15 to $25 per month for unlimited access to the Internet. I have also encountered some annual payment programs that provide unlimited Internet access for $99 to $150 per year. In some rural areas, monthly rates can be as high as $35 per month. A review of pricing information provided by over 3,700 Internet service providers revealed that the average 56K dial-up price is $19.95 per month for unlimited access.

Some ISPs are moving away from unlimited flat-rate service and heading toward a certain number of Internet access hours for x dollars per month. Additional hours are billed on a per-hour basis. Other ISPs offer unadvertised special pricing, so be sure to investigate pricing plans thoroughly.

You will discover that some ISPs offer two, three and sometimes four different pricing programs. Most will offer a flat monthly price for unlimited access. Many ISPs also offer alternative programs with monthly minimums often as low as $4.95 per month, with slightly higher hourly charges and fewer hours included in the base charge. $4.95 per month with 10 hours included and $1 for each additional hour is fairly typical.

Speaking of time spent online each month, I recently conducted a quasi-scientific study among the readers of my "Ask Mr. Modem!" newspaper column. The column reaches more than two million households every month. What my exhaustive study revealed is remarkably consistent with bonafide studies conducted by researchers who know what they're doing. These studies reveal the following amount of time spent online per month, broken down by age group—or time spent online per month by broken-down age group, in my case:

55 +	38 hours
45-54	34 hours
25-34	28 hours
18-24	22 hours

(**Source:** *Media Metrix Internet Research*)

The Internet is clearly a phenomenon within the seniors community. We utilize the Internet more frequently and for longer periods of time than any other segment of the population. And the best is yet to come.

Establishing an Internet Account

To obtain a dial-up connection to the Internet, you will need four things:

- Software for your computer to access e-mail, the World Wide Web, and other Internet resources

- A modem connected to your serial port (called a COM port or COMmunications port), or an internal modem

- A dial-up account with an Internet service provider
- A telephone line

If you are using Windows 95 or 98—and if you're not, you really should be—you already have the software you need to connect to the Internet. If your ISP requires something extra-spatial, as we say in Modemville, you will be provided with the appropriate software and instructions.

Establishing an account with an Internet service provider involves calling the ISP on the telephone (how archaic!) and providing them with some basic sign-up information and a credit card number—preferably your own. It may also involve configuring some software with some basic information provided by your ISP. In most cases, the ISP will send you a diskette or CD-ROM via U.S. Postal Service (referred to in Internet parlance as *snail mail*) with the requisite software configured for you.

It typically takes five minutes or less to establish an Internet account with an ISP. During this process you will select and receive your own unique e-mail address. Your ISP will handle the registration process and will probably ask you to choose three alternate "usernames" to submit for registration, so be thinking of names before you sign up. A traditional naming convention used by many Internet users consists of the first letter of your first name along with your surname. For example, *rsherman*, is followed by what is called the host and domain name, so the complete e-mail address would appear *rsherman@host.domain*. You are not limited to the traditional first letter and surname style by any means. Selecting a name for your e-mail account presents a wonderful opportunity to be creative, so have fun! For example, my e-mail address is MrModem@home.com. If you wish to contact me to tell me how much you're enjoying this book, this would be the appropriate e-mail address to use.

Every e-mail address is constructed in the same manner: Reading from left to right, first is the username, followed by the "at" sign, followed by the host and domain. That all sounds very technical, but it's really not. The username is you, the host is your ISP, and the domain will typically be .com indicating that your host is a commercial entity, .org if it's a non-profit organization, .net if it's part of a network, or .edu if it's an educational institution.

BPWI (Bonus Piece of Worthless Information): The "at" sign or @ sign is formally known as a *streusel*. Next time you want to impress your friends or bore them to tears, just trot out this little gem and you'll be sure to be the talk of the neighborhood.

Your Internet username can be your real name, a pseudonym, or just about anything you would like to use. One caveat: You might want to avoid being too cutesy with your username selection. Nicknames or pet names, for example, can come back to haunt you. Though you may start out using the Internet for fun and exploration just to see what all the Internet fuss is about, there are countless business, professional, and social opportunities that await your arrival. Just about the time you start discussing an opportunity with a prospective customer or client or you meet a very special person online, you may not want *Stinky* or *Muffin* to appear as your Internet identification.

On the other hand, if you're primarily going to be using the Internet for staying in touch with family members or socializing with other individuals who share similar interests—a cyberspace pen pal or *e-pal*, for example—take it from Mr. Modem: just choose a username that you're comfortable with, then sit back, relax and have fun!

What's Next?

Now that we've reviewed the basics and know how to get started, let's continue to the next chapter where we'll explore a typical Internet installation.

A Typical Internet Installation

An excruciatingly detailed tour through modem setup, configuration, and dial-up networking is the highlight of this chapter. Can't you just feel the excitement? Be careful not to get a paper cut as you move quickly to the next chapter.

Before you can dive into the Internet surf, you must first set up an Internet connection on your computer. There are actually several ways to establish this connection. If you have installed Microsoft Plus! you may already have the Internet Jumpstart Kit which will guide you through many of the steps we're going to go through in this chapter. Microsoft Plus! is an add-on program that isn't free, although some new computers do have it preinstalled. It is available at finer software stores everywhere.

If you already have Internet access and simply want to use that same ISP account on your new Windows 98 computer, please skip to the section cleverly entitled "Using an Existing Internet Account on a New Computer with Windows 98," later in this chapter. (I know what you're thinking: I can't believe how incredibly helpful this book is. That's okay, go right ahead and say it. You'll feel better. Now, here's an idea: Why not make yourself feel even better by telling everybody you know? Indulge yourself. You deserve it!)

Throughout this book, I utilize the ➤ symbol as an arrow or a visual instruction, indicating the next step or next selection in a sequence of selections, and bold for items you can click or select. For example, **File ➤ Open** indicates that you should click the **File** menu. When you do that, the File menu items are displayed, and among them you will see Open. Next, click **Open**. Similarly, **Edit ➤ Preferences** means to click the **Edit** menu, then click the menu item **Preferences**. Got it? Wonderful! Let's continue.

If you're using Windows 95 (not Windows 98), your computer may also have an Internet Wizard lurking within. You can easily check by clicking on **Start ➤ Programs ➤ Accessories ➤ Internet Tools**. If you see **Get on the Internet**, click it and just follow the prompts. The Internet Wizard will guide you through the connection setup process. Be sure to have the information discussed in the "Collecting Information From Your ISP" section of this chapter at hand before launching the Wizard.

After you locate an Internet service provider (see "Locating an Internet Service Provider" in Chapter 3) and establish an account, you will be provided with a start-up disk or CD-ROM that contains your ISP's setup program. Follow the instructions provided by your ISP unless you're feeling particularly frisky, in which case you should be as creative as you wish. After indulging your creative impulses and making a mess of things, you can always return to this chapter, follow my instructions and straighten everything out.

Since there are a number of ways to set up your connection to the Internet, I'm going to first walk through the steps any Windows 95 user can utilize without obtaining special software. It's an approach destined to warm the cockles of purist hearts everywhere.

I'll cover the Windows 98 approach later in this chapter.

Collecting Information from Your ISP

No matter which approach you take to set up your Internet connection, there are a few pieces of information you will need to obtain from your ISP before you begin. Be sure you have the following information close at hand before proceeding to the next section:

- Your Internet service provider's name.

- Your local telephone access number. This is the telephone number your modem will dial to connect you to the Internet.

- Your User ID, sometimes referred to as a Username, more often referred to as, "Holy Modem! I can't remember my $%&# username!"

- Your password. This is the password you provided to your Internet service provider when establishing your account. Your ISP may have provided you with an initial password. You can always change it later.

- Your IP (Internet Protocol) address, if any. When entering your IP settings later on, you'll have a choice of Server Assigned IP Address (referred to in geekspeak parlance as a *dynamically assigned* IP address), in which case you will not enter an IP address, or Specify an IP Address, (referred to as a *static* IP address), in which case your ISP will provide you with the correct IP address.

- Your DNS (Domain Name Server) address. Again, you will have a choice of Server Assigned Name Server Address, in which case you will not enter a Primary or Secondary DNS address, or Specify Name Server Address, in which case your ISP will provide you with the correct Primary DNS and possibly Secondary DNS addresses.

If your ISP provides you with a DNS address, it will appear as a series of numbers such as 198.24.68.10. If provided to you telephonically, you will hear someone cryptically articulate, "One-nine-eight-dot-two-four-dot-six-eight-dot-one-zero." Admittedly, it sounds a bit strange the first time you encounter geekspeak in its natural habitat.

As long as you're gathering information from your ISP, ask if there is anything else your ISP would recommend. Every ISP is different, so always defer to your ISP when it comes to these settings.

Setting Up Your Modem— Windows 95

The first thing you need to do is make sure that you have set up your modem properly and that your modem is functioning. You'll have better luck logging on to the Internet using two tin cans connected by a piece of string if you do not have a properly installed modem. If you already have a modem installed and configured, good for you! You can safely skip the following "Setting Up Your Modem" section—unless you have insomnia or another form of sleep disorder. Trust me, what follows is a major snoozer. However, if you haven't configured your modem or you just want to be absolutely sure it is correctly installed, feel free to follow along.

1. Click the **Start** button and select **Settings** ➢ **Control Panel**.

2. Double-click the **Add New Hardware** icon which brings up the Add New Hardware Wizard.

3. Click **Next**.

4. You will be asked if you would like Windows to detect whether the hardware (modem) is already installed. Click **Yes**.

   After Windows has done its detection work and discovered that you have a modem installed, the Verify Modem screen will appear and display The Following Modem Was Found on Communications Port (COM1 or COM2) and it will show the name of your modem.

5. If this information is correct, click the **Next** button, which will bring up the Install New Modem screen, then click **Finish**.

6. If the information is incorrect—if it doesn't list a modem or it lists a modem other than the one your computer has installed—click the **Change** button and the Wizard will let you select a modem manually from a list of manufacturers and models. After selecting the correct modem, click **Finish**.

If you want to change your modem settings at any point in the future, go to the Control Panel by choosing **Start** ➢ **Settings** ➢ **Control Panel** and then double-click the **Modems** icon.

There are currently 93 million Americans (34 percent of the U.S. population) accessing the Web.

Source: Jupiter Communications, http://www.jup.com

Teaching Your Modem to Dial

Now that your modem is configured to work in peaceful harmony with Windows 95, you must instruct it to dial the telephone number provided by your ISP so you can log on to the Internet.

1. Click the **Start** button and select **Settings** ➢ **Control Panel** to return to the Control Panel and click the **Modems** icon. The Modems Properties screen will appear.

2. Click the **Properties** button, which will display the configuration of your modem. Most of these will default to the most commonly used settings, but you may want to adjust your speaker volume (under the **General** tab) using the little slidey thing (sorry for the technical talk) or set your Maximum speed to 57,600 if you're using a 56Kbps or slower modem. Do not place a check mark in the **Only Connect at This Speed** field.

3. Click the **Connection** tab and confirm that your connection preferences are correct. Data bits 8, Parity none, Stop bits 1 is standard, but check with your ISP to determine if you should be using any other settings. Feel free to click the **Port Settings** and **Advanced** buttons, but my recommendation is to leave everything alone. In most instances, the default settings will be just fine.

4. Click **OK** to return to the Modems Properties screen and make sure you're looking at the General tab.

5. Click the large **Dialing Properties** button located in the lower portion of the screen. This is where you instruct your modem how to dial from your default location. Just fill in the blanks at this point: Type **Home** or leave **Default Location** in the **I Am Dialing From:** field.

6. Next, type in your area code and what country you're logging on from. You can click the little down arrow to the right of the country field to display a listing of countries.

If you're setting this up on a notebook computer and want to dial into your ISP while traveling, you can create a new location to call from by clicking the **New** button.

7. Fill in the appropriate fields in the lower half of the screen under How I Dial from This Location and click **OK** when you're done. This will return you to the Modems Properties screen.

8. Click **OK** again to return to the Control Panel.

You may be wondering why you didn't type in the telephone number provided by your ISP at this point. Rest assured you haven't missed anything. That comes later.

Congratulations! You have now configured your modem properly, so feel free to pause for a quiet moment of spiritual reflection, let out a whoop and a holler, or proceed to the next section so we can install and set up your dial-up networking.

Installing Dial-Up Networking in 39 Easy Steps

After you have run your ISP's setup program, sometimes referred to as a start-up disk, you will need to install Windows 95 Dial-Up Networking and configure it for use with your ISP.

For the sake of this excruciatingly detailed exercise, I'm going to assume ISPNet is my Internet service provider and my username is *ras* (my initials). Be sure to enter the correct information provided by your ISP for your Internet account, however.

1. We concluded the previous "Teaching Your Modem to Dial" section at the Control Panel, but if you are joining our magical mysterious tour at this point from your Desktop, return to the Control Panel by clicking the **Start** button, then selecting **Settings** ➤ **Control Panel**.

2. Double-click the **Add/Remove Programs** icon (shown in Figure 4.1).

3. Click the tab marked **Windows Setup**.

4. Click once on **Communications** and then click the button marked **Details…**.

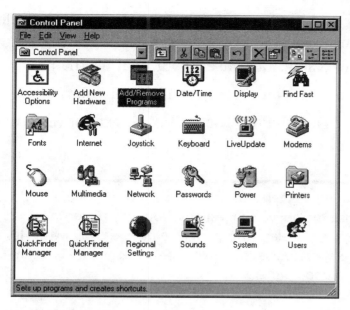

FIGURE 4.1: Control Panel, Add/Remove Programs icon

5. If the box directly to the left of Dial-Up Networking is already checked, then click the **Cancel** button in the Details... window and again in the Add/Remove Programs window and skip to step 7. Do not pass Go, do not collect $200.

6. If the box directly to the left of Dial-Up Networking is not already checked, then click in that box to place a check mark there. Click the **OK** button at the bottom of the Details... window and again in the Add/Remove Programs window. Your computer may prompt you for the necessary disk(s) or CD-ROM so that it can install the Dial-Up Networking component of Windows 95. Follow your computer's prompts until Dial-Up Networking is installed. Towards the end of this installation you may be asked for some identification information. As long as your computer is not on a Local Area Network (LAN), you can use the following information:

Computer Name: **ras** (insert your own username)

Workgroup: **ISPNet** (insert the name of your ISP)

Computer Description: **Richard A. Sherman** (insert your full name)

While you must enter something in each blank field, you do not have to use the above suggestions. You may dither for hours as you struggle to select the perfect entries, if you wish. It's all meaningless, of course, but if you are dither-prone, who am I to deny you a good dither?

Configuring Dial-Up Networking: Part I

After the Dial-Up Networking component is installed, you will need to configure it for use with your ISP's network.

7. Click the **Start** button and select **Settings** ➣ **Control Panel** to go to the Control Panel again. Double-click the **Network** icon.

8. When the Network window opens, you may see a list of network components already installed. Lucky you! If your computer is part of a Local Area Network (LAN), this would be a good time to awaken your LAN administrator and ask your LAN man or woman to make the rest of the changes in your Network window.

9. You may see Client for Microsoft Networks in the list of installed components. If you do, skip to step 10. If you do not, click the **Add...** button, then click **Client** and then again on the new

Add... button. From the Manufacturers list on the left side, select Microsoft. The list on the right side will change when you do this. Select **Client for Microsoft Networks** from the available list of network clients on the right side. Now click the **OK** button.

10. You will be back at the Network window now and Client for Microsoft Networks will be in the list of installed network components. Look through the list of components again and determine if you have Dial-Up Adapter installed. If you do, skip to step 11. If you do not, click the **Add...** button. Then click **Adapter** and then again on the new **Add...** button. From the Manufacturers list on the left side, select **Microsoft**. The list on the right side will change when you do this. It's déjà vu all over again. Select **Dial-Up Adapter** from the available list of Network Adapters on the right side. Now click the **OK** button.

11. You will again be back at the Network window and Dial-Up Adapter will appear in the list of installed network components. Look through the list of components to see if you have TCP/IP installed. If you do, skip to step 12. If you do not, click the **Add...** button. Then click **Protocol** and then again on the new **Add...** button. From the Manufacturers list on the left side, select **Microsoft**. The list on the right side will change when you do this, "yadda, yadda, yadda." Select **TCP/IP** from the list on the right. Now click the **OK** button.

12. You will now be back at the Network window and TCP/IP will appear in the list of installed network components. Look through the entire list of installed network components. You may have some items in your list other than those that you have just recently added. If you are not on a LAN, remove any additional items in your network components list. (If you are on a LAN, consult your LAN administrator before removing anything or risk being slapped silly for tampering with the network.)

Start at the top of the list and remove any component that is not Client for Microsoft Networks, Dial-Up Adapter, or TCP/IP. To remove a component, highlight it by placing your cursor on it and clicking once, and then click the **Remove** button (see Figure 4.2).

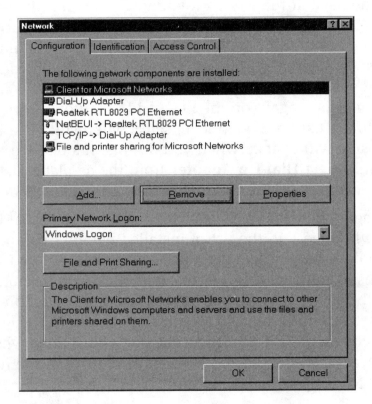

FIGURE 4.2: Installed Network Components

13. You will next be required to make changes in the TCP/IP configuration for your ISP. Highlight TCP/IP in the components list by clicking it once. Be gentle with your mouse. (Mice need love, too.) Click once again the **Properties** button.

14. You will see several tabs in the TCP/IP Properties window (shown in Figure 4.3). The IP Address tab should be in front. Make sure it's set to Obtain an IP Address Automatically. (Again, this is for use in our example only. Check with your ISP to confirm their requirements regarding this configuration.) Click the **WINS Configuration** tab and set it to Disable WINS resolution. (If you are seeking a detailed, highly technical explanation of the WINS configuration and its effect on the ozone layer, please keep reading. You won't find it here, of course, but if you keep reading, you'll forget about this WINS configuration mumbo-jumbo and we'll both be happier.)

Those tabs mentioned previously are the only tabs that you need to tweak. All others should be left at their default settings. Click the **OK** button at the bottom of the TCP/IP Properties window. This will take you back to the Network window.

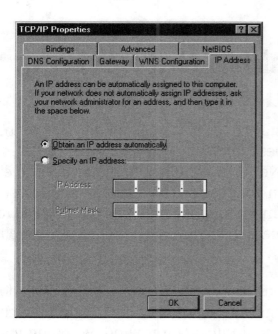

FIGURE 4.3: TCP/IP Properties

15. Click the **OK** button in the Network window. Windows 95 may ask you for your original Windows 95 floppy disks or CD-ROM. If you have them, you must produce them. What Mr. Gates wants, Mr. Gates gets and Mr. Gates is requesting your floppies or CD-ROM. Insert Disk 1 or your CD-ROM.

16. After your computer finishes copying selected files while you just sit there like a lump—my favorite computing position, by the way—Windows 95 will ask you if you want to restart. The question refers to your computer, not your life. You *must* restart Windows 95 for all these changes to take effect.

After Windows 95 restarts, you will need to enter the Dial-Up Networking portion of Windows 95 to finalize your ISP's configuration, so let's proceed to Part II and enjoy the exciting conclusion.

Configuring Dial-Up Networking: Part II (The Sequel)

After your computer has restarted, double-click on the My Computer icon on your Windows 95 Desktop. When My Computer opens, you will see an icon for the Dial-Up Networking folder. You may need to either scroll down to find it or open your eyes if they happen to be closed. If you absolutely, positively cannot find this folder, you may need to reinstall Dial-Up Networking (see steps 1 through 6). Then double-click the **Dial-Up Networking** folder.

17. If you have never used Dial-Up Networking before, Windows 95 will automatically begin the process of creating a new connection. You will see a small information window telling you what

Dial-Up Networking does. Click the **Next** button. If you have used Dial-Up Networking before, you must double-click the **Make New Connection** icon.

18. In the field labeled Type a Name for the Computer You Are Dialing, change the contents of the field by inserting the name of your ISP—e.g. **ISPNet**.

19. In the second box labeled Select a Modem, you should see your modem listed. If you do not see your modem listed or appearing in the drop-down menu, your modem is not properly installed. Couldn't you just die? You must install and configure your modem before continuing. See "Setting Up Your Modem" earlier in this chapter or consult your Windows 95 help system and modem manual for additional assistance. Once you see your modem listed (an indication that it has been properly installed), click the **Next** button.

20. You will now see fields for Area Code, Telephone Number, and Country Code. Type in the appropriate area code and telephone number. This is the telephone number provided to you by your ISP; the one your modem will dial so you can log on to the Internet. Then click **Next**.

21. You will then be face-to-face with a screen advising you that you have successfully set up a new dial-up networking connection for your ISP. Congratulations! It's too soon to gloat, so click the **Finish** button and let's keep moving forward.

22. After clicking **Finish** you will be returned to the Dial-Up Networking folder. Click once on the newly created icon containing the name of your ISP or whatever name you entered while completing step 18. Go to the Connections menu at the top of the window and select **Settings**. The General tab will be displayed (see Figure 4.4).

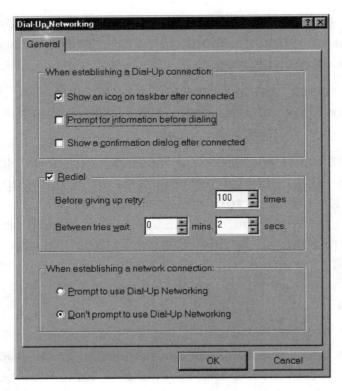

FIGURE 4.4: Dial-Up Networking, General tab

Mr. Modem's exhaustive and frequently inaccurate research reveals the General tab was named after the Gen. Phineas Tab, a respected Civil War hero who uttered the immortal words, "I have not yet begun to download."

23. Click the small box labeled **Redial**. Set the box labeled **Before Giving Up Retry** to the number of times you wish your modem to automatically redial if it cannot connect. Since your modem may require a few seconds to reset itself during redials, I would

recommend setting the **Between Tries Wait** field to three to five seconds. Your modem will not work without this delay, and it will file a grievance against you if you try to force it to work. I also recommend selecting the option **Don't Prompt to Use Dial-Up Networking** to avoid any problems. Click the **OK** button.

24. You will now be back at the Dial-Up Networking folder. Your ISP's icon should still be highlighted. Right-click and select **Properties**.

25. A window displaying the name of your ISP in the Title Bar will open. Click the tab labeled **Server Types** (shown in Figure 4.5).

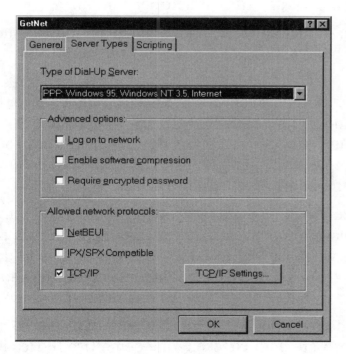

FIGURE 4.5: Dial-Up Networking Properties, Server Types

26. Check with your ISP for recommended settings, but generally the Type of Dial-Up Server should be set to PPP: Windows 95, Windows NT 3.5, Internet.

Under Advanced Options, there should be no check marks appearing next to Log On to Network, Enable Software Compression, or Require Encrypted Password.

Under Allowed Network Protocols, there should be no check marks appearing next to NetBEUI and IPX/SPX Compatible, but make sure TCP/IP does have a check mark appearing to the left.

Once you have these settings configured according to your ISP's requirements, click the **TCP/IP Settings** button.

27. At the top of the window, Server Assigned IP Address should be selected, but again, always defer to your ISP's recommended settings.

In the middle of the screen, select **Specify Name Server Addresses**. In this field you will enter the Primary and Secondary DNS (Domain Name Server) addresses obtained from your ISP. For our example we're going to use **123.456.7.89** and enter it in the field to the immediate right of Primary DNS.

In the field to the immediate right of Secondary DNS you will once again have to obtain this address from your ISP, but for our example we'll use **987.654.3.21**. Leave the fields to the right of Primary WINS and Secondary WINS exactly as they appear. Don't change a thing unless your ISP instructs you otherwise.

Make sure the two check boxes at the bottom of the TCP/IP Settings screen are both checked, one being Use IP Header Compression and the other being Use Default Gateway on Remote Network.

When you have entered the settings as described above or in conformance with your ISP's recommendations, click **OK** and return to the Server Types window.

28. Click **OK** to return to the window displaying the name of your ISP.

29. Click **OK** to return to the Dial-Up Networking window.

Deactivating Area Code Dialing

If you are connecting to the Internet using a local telephone number (as opposed to a long-distance number that requires 1- followed by the area code), you will need to modify the dialer setting which often defaults to dialing the area code. You won't know if your area code is going to be dialed automatically until you log on for the first time, but if it does, to prevent the area code from dialing, do the following:

You should still be in the Dial-Up Networking window. If not, from your Windows Desktop click **My Computer**, then click **Dial-Up Networking**. Highlight the icon displaying the name of your ISP, right-click, and select **Properties**. Remove the check mark to the left of Use Country Code and Area Code then click **OK** to exit.

Configuring Dial-Up Networking: Part II Continues

We've almost completed the 39 Steps to Internet Nirvana, so let's pick up where we left off prior to "Deactivating Area Code Dialing."

30. Create a shortcut on your Desktop to make it easy to connect to the Internet in the future. To accomplish this, go to the Dial-Up Networking folder and highlight your ISP's icon.

31. Click **File** located in the top left-hand corner and select **Create Shortcut**. Windows 95 will inform you that it cannot create a shortcut right there in the Dial-Up Networking folder, but it will thoughtfully ask if you wish to create it on your Desktop. Click **Yes**.

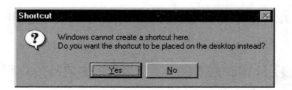

Windows 95 will create a Shortcut to (*YourISP*) icon on your Desktop.

Close the Dial-Up Networking folder by clicking the Close button (X) in the upper right-hand corner.

32. Double-click the newly created **Shortcut to (*YourISP*)** icon on your Desktop. This will open the Dial-up Connection dialog box (see Figure 4.6). In the User name field, type in the username you selected when you established your Internet account with your ISP. Typically, this will appear in all lowercase with no spaces between words. Some ISPs will require that you place a *P* (or other letter or symbol) before your actual username. For example, if my username is *MrModem*, I would enter **PMrModem** in the User name field. Follow your ISP's specific instructions regarding the entering of your username and password.

33. Enter your password in the Password field. For security reasons it will appear as a series of asterisks when you enter your password. Most passwords are case sensitive (uppercase and lowercase) and thus subject to irritation and chafing, so gently type your password exactly as you provided it to your ISP or as provided to you by your ISP when you established your account. Make sure that your CAPS LOCK is not on when entering your username or password.

FIGURE 4.6: Dial-up Connection dialog box

34. You may choose to check the **Save Password** box if you do not wish to type in your password each time you connect. Just be aware that this will allow anyone with access to your computer to access your Internet account without your password. Generally, this is not a problem and the convenience of not having to type in your username and password each time more than outweighs any potential security risk. Do whatever makes you most comfortable. If you don't trust your family, colleagues, or cellmate, it's probably best to require the use of a password each time you log on by leaving the Save Password box unchecked.

35. Your local ISP dial-up phone number should appear in the Phone number box. If the correct telephone number does not appear there, enter it at this point.

36. Click the **Dialing Properties** button. Check all the information to make certain that it is correct. If you have call waiting and do not want to be disconnected from the Internet when you receive a call on the phone line you are using, check the box labeled **This Location Has Call Waiting**. Different areas of the country use different codes to disable call waiting. Check with your local telephone service for the appropriate code for your area or select it from the drop-down menu.

Also, if you need to dial a particular number or code to obtain an outside phone line or if you want to dial with a calling card, make the appropriate changes on this screen.

Once you are finished with any changes, look at the Number To Be Dialed field near the bottom of the window and make sure it is correct. When you are finished, click the **OK** button.

37. The big moment is at hand, so wake the grandkids and call the neighbors. You are now ready to dial into your ISP for the first time. Kind of makes you feel tingly all over, doesn't it? If you're ready, double-check all wiring and connections and then click the Connect button. Your modem should being dialing, squealing with delight in the process, and connecting you to your ISP. You will see a Connecting to (*Your ISP*) screen during this process. If you are asked for your password, type it in. Again, most password systems are case sensitive. Make sure that your CAPS LOCK is off.

38. Once the connection is established, minimize the Connected to (*Your ISP*) window (it may minimize automatically) and use any Internet program (e-mail or Web browser, for example) that you wish. To manually minimize the window, click the Minimize button—the one that has a small dash in it—in the upper-right corner of the window. *Do not close* the Connected to (*Your ISP*) window unless you want to log off the Internet.

39. When you want to log off the Internet, click the **Connected to (*Your ISP*)** icon located on your Taskbar.

Instead of the name of your ISP appearing on an icon located on the Taskbar, you may see a small icon with a representation of two connected computers. Click whichever is displayed on your Taskbar so that you can see the entire dialog box again. To disconnect, click the **Disconnect** button.

Congratulations! Your computer is now ready to access the Internet and the grand adventure begins! When you want to connect in the future, just double-click the shortcut icon created on your Desktop. Once connected, you can launch any installed Internet program such as your e-mail program or World Wide Web browser. The world is now at your fingertips!

Using an Existing Internet Account on a New Computer with Windows 98

Okay, you've read through this chapter, you've studied it, and if you're like most readers, you've committed most of it to memory and possibly laminated some of the pages because it moved you so profoundly. But there's something missing. Your brain hurts from all the information, yet you're curiously unfulfilled. Perhaps you already have an Internet account, you've been happily surfing for a period of time already, and you simply purchased a new computer that's got a modem already installed and it's running Windows 98! Congratulations!

All you need to do is a little razzle-dazzle with your Dial-Up Networking and you'll be surfing your little heart out in minutes. Just follow these easy steps:

1. Double-click the **My Computer** icon on your Windows 98 Desktop. When My Computer opens, you will see an icon for the Dial-Up Networking folder. Double-click the **Dial-Up Networking** icon.

2. Double-click the **Make New Connection** icon.

3. In the field labeled Type a Name for the Computer You Are Dialing, insert the name of your ISP—e.g. ISPNet.

4. In the second box labeled Select a Device, you should see your modem listed. Click the **Next** button.

If you do not see your modem listed, it could mean that you either don't have a modem or it hasn't been configured, in which case you'll want to return to the "Setting Up Your Modem" section of this chapter. But since this section is for readers who do have a modem installed and configured, we'll forge ahead.

5. You will now see fields for Area Code, Telephone Number, and Country Code. Type in the appropriate area code and telephone number. This is the telephone number provided to you by your ISP when you originally set up your account, and that you've been using to connect to the Internet in the past. Click **Next**.

6. You will then be face-to-face with a screen advising you that you have successfully set up a new dial-up networking connection called ISPNet—or whatever you named this connection in step 3.

7. Click the **Finish** button to save this new connection in your Dial-Up Networking folder. You can double-click this new icon now to connect to the Internet if you just can't stand the excitement. However, practitioners of delayed gratification would be advised to hold off just a little bit. Let's fine-tune a couple of little odds and ends and then create a shortcut to your Windows 98 Desktop to make future connections as easy and convenient as possible.

8. After clicking **Finish** you will be returned to the Dial-Up Networking folder. Click once on the newly created icon to select it (but not open it).

9. Click the **Connections** menu located in the toolbar at the top of the window and select **Settings**.

10. Looking at the General tab, you'll see three options listed under When Establishing a Dial-Up Connection that you can activate or deactivate by placing a checkmark in the appropriate box:

   ■ Show an icon on Taskbar after connected.

   ■ Prompt for information before dialing.

   ■ Show a confirmation dialog after connection.

   Be adventuresome and try each option. Personally, I have Options 1 and 2 selected, but not Option 3. It's not that I begrudge Option 3. Option 3 is a very nice option and it's been very good to me in the past. I just don't feel like Option 3. Go with your feelings here and whatever options make you happy, those are the right options for you.

11. Further down on the General tab you'll see a small box labeled Redial. Put a checkmark in the little box to activate this feature. Then set the box labeled Before Giving Up Retry to the number

of times you would like your modem to automatically redial if it cannot connect. Since your modem may require a few seconds to reset itself during redials, I would recommend setting the **Between Tries Wait** to three to five seconds. I also recommend selecting the option **Don't Prompt To Use Dial-Up Networking** to avoid any problems, but having tried both settings, I can't say that I really noticed any big difference. Click the **OK** button.

12. You will now be back at the Dial-Up Networking folder. Your ISP's icon should still be highlighted. Right-click and select **Properties**.

13. A window displaying the name of your ISP in the Title Bar will open. Click the tab labeled **Server Types**.

14. If you're simply moving your existing ISP access to a new computer, you can follow these steps on your old computer and copy the server information from your old Dial-Up Networking folder. If you're feeling insecure about your old settings or you have a nagging, burning, gnawing, haunting feeling that your ISP may have updated its settings without telling you—they're like that, you know—call your ISP and review their recommended settings.

Generally, the Type of Dial-Up Server should be set to PPP: Internet, Windows NT Server, Windows 98.

Under Advanced Options, follow your ISP's recommendation, but typically there should be a check mark appearing to the left of Enable Software Compression. There either will be or there won't be. How's that for precise instruction?

Under Allowed Network Protocols, make sure TCP/IP has a check mark appearing to its left, but make sure the others, meaning NetBEUI (pronounced *NET-buoy*) or IPX/SPX Compatible (pronounced *com-PAT-able*) are not checked. Nobody really understands what either of these terms mean, so you're in good company.

Once you have these settings configured according to your ISP's requirements, click the **TCP/IP Settings** button.

15. At the top of the window, Server Assigned IP Address should be selected, but again, always follow your ISP's recommended settings.

    In the middle of the screen, select **Specify Name Server Addresses**. In this field you will enter the Primary and Secondary DNS (Domain Name Server) addresses, obtained from your ISP. For our example we're going to use **123.456.7.89** and enter it in the field to the immediate right of Primary DNS.

    In the field to the immediate right of Secondary DNS, you will once again have to obtain this address from your ISP, but for our example we'll use **987.654.3.21**. Leave the fields to the right of Primary WINS and Secondary WINS exactly as they appear. Don't change a thing unless your ISP instructs you otherwise.

    Make sure the two check boxes at the bottom of the TCP/IP Settings screen are both checked, one being Use IP Header Compression and the other being Use Default Gateway on Remote Network.

    When you have entered the settings as described earlier or in conformance with your ISP's recommendations, click **OK** and return to the Server Types tab of the window with the name of your ISP (ISPNet, in this example) at the top.

16. Click **OK** to return to the Dial-Up Networking window.

Creating a Shortcut

Let's create a shortcut on your Windows 98 Desktop to make it easy to connect to the Internet in the future.

1. Go to the Dial-Up Networking folder and highlight your ISP's icon (**My Computer** ➤ **Dial-Up Networking**).

2. Click **File** located in the top left-hand corner and select **Create Shortcut**. Windows 98 will bluntly inform you that it cannot, will not, and absolutely refuses to create a shortcut at that location:

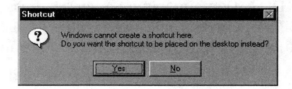

It will, however, graciously inquire if you wish to create the shortcut on your Desktop. Click **Yes**, politely.

3. Windows 98 will create a Shortcut to (*Your ISP*) icon on your Desktop.

4. Close the Dial-Up Networking folder by clicking the **Close** button (X) in the upper right-hand corner.

5. Double-click the newly created **Shortcut to (*YourISP*)** icon on your Desktop. This will open the Connect To window. In the User Name field, type in the username you selected when you established your Internet account with your ISP. Typically, this will appear in all lowercase with no spaces between words. Some ISPs will require that you place a *P* (or other letter or symbol) before your actual username. For example, if my username is *ras*, I might have to enter *Pras* in the User name field. Follow

your ISP's specific instructions regarding the entering of your username and password.

6. Enter your password in the **Password** field. For security reasons it will appear as a series of asterisks when you enter your password.

7. You may choose to check the **Save Password** box if you do not wish to type in your password each time you connect.

8. Your local ISP dial-up phone number should appear in the Phone number box. If the correct telephone number does not appear there, enter it at this point.

9. Click the **Dialing Properties** button. Check all the information on the My Locations tab to make certain that it is correct. If you have call waiting and do not want to be disconnected from the Internet when you receive a call on the phone line you are using, check the box labeled **To Disable Call Waiting, Dial:** and insert the appropriate code for disabling call waiting. In most areas of the country it's *69, but check with your local telephone service for the appropriate code for your area, or select it from the drop-down menu.

   Also, if you need to dial a particular number or code to obtain an outside phone line or if you want to dial with a calling card, make the appropriate changes on this screen.

   You will also see a field that permits you to enter calling card information. Enter your calling card information in this area if you need your modem to dial a long-distance number to gain Internet access and want to use your calling card for billing purposes.

   Once you are finished with any changes, review all the information to make sure it's correct, then click the **Apply** button, followed by **OK**.

10. That's all there is to it. You have now successfully transferred your Internet access dial-up information from your old computer to your new computer running Windows 98, and you're ready to log on once again.

Installing a New Modem

If you upgraded your system from Windows 95 to Windows 98 and you already had a modem installed, chances are the Windows 98 upgrade discovered your modem and you won't need to do anything else—other than enjoy the ability to be rightfully smug about this wonderful development.

Before you wake the kids and call the neighbors, better check to be sure your modem is present and accounted for. You can do this by clicking **Start ➢ Settings ➢ Control Panel**. If your physician has suggested you try cutting down on your clicking, you can save a click by double-clicking the **My Computer** icon on your Windows 98 Desktop, then double-clicking the **Control Panel** icon. Either way, you'll end up at the same place.

Double-click the **Modems** icon. You'll see a little window with two tabs at the top, one labeled General and one labeled Connection. You should see your modem listed under the General tab, shown in Figure 4.7. If you don't see it, you've got big troubles. Big troubles! Okay, so Mr. Modem has a flair for the dramatic. It's really no big deal at all. If you don't see your modem listed, it simply means you have to install it. Say it with me, "Piece of cake!"

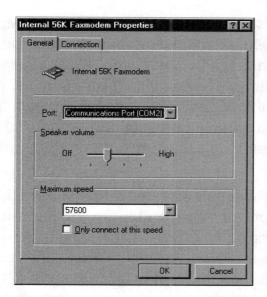

FIGURE 4.7: Modem Properties

If you're using an external modem, just make sure you've got the cable plugged in and the power on. How do you know if you've got an external or an internal modem? Well, if you can see it, feel it, move it, smell it, and knock it to the floor, that's an external modem. If all you see is a little telephone jack-like opening on your computer, you've got an internal modem.

Click the **Add** button. The Install New Modem Wizard will ask you whether you would like the Wizard to detect or "see" your modem. Never refuse a generous offer like that, so go ahead and click **Next**.

Next you'll see the Wizard hard at work poking around the nooks and crannies of your computer, looking for a modem. If you put your ear to your computer, you may actually hear the Wizard shouting, "Yo, Modem!" After a few seconds, the Wizard will report to you and tell you which modem it found and where. You don't have to do anything with this information, so just click **Next** and move on.

If your modem isn't found, try the process again by shutting everything off—well, except the lights in the room. Start by powering your computer back up, and then go through the above process again. Chances are your modem will be detected fine and dandy. If it isn't found and you have the paperwork, manual, or other support documentation that came with the modem, look for a toll-free tech support number and give them a holler. Remember, you don't have to figure out everything yourself, and you're certainly not alone.

It's also possible when your modem is detected by the Wizard that a prompt or message will appear on your screen advising you that you're lacking a certain driver. The name of the driver will be provided to add additional stress to the situation. A driver is a file that's actually a small software program. Its singular purpose in life is to translate commands or instructions between a piece of hardware, such as a modem, and the software that uses that hardware, so everything hums along in digital harmony.

If you're suffering from a modem driver deficiency, the message on your monitor will most likely instruct you to insert the disk or CD-ROM that arrived with your modem and copy the named driver file as directed. It's a terrible thing to say to anybody but in this case it's true: "follow the prompts." The Wizard won't lie. If the driver isn't found or you don't have the original disk or CR-ROM, call the modem manufacturer's tech support number. If you don't have the paperwork or manual that provides the modem manufacturer's contact information, call a local computer repair facility and pour your heart out to them.

The next thing you should see is a message that congratulates you upon the successful installation of your modem. Congratulations!

What's Next?

E-mail is the most frequently used feature of the Internet with more than 100 million e-mail messages being sent every day. In the next chapter we'll take a look at this communications phenomenon and see how you can be part of it!

The ABCs of d'E-Mail

Rumor has it there was life before e-mail, but you couldn't prove it by me. In this chapter, you will learn about e-mail software programs, sending and receiving attachments, viruses and free e-mail services. Your life will never be the same.

E-mail, or *electronic mail*, is the most popular feature of the Internet, by far. Just how popular requires the bandying about of some numbers. Big numbers. More sensitive readers or those easily offended by public bandying would be advised to divert their attention or shield their eyes before reading further.

According to Forrester Research (`http://www.forrester.com`), Americans send approximately 100 million e-mail messages daily. According to the Inverse Network Technology E-mail Study, 91 percent of e-mail messages arrived at their intended destination within 5 minutes; 5 percent arrived within 30 minutes; 1 percent arrived within 1 hour. Maybe it's just me, but I think that's pretty darned impressive. How about a round of applause for e-mail? Give it up for e-mail! Of course, those percentages only add up to 97 percent. It's my opinion that the remaining three percent are get-rich-quick schemes that most likely wound up in my e-mail box.

Worldwide, there are now an estimated 263 million e-mail boxes. Make that 264 million. Oops, 265. Well, let's just say that the number of e-mail addresses is growing rapidly and e-mail is transforming the way people communicate around the world.

What Is E-Mail?

E-mail started out as fairly simple technology for sending messages from one computer to another. In recent years, a few more bells and whistles have been added and today's e-mail programs make life a lot easier for those of us who have come to know and depend upon e-mail communication. Documents of all kinds—text, numeric, graphic and specialized items such as spreadsheets and reports—are easily transmitted via e-mail as attachments.

By definition, an Internet e-mail system is one that uses an SMTP (Simple Mail Transfer Protocol) mail server (computer) to send mail, and a POP (Post Office Protocol) server to receive mail. The SMTP server is the one your e-mail program needs to connect with when you're sending a message. Its singular mission in life is to move your message to a POP server where it will be stored and forwarded to the intended recipient. When you check for incoming Internet mail, your e-mail program logs on to the POP server and politely sends a request to see the messages that have accumulated in your mailbox.

Due to the relative simplicity of this technology, new Internet e-mail features tend to be included within e-mail programs rather than reside on your ISP's server. What this really means is that if you're using an e-mail program that's several years old, chances are you won't be able to take full advantage of recent developments unless you upgrade. Most popular e-mail programs can be easily upgraded by downloading the appropriate update files from the program's Web site. Web site addresses are noted later in this chapter for your updating convenience. In real estate, the three essentials are location, location, location. The Internet version of that truism is upgrade, upgrade, upgrade. The bottom line: Make sure you're using a current version of your favorite e-mail program.

The number of e-mail mailboxes worldwide reached 112.4 million in 1998, up from 48.7 million in 1997.

Source: Frost & Sullivan, April 1999, http://www.frost.com

E-Mail Basics

All e-mail programs have several components in common and all have three primary functions: composing or writing e-mail, sending e-mail, and checking for incoming or new e-mail.

Every e-mail program will have an Outbox, an Inbox, and a trash receptacle of some type (see Figure 5.1). The Outbox is an area (called a *mailbox*) where e-mail you send is stored after it's been sent. This comes in handy if you can't remember if you actually sent an e-mail to somebody or you simply want to review something you previously sent.

The Inbox is the area where incoming e-mail is stored until you decide to read it.

The trash basket, wastebasket, or cyber dumpster is where deleted e-mail messages are stored until you exit the e-mail program.

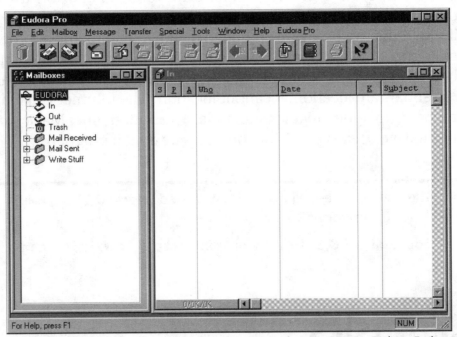

FIGURE 5.1: E-mail mailboxes

Composing or Writing E-Mail

To compose or write an e-mail, you can either establish your Internet connection first, then launch your e-mail program, write, and send the e-mail, or you can boot up your e-mail program, compose your e-mail, *then* establish your Internet connection and send the e-mail. I usually establish my e-mail connection first, then check for new e-mail, write any replies necessary, compose new e-mail, set my hair on fire, and call it a day.

To compose an e-mail, after launching your e-mail program look for a Compose E-mail, Write, New Message, or similar button. Click it and a blank e-mail form will appear. You will need to supply an e-mail address for the intended recipient. Most e-mail programs have an address book feature that will store your addresses, providing an easy method for retrieving e-mail addresses and inserting them into the To field of any outgoing e-mail.

After composing your e-mail, with your finger hovering over your mouse button and ready to click, look for a Send or Send Now button in order to whisk your e-mail off into cyberspace where it will arrive at its destination in split seconds. On a good day. With a tail wind.

Figure 5.2 displays the anatomy of a typical e-mail viewed through the Eudora e-mail program. Note the Toolbar buttons above the body of the e-mail message. Whatever you do, do not be intimidated by all the buttons! Each one has a very specific purpose. Resting your cursor on any toolbar button will usually  reveal the function of that button. And when you're not sure what a button does, what better way to find out than by clicking it? You can't hurt anything, so click away and indulge that wild and crazy spirit of adventure lurking within you.

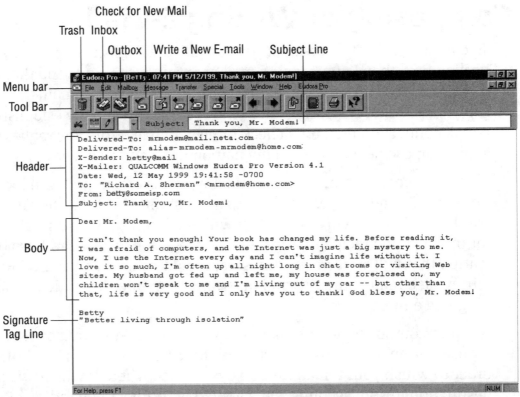

Check for New Mail

Trash Inbox

Outbox   Write a New E-mail   Subject Line

Menu bar

Tool Bar

Header

Body

Signature
Tag Line

FIGURE 5.2: E-mail message

Checking for Mail

While sending e-mail is fun, there's nothing quite like the thrill—the pure, unbridled joy—of receiving e-mail. Well, maybe I'm overstating it just a bit, but it is kinda cool.

The process of checking e-mail is the same no matter which e-mail program you're using. In fact, it's as easy as 1-2-3:

1. Establish your Internet connection.

2. Launch your e-mail program.

3. Click **Check Mail**, **Get Mail**, or something similar, depending on your e-mail program.

For some real fun, be sure to scream "Incoming!" and hurl yourself to the floor when downloading new e-mail. Your friends, neighbors and mental health care attendant will howl with laughter.

What to Look for in an E-Mail Program

While evaluating any e-mail program, make sure it permits you to maintain a private address book, send cc's (formerly referred to as carbon copies, currently referred to as cyber copies or courtesy copies), and automatically append your own signature text to any outgoing correspondence.

An e-mail program will typically place incoming messages into an *inbox* and place outgoing messages into an—anybody care to guess?—that's right, an *outbox*. For permanent message storage, your e-mail program should permit you to create folders (or mailboxes) and name them according to any organizational or naming convention you wish. Bear in mind that it doesn't really matter what type of naming convention you develop because chances are you won't be able to find anything anyway, and you'll still end up using the Find command like the rest of us.

Some programs permit you to sort mail messages into folders by clicking and dragging the actual message header. Many programs also include a spell-checker, which can be a big help, particularly if you're using e-mail for business or professionally related correspondence and you want to avoid loking lik a fooll.

Just about every e-mail program I've ever had the pleasure to meet also has the ability to check for new e-mail every few minutes, depending upon your instruction. This is very convenient if you have a full-time connection to the Internet or if you're just online for long periods of time. So be sure to check your e-mail program's options and look for a Check for E-Mail Every (Blank) Minutes and fill in the blank.

I find the e-mail filtering feature of Eudora Pro extremely useful. The ability to create filters allows incoming e-mail to be sorted automatically and placed into specific folders upon arrival. In the early days of e-mail, this type of filtering was simply a convenience. Today, it's rapidly becoming a necessary cyberspace survival tool for anyone who receives large volumes of e-mail. I receive 200 to 300 e-mails each day and having them sorted and filed into individual mailboxes when they arrive is a tremendous time-saver. Using this feature, I can ignore or overlook huge volumes of mail on a daily basis. Very handy, indeed.

Eudora also permits me to assign certain sounds to particular incoming messages, so even though I may be working on something very important or taking a snooze at the keyboard, I will be notified by sound when a specific e-mail arrives. Your e-mail program must be running and you must be connected to the Internet before you can be notified that an e-mail has arrived.

In the year 2000, 108 million Americans will have access to e-mail.

Source: Electronic Messaging Association, `http://www.ema.org`

Microsoft Outlook is fully integrated with other Office 97 and Office 2000 software, including a wonderful calendar that tracks single and recurring events, a contacts manager, an address book, a task list feature, and much more. Unlike Eudora Pro, Outlook is not exclusively an e-mail program—which is a big plus and provides greater flexibility and utility.

One of my favorite features of Microsoft's Outlook e-mail program is its ability to check multiple e-mail addresses conveniently and efficiently. Let's say you have access to the Internet via an Internet service provider (ISP), you're a member of CompuServe, and a member of America Online—which is clearly the cybergods' way of telling you to get a life if you have that many e-mail addresses. You can check your e-mail at all three locations (or more) without ever leaving Outlook. You don't have to log on and log off each service to check your e-mail. Once you establish your Internet connection via your ISP, for example, you can configure Outlook to check your other e-mail boxes at varying schedules throughout the day or night. Could it be more convenient? I think not.

Microsoft's Outlook Express is included in Internet Explorer 5, Microsoft's Web browser, which makes it convenient and always a mouse-click away. One particularly useful address book feature of Outlook Express provides the ability to create contact groups for related addresses. For example, you might create a group for your bowling league, your golf buddies, or your skydiving colleagues. Each contact group functions as its own mini-address book and can be sorted and printed individually.

A full-featured e-mail program will also provide the option of forwarding copies of messages to a specific e-mail account as well as replying to All. This feature comes in handy if you are the recipient of a message and other people are also copied on the message. Clicking the Reply to All button permits you to write your reply, then automatically send your reply back to everybody on the original mailing list.

With an integrated pager system, you can also use forwarding to set up an emergency alert process. For example, if you have a pager, you can forward messages to the e-mail address that comes with your pager account. Then when a message arrives at the pager's e-mail address, the subject of the message appears on the pager display. There's just no escaping, is there?

Test Driving New E-Mail Programs

Many people ask me how they can try out different e-mail programs without canceling their existing mail account or missing incoming e-mail. You can actually do this quite easily. All you'll need are four pieces of information: your e-mail name (sometimes called a *username*), your password, and the names or numbers of the two servers (POP and SMTP) maintained by your Internet e-mail provider. If you have an existing e-mail account and you're using e-mail software, you probably have this information readily at hand.

- If you're using Eudora Pro, for example, look under **Tools** ➤ **Options**. Click **Checking Mail**; the first line will reveal your POP Server address. Then click **Sending Mail**; the third item down will be your SMTP server identification.

- If you're using Outlook, choose **Tools** ➤ **Services**. Select your existing e-mail account from the list of information services presented, then click **Properties**.

- If you're using Netscape, choose **Edit** ➤ **Preferences** ➤ **Mail & Newsgroups** ➤ **Mail Server**. You'll see the Incoming Mail Servers and Outgoing Mail (SMTP) Server fields containing the necessary information. If you don't find this information in these fields, you can always call or e-mail your ISP and request the specific numbers.

- If you're using Big Tony's JiffeeMail, you're on your own.

To become familiar with the various goodies (term of art) incorporated within each e-mail program you're trying out, send a barrage of test e-mail messages to yourself so you can see what it's like to both send and receive mail with the new program. Because mail must be transferred from one server to another at your ISP's location, it may not arrive immediately, taking up to a minute or longer, so be patient.

If you decide to keep a new program, don't delete (uninstall) your old one right away because you might want to refer to previously received e-mail residing in your old program. If you prefer, you can copy these message oldies to a separate file or folder for safekeeping. Regardless, you will want to disable or deactivate your old e-mail program so it won't download your new messages when you launch it to review old messages.

To disable your old e-mail program, select the configuration or options menu from the Toolbar and remove your e-mail name or the mail server name from the appropriate field. You will still be able to use the other commands to manage your old e-mail.

If you would rather move your old mail to the new e-mail program, just remove the POP server name from your old e-mail program, but keep the correct SMTP server name. This will permit you to send mail, but not receive it. Then simply forward the old messages to yourself. The mail will arrive in your new e-mail program and you'll be off and running. Kind of makes your head hurt, doesn't it?

Additional Information about E-Mail Programs

To learn more about some of the leading e-mail programs and utilities, visit the following Web sites:

Attachment Opener 1	`http://www.dataviz.com`
Eudora Pro 4	`http://www.eudora.com`
Netscape Navigator Mail	`http://www.netscape.com`
Outlook Express	`http://www.microsoft.com`
Pegasus Mail	`http://www.pegasus.usa.com`

Multiple E-Mail Addresses

There may be occasions when you want more than one e-mail address, just as you may need more than one telephone number. The most common reason is the desire for both a business and a personal e-mail address. If you do want an additional e-mail address, you have a number of options, described in the following sections.

Paid E-Mail Addresses

Additional e-mail addresses are typically available from your ISP for a few dollars each month. The cost is low, and the convenience high. Many ISPs have package plans available where you can purchase five or six additional e-mail addresses for a set fee. Call or e-mail your ISP and inquire about the variety of e-mail options available.

Free E-Mail

A number of services have emerged on the cyberscene in the past few years that provide free e-mail accounts. The downside—and there's always a downside—is that advertisements will be attached to your e-mail. For many individuals, the advertisements are not a problem and the one thing that can't be beat about free e-mail is the price.

It's Free!

The following list contains a lovely assortment of popular, free e-mail services available on the Internet today:

Email.com	http://www.email.com
Hotmail	http://www.hotmail.com
Juno	http://www.juno.com
NetAddress	http://www.netaddress.com
NetZero	http://www.netzero.com
Rocket Mail	http://www.rocketmail.com
Yahoo! Mail	http://www.yahoo.com

Web-Based E-Mail

Web-based e-mail permits you to send and receive e-mail using a Web browser such as Netscape Navigator or Internet Explorer. You don't need any additional software. Your e-mail resides on a Web site and you simply navigate to the Web site and enter your username and password to view your e-mail. Many of the free e-mail services referenced utilize Web-based e-mail.

Setting up a Web-based e-mail account is as easy as visiting a Web-based e-mail Web site. For this example, let's use MSN's (Microsoft Network's) Hotmail, shall we? Hearing no objection, just point your browser to `http://www.hotmail.com`.

1. Click **Sign Up Here!** For your eyestrain pleasure, you will be presented the Hotmail Registration page containing the Hotmail Terms of Service (TOS). Why it's necessary to refer to Terms of Service as TOS is BM (Beyond Me). At your leisure you are welcome to scroll through pages of mind-numbing fine print that only an attorney with excellent vision could love.

2. When you reach the bottom of the TOS page, anticipating that your vision will be pretty well shot by this point, the good folks at Hotmail provide two large buttons, I Accept and I Decline. If you click **I Accept**, you will be transported to the Hotmail Registration form. If you click **I Decline**, you will be taken to the Why Sign Up for Hotmail page, slapped around for a few minutes, and then given another opportunity to sign up. Just click **I Accept**. It's easier and less bruising.

3. The Hotmail Registration form will require you to create a login name and password for your account. You will also be required to provide additional information such as your name, state, country, occupation, unusual birthmarks, hallucinations, disturbing dreams, and intrusive thoughts. You will also have the option of listing your new e-mail address in the Hotmail directory making it accessible to the general public, or of keeping your e-mail address private.

Your login name will become part of your e-mail address so choose your login name carefully. If you select StudMuffin, your e-mail address will then be `StudMuffin@hotmail.com`.

4. When you have filled out the registration form, click **Submit Registration** and your account will be created. There is no charge for this service, but you must log into your account once within the first ten days after creating the account and at least once every 120 days thereafter to keep the account active.

5. To check your e-mail in the future, simply navigate to `http://www.hotmail.com`, enter your login name and your password, and you'll be able to send and receive e-mail from the safety, security, and comfort of your Web browser.

Web-Based Access to Your Regular E-Mail

Just when you thought there couldn't possibly be any more options for checking e-mail, along comes something new! MailStart (see Figure 5.3) is a free service that permits you to enter your regular e-mail address and password, and the site will convert your e-mail into Web pages and display them for your reading pleasure. When you reply to e-mail from the MailStart site, your regular e-mail address appears, so this service is completely invisible to the recipient.

This is an extremely convenient service to use when traveling because you're not retrieving your regular mail. All your e-mail remains on your ISP's mail server, so when you get home and check your e-mail, all your mail, including the things you've read and responded to, are available to you in the normal manner.

While other free e-mail services offer access to your regular mail in this manner, most will stamp your e-mail with the name of their service, such as Hotmail or Yahoo! Not so with MailStart.

On the downside, sometimes the service is a little sluggish as it converts your e-mail for Web viewing, and you cannot receive attachments at this time—though who knows what the future will hold. This service will not work with a proprietary mail system such as AOL or MSN.

For additional information, visit MailStart at `http://www.mailstart.com`.

FIGURE 5.3: MailStart.com home page

Redirection Services

E-mail redirection or forwarding services provide you with what is often characterized as a *lifetime* e-mail address. All e-mail addressed to you at your redirection service e-mail address will be forwarded to your current e-mail address. Using a forwarding service is convenient because your e-mail address remains constant to the outside world, yet you have the ability to change ISPs whenever you wish.

These services also generally permit you to select your complete e-mail address—the username before the @ sign, as well as what appears after the @ sign. So if I owned Big Ernie's House of Linoleum, I could have as my e-mail address `BigErnie@HouseofLinoleum.com` or `BigErnie@HOL.com`.

Redirection Services

Redirection services vary in pricing, but most are less than $20 per year. Some of the most popular redirection or forwarding e-mail services include:

Forever Mail	`http://www.forevermail.com`
iName	`http://www.iname.com`
StarMail	`http://www.starmail.com`
NetForward	`http://www.netforward.com`

Spam

Junk e-mail or unsolicited e-mail is called *spam*. It is the scourge of the Internet. If you have an e-mail address, you will receive spam, much of it emanating from junk e-mail 'bots or robotic programs that harvest e-mail addresses from the Internet in drone-like fashion.

For most of us, the worst thing about spam is that it clutters up our e-mail boxes and requires at least a quick glance before being deleted. Spam is increasing because it's a lot less expensive to send than U.S. mail or *snail mail*, and it doesn't kill trees. But for the most part, whether it's promoting something x-rated or some harebrained, get-rich-quick scheme, it's junk. And junk by any other name is still junk.

Coping with Spam

While you cannot completely eliminate spam from your life, there are a few things you can do to help minimize the amount you receive:

- Ask to be removed from the list that sent you the spam. Usually, within any robot-generated message is information on how not to receive more similar junk. Follow those instructions to be removed from the list of recipients. This method of dealing with junk e-mail is by no means foolproof, and may actually contribute to the problem. Some unscrupulous spammers *want* you to reply to their spam because it serves as verification to them that your e-mail address is valid. Your address may then be sold to other spammers and as Sonny & Cher once intoned, "The beat goes on."

- Look within the body of the spam for a postal address, phone, or fax number. Contact the sender and ask that they stop sending any further messages to you.

- Use filters. Many e-mail programs permit you to create rules or filters that will automatically delete e-mail from particular senders or with certain words in the header of any given e-mail. I have filters set up to route any e-mail received with "XXX," "X-rated," "Get rich," or "Earn money" in the header directly to my trash bin. If you consistently create a filter for every piece of junk e-mail you receive, in time you will significantly reduce the amount of spam you will be forced to view.

- Get unlisted. The Internet E-mail Marketing Council (`http://www.iemmc.org`) enables you to put yourself on one list to remove yourself from another list. Sounds strange, I know, but it does work.

- Delete your return address. The best way to avoid spam is to keep your e-mail address away from spammers in the first place. Address lists are often obtained by scanning newsgroups. One way to avoid being scanned is to delete your address from messages you may post in newsgroups or other interactive areas on the Internet. If you want to include an e-mail address so other members of the group can contact you, just place your e-mail address near your signature line or elsewhere in the body of your message.

- Remove your e-mail address from Internet directories. Contact Internet directories such as Bigfoot (`http://www.bigfoot.com`) and Yahoo! (`http://www.yahoo.com`) and request that your name be removed from their directories. You can find an A–Z list of these directories at Search.com (`http://www.search.com`).

- Contact the spammer's ISP. Look in the header information of any spam you receive. Although it is possible to fake this information, this is worth trying if you're really getting fed up with spam. Somewhere in the header, you should see some text that displays who sent the offending e-mail. If you see something like `john@xyznet.com`, that tells you that the sender's ISP is xyznet. Using your Web browser, go to `http://www.xyznet.com` and see what appears. If you're lucky, you'll arrive at the home page of the spammer's ISP. Using the contact information provided on the site, copy the spam you received and notify the Webmaster. You can also try addressing an e-mail to `abuse@xyznet.com`. ISPs are not appreciative of their services being utilized for spamming purposes. If enough people complain, the spammer may be run out of cybertown.

Fighting the Good Fight

For more information about fighting spam, visit any of the following Web resources:

Fight Spam on the Internet	`http://spam.abuse.net/spam`
Getting Rid of Spam	`http://www.thisistrue.com/spam.html`
The Netizen's Guide to Spam and Abuse	`http://com.primenet.com/spamking`
The Spam Tools Mailing List	`http://www.abuse.net/spamtools.html`
Stop Junk E-mail	`http://www.mcs.com/~jcr/junkemail.html`

Transmitting Attachments via the Internet

E-mail is the most frequently used feature of the Internet, but communicating by e-mail is not limited simply to text messages, or to simple text messages (in my case). As I already mentioned, for those of you paying attention, you can also send documents, presentations, spreadsheets, graphics, or tuna melts, as long as what you want to transmit exists in electronic format. No matter what it is, if it tags along with an e-mail, it's called an *attachment.* And if you've never had an electronic tuna melt, you don't know what you're missing. If it exists in a file or folder on your computer, you can transmit it. And how do you do this? Didn't you read the first paragraph? What do you think, words grow on trees? Okay, let's review it once again. You do this by sending a file as an attachment to an e-mail message.

To actually send an attachment—after composing a message that will serve as your cover letter—look for a menu item called Attachments or a button with a little paperclip. Darker, edgier programs may have a picture of an ex-spouse, a houseguest who overstayed his or her welcome, or an ever-present neighbor to signify an "attachment." Click that item and it will present to you a list of directories, files, and folders residing on your hard drive, floppy disk drive, or any other storage device you may be using. Take a leisurely scroll around your hard drive and locate the file you want to attach. Once you find the file, just click it. That's all there is to it. When you send your e-mail, a copy of the selected file will be attached to it, and the "original" will remain on your computer. So when we speak in terms of *sending* a file or folder, we're actually just sending a copy of the file.

Compressing Files

In order to shorten the time it takes to send a file and to avoid consuming large amounts of disk space, larger files are typically compressed via a process called *zipping*. When a recipient receives a zipped file, he or she then unzips the file and it's ready to use. I generally zip any file larger than 100KB. To check the size of a file, select or highlight the file with your cursor, then right-click and choose Properties. Under the General tab you will find the size of the file in kilobytes (KB) displayed.

One of the most popular compression programs is WinZip (see Figure 5.4), which is a shareware program available on the Web at `http://www.winzip.com`.

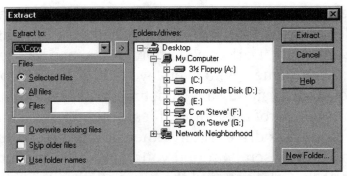

Copyright ©1991-1997, Nico Mak Computing, Inc.
Printed with permission of Nico Mak Computing, Inc.

FIGURE 5.4: WinZip File Compression Software

Shareware, as distinguished from *freeware*, is software made available to you on the honor system. You are welcome to try it, but if you decide to use it on a regular basis, you're on your honor to send in the registration fee requested, as explained in an accompanying text file.

WinZip integrates beautifully with Windows 95 and Windows 98 and makes compressing (zipping) and decompressing (unzipping) files so easy you'll be singing "Zippity Doo-Dah" before you know it.

To use it with Windows 95/98, simply right-click the name of a file or folder you wish to zip (compress) and select **Add to Zip**. The Add dialog box will appear.

In the Add to Archive field you will see the path (example: `C:\ Folder\Filename.zip`) to the file you have targeted for zipping. Note that the file extension will be changed to ZIP. So if you selected the file `Ilovemrmodem.txt` as the file to be zipped, it will appear in the Add to Archive field as `Ilovemrmodem.zip`. This is normal, so don't be alarmed.

If everything looks hunky-dory to you, click the **Add** button and the file you selected will be compressed in a split second. The newer, zippier version of the file will reside in the same folder as the non-zipped version of the file.

There are a number of options available to you on the Add to Archive screen, so spend some time exploring and experimenting. The best way to develop functional skills—and that's the objective here—is to practice. Use your word processor or other favorite program to create a test file and then zip it. For fun, move the zipped file to a new folder or be even more adventuresome and create the zip file in a new folder. (Hint: Choose **Add to Archive** ➢ **Open** to select a new location.) Then launch your e-mail program and try sending the zip file to yourself.

When it arrives, be sure to shout the obligatory file compression cheer, *Here comes Zippy! Here comes Zippy!* and then unzip the file. How do you unzip? Think it through: If you had to right-click to zip a file, try right-clicking to unzip a file and see what happens!

The more you experiment and explore all the little nooks and crannies of any software program, the more comfortable you will become with it. You don't need to *master* any of these programs, you just need to know how to use any program well enough to meet your basic needs. Most software programs provide many more bells and whistles than most of us will ever use. I've been using WinZip for years and I know how to zip and unzip files. Though the program can do a lot more than that, that's all I need, so that's all I've ever learned. I've only got four neurons left, so I'm trying to be as gentle as possible with them and not fill them full of unnecessary information.

Viruses and E-Mail

No discussion about the Internet would be complete without mentioning the dreaded V-word, viruses. A virus is a nasty little computer program that can do everything from destroying the data on your computer to deflating the tires on your car. A virus can be transmitted between computers by sharing or exchanging files. In other words, if a file is created on a computer that is infected with a particular virus and that file is sent to you as an attachment to an e-mail, you can become infected. What would your neighbors say? Oh, the shame of it all. You can also get a virus by downloading files from a Web site, so it's important to understand what all the fuss is about regarding viruses and to take a few basic precautions to minimize your risk.

Myths abound about viruses, and one of the most popular misconceptions is that you can catch a virus by reading e-mail. Not true! Viruses cannot be transmitted via text e-mail messages anymore than you can catch the flu by talking to somebody on the telephone. However, viruses can be transmitted via attachments to e-mail, so beware of geeks bearing gifts. Never…NEVER launch or execute a file received via e-mail without checking it for viruses first.

The reality is that most viruses are little more than pesky annoyances rather than catastrophic events, but all require an investment of time and energy. Education and preparedness can make all the difference in the world.

Your choices for dealing with viruses are limited, which makes the decision-making process rather easy. You can wait until you contract a virus and then go into panic mode—sometimes referred to as a Techno-Tizzy, or you can educate yourself now and prepare for a possible virus attack in advance of the actual event. Mr. Modem's Golden Rule of Computing is this, "If you use a computer, you will get a virus. And if you haven't yet, it's just a matter of time." You can count on Mr. Modem when it comes to comforting words.

Prevention is really simple if you follow this one little rule: Always virus-check any file or software program not received directly from a manufacturer or distributor. If you follow this rule, your chances of becoming the victim of a computer virus will be significantly minimized.

Practice Safe Computing

Be sure your computer has a current anti-virus program, and even more importantly, make sure you're using it! It's important that you update your virus-checking program periodically because hundreds of new strains of virus—or is it virii—are discovered each month, and your virus-checking software can only check for viruses it is programmed to detect. There are an estimated 40,000 viruses in circulation today, so you can stay safe by staying current.

Two of my favorite virus-checking software programs are McAfee's VirusScan (`http://www.mcafee.com`), shown in Figure 5.5, and Norton Antivirus, by Symantec (`http://www.symantec.com/product`). Both offer shareware versions that you can download and try before you buy. Is that thoughtful or what?

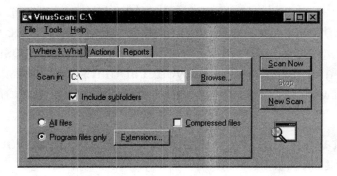

FIGURE 5.5: McAfee ViruScan Virus-Checking Software

Keeping your virus-checking software current is not difficult. Using a registered version of any popular virus-checking program will typically result in an e-mail notification when it's time to update. Updating the software is as simple as navigating to the software publisher's Web site, then downloading and installing the update file. The installation "ordeal" generally consists of one mouse-click, and the update file will install itself into the appropriate folder or directory on your computer. If I can do it, you can do it. Mr. Modem would never lie to you. Detailed instructions will be provided on each site, should you experience difficulty, discomfort, nausea, or cramping.

Your virus-checking program will permit you to schedule virus-checking at regular intervals. Even if you set up your schedule to check for viruses at 2:00 A.M. every Tuesday morning, be sure to also check individual files whenever they arrive as attachments or as you receive them online or offline.

What if a virus is detected? After you regain consciousness, you'll be able to use that same program to rid yourself of the pesky critter! Virus-checking programs permit you to get back on the road to good computer health in no time! In fact, most programs will either ask you during the initial installation or by user preference option if you would like the program to eliminate any viruses as soon as they're discovered. I don't know why they even ask because I can't imagine anybody wanting to keep a virus as a treasured keepsake, but the option does exist to simply receive a notification, should you be a little squeamish or are feeling compassion for viruses. If you have a bumper sticker on your car that says, *Viruses need love, too,* I suspect you'll not want to utilize the "Vaporize the Vermin" option.

As a matter of general practice, it's a good idea to virus-check your entire hard drive at least once a month.

Virus Hoaxes

As if viruses weren't bad enough, some cyber hooligans delight in frightening millions of people by sending virus warnings via e-mail. So if you receive e-mail, sooner or later you'll receive some messages warning you not to open e-mail with certain subject headings. Most of these types of e-mails are nothing more than hoaxes, created to scare the heck out of you. The sicko hoax perpetrators are depending upon your good nature and concern for others to spread the warning and thus the hoax, so don't fall for it.

As you become more comfortable online, you'll be able to spot hoax messages a smile away because they typically display the same four characteristics:

Urgency   These e-mail chain letters typically have a breathless, "The sky is falling! The sky is falling!" quality to them.

Request for distribution   You are encouraged to tell everybody you know about the alleged virus. You may be asked to help the sender spread the word in order to protect all citizens of cyberspace.

Consequences   You will be warned of dire consequences if you do not pay heed to the message and fall victim to the digital scourge. Typical dire consequences include destruction of all data, failure of your computer to ever boot up again, spontaneous bouts of uncontrolled weeping, redness, irritation, and a host of other afflictions.

Authentication   The message will also be "authenticated" by quoting a big-shot/muckety-muck CEO of a major computer company, somebody within the government, Microsoft, IBM, Intel, etc.

Remember, 99 percent of the time it's all pure nonsense, so don't get caught up in it! These hoaxes are written to incite you to take immediate action, so most importantly, don't panic!

If you do receive a warning message of this type, *before* you inadvertently perpetuate the hoax by sending the message to everybody you have ever met in your life, visit one of the virus hoax Web sites listed in the box. Confirm for yourself that what you received is a hoax. It just takes a few seconds to check, and you can really make a significant contribution to the global Internet community by helping stamp out virus hoaxes by not passing them along.

Once you determine that the message you received is indeed a hoax, be sure to contact the person who originally notified you. Advise them that it's a hoax and provide them with the URL of the page that contains the hoax information. Ask them to in turn notify everybody to whom they sent their original warning message.

Virus and Hoax Information Sites

Please feel free to share any or all of the Web sites listed here with your friends so they can be hoax busters, too!

Computer Virus Myths	http://kumite.com/myths
Data Fellows	http://www.datafellows.fi/news/hoax.htm
Dr. Solomon's Hoax Page	http://www.drsolomons.com/vircen/vanalyse/va005.html
McAfee's Virus Information Library	http://vil.mcafee.com/villib/alpha.asp
Networks Associates' Virus Alerts	http://beta.nai.com/public/datafiles/valerts
Symantec's AntiVirus Research Center	http://www.symantec.com/avcenter/hoax.html
U.S. Dept. of Energy's Computer Incident Advisory Capability	http://ciac.llnl.gov/ciac/CIACHoaxes.html

What's Next?

Among the post popular activities of Internet enthusiasts is the ability to chat or engage in real time conversations with other individuals. In the next chapter we'll take a look at Internet chat, why it's so popular and how to participate.

Internet Chat

The global Internet community is made up of vibrant, animated individuals conversing with their CyberNeighbors, sharing thoughts, feelings and opinions. In this chapter, you will learn how to participate in these live conversations in their native habitat on the Internet. Everyday, millions of people enjoy the camaraderie provided by chatting online; some are meeting old friends and colleagues at a designated time and location, others are simply stopping in to visit what has evolved into a neverending social gathering.

What Is Chat?

Think of online chat as a text-based telephone conversation, or conference call. Instead of engaging in verbal conversation, words are exchanged on computer monitors. As few as two people can participate in a chat. The maximum number of participants is determined by the chat site itself. Some chat areas are licensed for 25 participants, others for 50 and others for thousands. It's very rare that you won't be able to join a chat session because it's full to the brim. If you ever do find yourself on the outside looking in, don't take it personally. It happens to the best of us.

In its simplest form, Internet chat is a form of instant written communication transmitted via computer, by people who have a shared interest in a given topic. In its most complex form, Internet chat is a form of instant written communication transmitted via computer by people who have a shared interest in a given topic.

Unlike e-mail communication, chat is *realtime* conversation. Whatever you type on your keyboard instantly appears on the monitors of everybody else participating in that chat.

The chat room of today is what a telephone party line was to many of us years ago. And true to form, sometimes it does feel a bit strange eavesdropping on a conversation. Chat has many complexions. At times, the quality of communication can be disappointing, but at other times it can be intellectually stimulating, exciting, and even provocative. Anyone with Internet access can chat, so you can and should expect the unexpected— chat is never predictable.

Chat Rooms

A chat room is an area set aside for the purpose of people getting together to chat. Think of it as an online meeting room, only visualize thousands of such areas. Some chat rooms are predefined, meaning that they exist whether anybody is using the room or not. Other chat rooms are created by Internet users any time they want to create a private or topic-specific chat room. The room is created by using certain chat software, which we'll discuss later.

Once inside a chat room, a small window will appear on your computer monitor. It is within this area that you can type your messages so other individuals in the chat room can instantly read your words on their monitor. They will then reply, and you will see their words scrolling across your monitor in a larger window, usually above the window where you've entered your words of wisdom.

Chat rooms are generally fun places, and typically allow participants to change the color of their text or attach small pictures or caricatures called *avatars* to their messages that will be seen by other participants.

Although there are many general purpose chat rooms, most tend to have a particular focus. Whether the discussion is current events, hobbies, travel, camping, investments, music or fine wines, anything is fair game, and most chat sessions are thoroughly enjoyable.

Types of Chat Rooms

Chat rooms come in a variety of shapes and sizes, typically small, medium, and large. Sometimes it's a one-size-fits-all venue, but I have yet to encounter a garment or other one-size-fits-all product that actually fits. Still, the concept is refreshing.

The largest of the chat rooms are the *auditoriums,* most generally used for guest interviews, lectures, or other such events. The primary difference between an auditorium and a regular chat room, besides the spelling, is that the person being interviewed and the chat room host or moderator converse separately from the main viewing audience. The audience can interact by sending questions to the guest speaker or sometimes a moderator, who will screen questions and comments for appropriateness before they appear on screen for the world to see.

Auditoriums are usually reserved for special events or topical subjects that are expected to draw a very large audience. Medium-sized chat rooms may also be set up as auditoriums, but they usually limit the number of participants.

A number of variables determine the capacity of a chat room, not the least of which is the type of license the chat room owner has from the company providing the chat software, as well as the capacity of the host server (computer) upon which the chat host (software) resides. Small chat rooms are the most popular on the Internet and typically can accommodate from 1 to 30 or even as many as 50 people.

Public vs. Private Chat Rooms

Two types of chat rooms are available, and as the title of this section suggests to all but the most cerebrally challenged readers, those types are public (or open) chats or a private chat, only accessible by invitation or password.

Most chats are public chats where anybody with Internet access can join in. Public chats can be fun, and topics can cover anything of interest to participants. At any given time there are people chatting about the weather, travel, cars, camping, hometowns, restaurants, gardening, pets, relationships, UFOs, television, movies, current events—you name it!

As popular as public chats are, there will be times when it's more comfortable to meet privately with one or more individuals, much as you would in a telephone conference call situation. Private chats are very useful for friends to gather or for club meetings, committee meetings, or for online family gatherings. Any participant can "capture" or save the dialog of the gathering and later edit it, print it out, or distribute it to the participants via e-mail. So it's a wonderful way to preserve the minutes of any online meeting.

Finding a Chat Room

Locating a chat room on America Online is as simple as clicking the **People Connection** button located in the **Channels** window. Every other online service has chat rooms as well.

Finding a chat room that focuses on a particular topic on the Web is as easy as using your favorite search engine. Try entering **chat AND travel** or whatever topic interests you. When search results are returned, you will have a number of chat rooms to choose from. Just click any of the links presented and follow the instructions. You will have to provide a username or ID that will be your online identification, and possibly provide your e-mail address as part of the registration process.

Anonymity

Chat has rapidly evolved into an inexpensive alternative to long-distance telephone calls. Participating in an online chat is like participating in an extended conference call, but oftentimes anonymously. One of the reasons that chat is so popular is that you can assume any identity you want, so unlike Mr. Bond, your reputation need not precede you.

Being anonymous presents a double-edged sword. In most seniors-oriented community chat rooms, people are generally honest and forthright. Chatting with members of our peer group is more focused on socialization, but whenever interacting with strangers, it's always best to be cautious. When in a chat room, *never give out personal information about yourself,* such as where you live. That's nobody's business. Apply the same rules about meeting people in the offline world as you would to the world of chat. Don't let down your guard or be lulled into a false sense of security.

A cartoon appeared in the *New Yorker* several years ago that perhaps best captures the reality of chatting online. The cartoon depicts two dogs sitting in front of a computer. The dog at the keyboard turns to the other dog and says, "On the Internet, nobody knows you're a dog." Truer words were never spoken.

If you decide to chat, have fun, but be careful.

Chatting on the Web

The easiest and most popular form of chat requires no special software other than your Web browser. If a small plug-in program called an *applet* is required, it will be installed painlessly during the chat sign-up process and will not require any intervention on your part.

Plugging into Plug-Ins

Ichat is one of the most popular chat platforms on the Internet, so we'll use ichat as an example of a typical plug-in installation. When visiting a Web site's chat area that features ichat, you will be invited to **Get the**

plug-in. This is not mandatory, however. Most sites will advise you that chat is usually more enjoyable and provides more customization and personalization features if you do use the plug-in, but you can also participate in chat using your plain ol' Web browser of choice. If you decide against it, you may take comfort in knowing that other chat participants won't necessarily be able to tell that you weenied out and didn't get the plug-in. That alone will spare you years of emotional scarring caused by chat-based hoots, taunts and jeers—which I believe, coincidentally, is the name of a law firm just outside of Cincinnati.

But what the heck, let's throw caution to the wind and get the ichat plug-in. It's free, it's fun, and it's very simple to install, so let's go for it! I can hear the strains of Steppenwolf's "Born to be Mild," in the background: "Get your modem running…head out on that I-way…"

If you're visiting a site that uses ichat, you will see a hyperlink that says **Get the plug-in** or words to that effect. Click the link or better still, click your heels together, Dorothy, and you'll on your way to the land of *ahs*. (Kindly hold your groans until the end of the chapter, please.)

You will then be transported to the ichat Web site where you will be presented with a list of operating systems—Windows 3.1, Windows 95/98, Macintosh, etc. to choose from, as well as a list of browsers. Select the operating system and browser you're using.

Mr. Modem Hint: If you're not sure which browser version you're using, open your browser, click on the **Help** drop-down menu located in the toolbar at the top of your screen, then select **About**. The name of the software and its version number will be displayed.

The **Download** page will next appear before your eyes. Don't be alarmed. This is a good thing. Repeat after me, "The download page is my friend." At this point you can download the plug-in file to your computer by clicking the **Download Now** link. You will be prompted to provide a destination location for the downloaded plug-in file on your computer, so click **Save to Disk**. Next, click the little down arrow to the right of the **Save In** field and select where you would like to save the plug-in.

Mr. Modem Bonus Tip: I always recommend downloading to your Desktop which makes it easy to find any file you download. Plus, once you have completed the installation of any program you can easily tidy up your Desktop by deleting the icon placed during the download.

If you select the Desktop as your designated location for the download, click the Save button and the plug-in will download. It will have a filename approximating *icnp222.exe*. The numbers on your screen may be different reflecting a more recent version of the plug-in program.

When the plug-in file has completed downloading, close your browser and double-click the new icon that appears on your Desktop. The Installation Wizard will greet you warmly and escort you through the rest of the installation which will install the plug-in in the appropriate folder for you in a matter of seconds. You won't have to make any life-altering decisions during the remainder of the installation.

Once the plug-in is installed, return to the chat room. You will be requested to create an account. This is your chance to select a nickname or *handle* for yourself that other chat participants will see. You will also be requested to select a password.

If you have any difficulty at all, a wonderful troubleshooting guide for ichat is available at all times on the Web at `http://www.ichat.com/plugin/download/win95nt/win95_ts_guide.html`. (I love these nice, short URLs. Very easy to remember.)

A Typical Chat Sign-Up

The process of joining an ongoing chat will vary depending upon the chat community, but overall the process is very similar throughout the Internet. You will be asked to agree to certain terms and conditions governing chat participants and you will be asked to select a username or User ID for yourself, which will be your identity in the chat room as well as a password. You will also be asked for your e-mail address. Beyond that, most other information you may be requested to provide will likely be optional.

In the following example, we'll join a Yahoo! chat room, but the process is very similar for any Web-based chat.

1. First, navigate to `http://www.yahoo.com`.

2. Click **Chat**.

3. On the Yahoo! Chat Page, click **Sign Me Up!**

You'll next be presented with the Yahoo! Chat Terms of Service Agreement that you probably won't read, but if you did, you would see that it requires you to, among other things, agree not to "harass, threaten, embarrass or cause distress or discomfort upon another Yahoo! Chat participant, user, or other individual or entity." So if that's your objective, you would be well-advised to head for the hills now before the Chat Police appear at your door.

Though most people never read agreements of this type, it is a good idea to at least read the Chat Rules portion of the agreement. The agreement further addresses "Intellectual Property, Content, Privacy, Disclaimers, Limits of Liability, Special Admonitions, Termination, Minors, Miscellaneous issues," and contains enough caveats to warm the hearts of attorneys everywhere. At the conclusion of the document, after being assaulted by a litany of warnings and dire consequences, you are encouraged to "Enjoy!" Enjoy? Never mind "enjoy"! I haven't had a good night's sleep since reading it.

4. If you decide to read the agreement, once your insomnia is in remission or medications have kicked in—whichever occurs first—click the **I Accept** button located at the bottom of the page.

5. On the following **Sign Up!** page you will be invited to sign up for your very own Yahoo! ID and Password, followed by some personal account information. Fill in the fields as requested, and note that some of the personal information requested is optional.

6. When you have completed filling out the information, click the **Submit This Form** button. That's all there is to it. No physical is required, no salesman will call.

Once you've filled out the form, you'll be face-to-face with the **Welcome To!** page which will include confirmation of your Yahoo! ID and your password. A confirmation message which includes your password will also be e-mailed to you. Be sure to write down your Yahoo! ID and password for future reference. If you do forget your ID or password at some point, there's an area where you can enter your e-mail address and, by return e-mail, receive your ID and password.

7. Next, click the **Go to Yahoo! Chat** link. You will be asked to select a topic area (see Figure 6.1) where you would like to begin chatting. Available topic categories include 40+, Sports, Stock Talk, Romance, Movies, General Chat, Computers, Music and Current Events. You can change selections at any time, so just select something that looks interesting for starters.

Following the chat categories appears the cryptically worded **Choose Software** box. Don't panic! You won't be asked to do anything beyond making a selection. The choices presented are **Java—Best Choice** and **HTML**. If you're using AOL, select **HTML**. Select **Java**, though, for the most stable and dependable chat client. *Client*, in this context refers to the software you're about to receive. Yahoo! is the *host* or *server*, and you are the *client*. Follow Yahoo!'s recommendations. Yahoo! wouldn't lie to you.

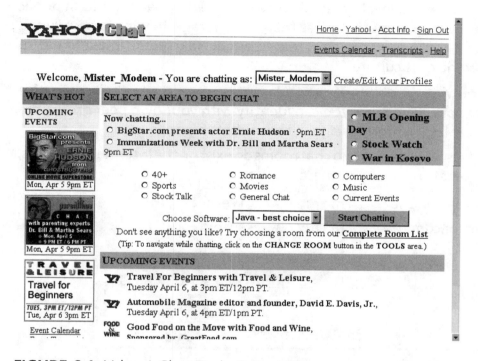

FIGURE 6.1: Yahoo! Chat Topic Categories

8. Once you've made your selection and you're ready to chat, click the **Start Chatting** button. You'll be transported into the chat room you selected where you'll see lots of other people merrily chatting away. Yahoo! ID names or *handles* of participants will appear in the **Chatters** box.

The scrolling chat window will contain the ongoing chat conversations. Each participant is identified by his, her, or its Yahoo! ID name.

Explore the **Preferences**, **Friends**, and **Emotions** buttons. Try each of them out and have fun experimenting!

A Word of Caution

Many times the level of intelligence displayed by participants in public chat rooms is something less than the average turnip, so be advised that all chat rooms are not created equal. Take your time and get to know the chat culture.

As you visit Web sites of particular interest, stop into their respective chat rooms. The more you can identify with your own peer group, the greater the comfort level you'll have chatting online.

Intellectually stimulating chat rooms do exist on the Internet for seniors, so try chatting in any of these locations:

Caregiver Chat	http://caregiverchat.com
Senior.com	http://www.senior.com

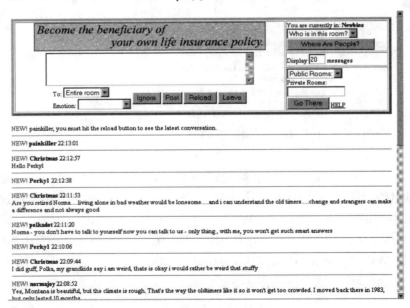

Seniors.com	http://www.seniors.com
Third Age	http://www.thirdage.com
Yahoo! Seniors	http://dir.yahoo.com/Society_and_Culture/ Cultures_and_Groups/Seniors/Chat/

What Can You Expect?

Asking what you can expect in a chat room is a lot like asking, "What can I expect if I walk into a building?" Just as it depends on which building you enter, so does it depend on which chat room you enter. The best advice I can offer is to expect the unexpected. The ability to communicate anonymously with others occasionally brings out the worst in a few people. Some will use provocative language or attempt to be controversial.

If you do cross paths with somebody whose language offends you, just leave. Don't respond; just leave. You can limit your exposure to offensive material by visiting chat rooms that have a particular focus or are created for a particular group of individuals, such as seniors. If it's a chat room for seniors or a chat room for needle-point enthusiasts, or golfers, the odds are heavily in your favor that you won't encounter any homosapienus idiotus. To help you ignore obnoxious chat participants, most chat platforms provide an Ignore button or other means of blocking messages from one or more participants. All you need to do is enter the username or names of the individuals you wish to ignore, then relax and enjoy your chat session. If only offline life could provide us with an Ignore button.

It's always best to lurk before you leap into any chat room. Lurking in this context means to take a few minutes and read what other participants are saying and how they're communicating with each other. This will provide an opportunity to decide if the chat room is your kind of place or not.

Most chat rooms or chat platforms have an associated Frequently Asked Questions file (FAQ), so be sure to take a few minutes and read that information. Participation guidelines will be spelled out in the FAQ, as well as general rules of conduct, so it's a good idea to become familiar with these before participating.

Approximately 5 million children younger than the age of 12 are online; 21 million are predicted to be online by the end of 2002. **Source:** Jupiter Communications, `http://www.jup.com`

Internet Relay Chat (IRC)

During your excursions into the Internet, you may encounter one of the oldest platforms for Internet chat called Internet Relay Chat or IRC. A group of people on IRC is called a *channel*. Today, thousands of channels exist, each one typically focusing on a particular topic, though many are simply informal chat lines.

Most standard Internet software packages, such as those provided by an Internet service provider, don't include a standard IRC software program. If you need one, mIRC is one of the most popular IRC programs for Personal Computers (PCs), and is available at `http://www.mirc.co.uk/get.html`. At that location, select a download site from the list presented. It's always best to select a site that's as geographically close as possible.

Once you download the file and install it, be sure to read the associated help files. Remember that once you connect to a chat channel, you're not invisible anymore. Your presence will be announced to all other participants and the nickname you select for yourself will remain in the names list or list of chatters for as long as you remain in a given chat room.

Since Web-based chat is infinitely more popular with our peer group than IRC chat, I'm not going to discuss IRC in any more depth. IRC was all the rage at one time on the Internet, but with more than 100 commands to learn, it wasn't the easiest thing to master. Thank the modem muses for newer technology.

ChatSpeak

Like the CB radio craze of a few years ago, chat also has its own vocabulary. Chat is a fast-paced medium where messages are quick and to the point and responses are equally fast. Unlike CB enthusiasts, you won't see online chatters talking about "smokies," "Buster Browns," and "rubber duckies," yammering about convoys, or asking, "What's your 20?" But you will see a great many cryptic abbreviations, acronyms, and text-based smiley-faces depicting a variety of emotions.

Because the objective is to keep the dialog flowing, a form of online shorthand has emerged over the years that permits participants to use phrases and express emotions with a minimal amount of typing. As an example, BTW translates to *By the way*, and GIWIST means *Gee, I wish I'd said that*. ITYGTP. (*I think you get the point.*)

See Appendix B, "FUIA: Frequently Used Internet Acronyms," and Appendix C, "An Extravaganza of Emoticons," for a comprehensive overview of this strange yet amusing language. Be forewarned, however, that some of the language can be a bit coarse.

Though chat is a free-wheeling, free-flowing form of communication, there are a few basic rules that, if observed, will enhance your chatting experience. Helpful guidelines for online communications can be found in Chapter 13, "Effective Online Communication."

What's Next?

Now that you know that an online chat session is like a big telephone conference call that you can jump into at any time, what about the times when you really don't feel like engaging in sparkling conversation with others? Have you ever wished you could just leave somebody a note or have them leave a message for you? Coming up in the next chapter we'll discuss how to exchange messages with others on the Internet's community bulletin boards, called *newsgroups*.

Newsgroups

More than 25,000 discussion groups welcoming 250,000 articles a day await your arrival on the Internet, so you've got a lot of catching up to do. In this chapter, you will learn about Usenet newsgroups and how to participate in them.

When it comes to communicating with others, no other vehicle has the capacity to bring as many people together than the Internet does. There are many places on the 'Net where people can talk with each other about topics of mutual or shared interest, but the most popular area is the Internet's *Usenet* (Users Network) newsgroups. Sometimes called *forums* or *bulletin boards*, today there are more than 25,000 of these discussion groups that allow participants to place or post messages (called *articles*) which can then be read and replied to by others. Usenet newsgroups are arguably the largest information resource in the world, with more than 250,000 articles posted each day. I don't know who you would argue with about it, but it arguably does provide a delightful author's loophole in case I'm wrong.

Keep in mind that no topics are off limits in newsgroups, so don't be surprised if you find things that are offensive to you. In fact, you can count on it! If you encounter something that isn't your cup of tea, just keep moving along your merry way and ignore it. Newsgroups are generally uncensored, free-flowing discussions. Every imaginable and unimaginable topic is under discussion, even as you're reading this. So whether your interest is in aardvarks or zithers, there's a newsgroup out there with your name on it, just waiting for your arrival.

Those aged 35–54 comprise more than half of all Internet users.

Source: eStats.com, http://www.estats.com

How newsgroups came into existence is semi-interesting, though you will certainly be the judge of that. In 1979, long before there was such a thing as the World Wide Web, a group of computer enthusiasts at Duke University created a system for sharing articles between several computers. The thought was that this system would be used for communication among the more cerebrally gifted, for sharing research and for other noble endeavors. An admirable ambition for sure, but rumor has it that it was used for social chitchat from the very beginning because it was such an easy way for participants to keep in touch with each other.

Up to that point in time, this initial group of cyber pioneers had been communicating via e-mail, which proved to be too awkward as the group of participants began to grow. It was decided that to be most effective, they needed some kind of structure within which articles could be posted so that many topics could be discussed on an ongoing basis at the same time. As this evolved, it was envisioned that anybody wishing to partici- pate could obtain a list of topics under discussion and review what others had to say within each respective topic. Thus was born what evolved into the phenomenon we know as Usenet newsgroups.

Your Internet service provider subscribes to the Usenet system and decides which of the 25,000 + newsgroups will be available to you. Most ISPs provide a huge selection of newsgroups, so it's very unlikely that you won't find anything of interest. Because newsgroups are open to anybody with Internet access, you can read any article, in any newsgroup, as long as your provider has included it in the newsgroups available to you.

Sometimes newsgroups are excluded from those available to you because they're deemed pornographic, offensively provocative, or just moronic. The decision to exclude a newsgroup lies with the entity that subscribes to the Usenet newsfeed, and for most of us, that's our ISP.

How Newsgroups Work

Just think of a Usenet newsgroup as you would a cork and thumbtack bulletin board located in a local supermarket where people post ads fea- turing items for sale, services offered, etc. If you put up an ad, anybody who comes along and looks at that bulletin board can see your ad. And of course, that's the idea. (See Figure 7.1)

Similarly, when you send (post) an article to a newsgroup, everyone who is reading that newsgroup can see your article. When someone replies to your article, everybody can see that, also.

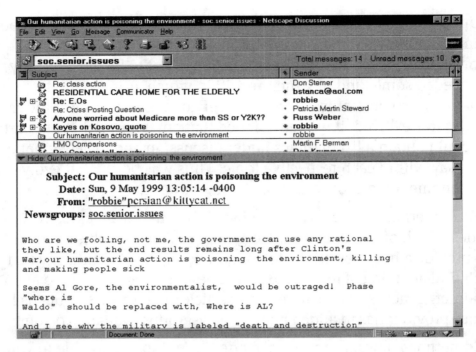

FIGURE 7.1: Newsgroup

Articles posted to newsgroups are like e-mail messages, but slither through a different system called *NNTP* (Network News Transport Protocol). Your ISP keeps a database of newsgroup articles that it updates periodically.

During the updating process, any articles you post are sent out to the newsgroup community worldwide, and at the same time, new postings from others are retrieved and then become available to you. The frequency of this updating process determines how quickly your article is available for others to see.

Most providers update continually, others update at periodic intervals. An article you post may be instantly available to some newsgroup participants, but only available to others on a delayed basis as a result of this process, depending on the updating schedule of others. This process of spreading throughout the Internet is called *propagation*.

Moderated Newsgroups

While newsgroups are generally verbal free-for-alls, some groups screen articles before making them available to others. Articles posted to moderated groups are screened by whoever oversees the group. Now, there's a job. Moderated newsgroups tend to stray off topic less frequently than unmoderated groups. It can be annoying to subscribe to a newsgroup about gardening, for example, only to find people talking about movies or sporting events, etc. Generally speaking, responsible members of unmoderated groups try to keep the focus of the group as the primary topic. Peer pressure is a wonderful thing.

In a moderated group, it is also possible that articles will be removed if they're obscene or contain material deemed offensive by those moderating the group. That is not the case with unmoderated groups, so be prepared. It can be ugly.

Newsgroup Names

The founding Usenet fathers and mothers defined a set of rules for maintaining what were referred to as newsgroups, and a hearty group of volunteers oversaw the fledgling infrastructure. Within its overall framework, they designed a hierarchy of newsgroups centered around eight major topical areas or categories: `alt.`, `comp.`, `misc.`, `news.`, `rec.`, `sci.`, `soc.`, and `talk.` Don't be concerned if these cryptic categories mean nothing to you. I'll explain each of them a little later.

Newsgroups were very popular from the get-go, and because they were so popular, it was quickly realized that this first hierarchy was too confining. Too many topics just didn't fit within the narrow, topical classification system. Necessity is indeed the mother of invention, so many additional categories were created, and others evolved over time.

One of the fun things about newsgroups is trying to figure out what the topic of a newsgroup is by observing its name. You can usually tell what the focus of a particular newsgroup is by looking at its full name. The first part of the name is the broad category or hierarchy that the group falls under.

Try reading the full name of a newsgroup from left to right, and you'll probably get a good sense of what the newsgroup is all about. For example, the newsgroup `rec.pets.cats`, reading left to right, tells us it's a recreational newsgroup, about pets, and a further subcategory is cats. See how easy? You probably didn't even know you knew newsgroupspeak!

What follows is a listing of some of the top-level hierarchies and a miniexplanation (or explanette), about the focus of each category:

`alt.`	Alternative newsgroups are considered the wild and crazy area of newsgroups. Sometimes referred to as FringeNet, try not to be surprised by anything you observe here. The `alt.` newsgroup hierarchy was created as a home base for a looser newsgroup structure. "Loosey-goosey" describes it perfectly. Anything goes in the `alt.` groups, so be advised that you probably won't want to explore these with your easily-offended Aunt Agnes watching over your shoulder. If so, you might want to have some smelling salts standing by.
`bionet.`	If biology is your bag, this is the place.
`bit.`	BitNet or Listserv mailing list topics.
`biz.`	Commercial advertising articles.
`clari.`	ClariNet subscription news service.
`comp.`	Very popular. Anything and everything about computers.

`k12.`	Newsgroups for K-12 teachers.
`microsoft.`	Product support and discussion. Very helpful.
`misc.`	Topics that don't fit anywhere else.
`news.`	Discussion about Usenet itself, including announcements about new newsgroups.
`rec.`	Recreation: sports, games, hobbies, arts, crafts, and similar topics.
`sci.`	Research, applied science, engineering. Cerebral stuff, in general.
`soc.`	Social, cultural, political, religious topics.
`talk.`	Current "hot topic" events or controversial topics. Political debates are all the rage.

Joining a Newsgroup

While surfing the Internet, you may encounter a Web page that refers to additional information located within a newsgroup. Don't panic if you haven't had occasion to visit a newsgroup previously. There's a first time for everything, so take this opportunity to try something new on the Internet.

Before you can access a newsgroup, there are a few steps you'll need to take. First, you will need a newsreader. If you use Netscape Navigator as your Web browser, you already have a newsreader named Collabra. We'll discuss using Collabra later in this chapter. Promises, promises.

Even if you are using Netscape, you can also use any of the newsreader programs available on the Web. It's most convenient to use your browser's built-in newsreader, but if you really get into newsgroups, you might want to try one of the newsreader software programs listed in the box below.

If you're using Microsoft's Internet Explorer as your browser, you'll need to use Outlook Express or any of several other newsreaders available for download from the Internet.

Newsreader Software Programs

Agent/Free Agent   `http://www.forteinc.com/agent/freagent.htm`

Anawave's Gravity (Mr. Modem's personal favorite)   `http://www.microplanet.com`

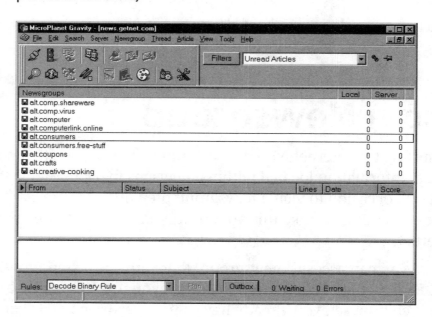

Lurker 32   `http://www.stsi.com/lurker.htm`

Newsmonger   `http://www.techsmith.com/products/nmonger/overview.htm`

OUI Message Reader   `http://www.zdnet.com/swlib/` (search for "Oui Message Reader")

Configuring Your Newsreader

Once you've decided on a newsreader program, you'll need two pieces of information to configure it.

- First, you'll need the address of your Internet service provider's SMTP (Simple Mail Transfer Protocol) server, which lets you send e-mail. Look in your e-mail program's settings. You probably already have this information at hand, but if you can't locate it, just call or e-mail your provider.

- Secondly, you will need the NNTP (Network News Transfer Protocol) address, which is the system used to transfer newsgroup articles between your Internet service provider's news server and your newsreader software.

Both the SMTP and NNTP are usually just variations of your Internet service provider's address. If your ISP's address is `cupcake.com`, for example, then the SMTP address is typically `mail.cupcake.com` and the NNTP address is usually `news.cupcake.com`.

Once you obtain the SMTP and NNTP information, just look for an **Options** or **Preferences** button or menu and enter the SMTP and NNTP information into the appropriate areas. You will also need to provide your own identity, but you're on your own for that one.

After you enter the above information, you'll probably see far too many options that will ask you intrusive questions such as how long you would like to retain articles after you've read them, the number of articles you would like to retrieve each time you go online, what colors you would like to use, etc. Far too many questions, in my opinion.

My recommendation, particularly if it's your first time venturing into the netherworld of newsgroups, is to accept the default settings. Whatever exists when you're setting things up, just leave them alone. Why look for trouble? You can always tweak the settings later, once you're a bit more familiar with newsgroups in general and have a sense of what might work best for you.

Retrieving Newsgroups

When you fire up your newsreader, you will automatically connect to your Internet service provider's news server and the process of downloading thousands of newsgroups will begin. Since there are so many newsgroups, this process could take several minutes, depending upon the speed of your Internet connection and the number of newsgroups your Internet service provider has subscribed to. Just be patient. You will only have to go through this process the first time.

Once the downloading process is complete, you should see hundreds of newsgroup folders with the number of groups contained within each folder. Each folder contains newsgroups categorized by type, such as alt., comp., etc., as we discussed earlier in this chapter. This newsgroup listing only contains the group names, not the actual articles contained within each group. To view articles, you need to retrieve the articles, and to do that you will need to *subscribe* to one or more groups of interest.

Finding Newsgroups of Interest

To locate newsgroups that discuss topics of interest to you, your newsreader program will contain a search mechanism so you can search for a keyword within a newsgroup name (such as `cats`). Scrolling through the hundreds of newsgroups available to you is an excellent way to become familiar with newsgroups, in general, as well as newsgroup hierarchies.

Several searchable newsgroup directories are available on the Web and are well worth a visit if you're looking for a newsgroup discussing a particular topic of interest to you:

CyberFiber Newsgroups   A comprehensive directory to Usenet and `alt.` newsgroups.

   `http://www.cyberfiber.com`

DejaNews   Archives containing more than 100 million articles dating back to 1995. An excellent way to avoid subscribing to newsgroups and newsreader software if you simply want to search newsgroup postings about a specific topic.

   `http://www.dejanews.com`

Liszt   Search directories by topic or by newsgroup name. Mailing lists, too.

   `http://www.liszt.com/news`

Reference.com   Search for data within newsgroups as well as by newsgroup topic. Also search mailing lists.

   `http://www.reference.com`

RemarQ   Search by keyword among newsgroup titles or posted articles.

   `http://www.remarq.com`

Tile.net　An Internet resource guide that includes an excellent newsgroup search.

```
http://www.tile.net
```

Starter Newsgroups

The following newsgroups represent just a small sampling of the thousands of newsgroups available, but they are good places to begin exploring the information-laden world of newsgroups:

`alt.computer`	`misc.health`
`alt.fifty-plus.friends`	`misc.invest.stocks`
`alt.government`	`rec.arts.movies`
`alt.health.alternative`	`rec.marketplace.travel`
`alt.health.hmo`	`rec.sport.golf`
`alt.investors`	`rec.travel.cruises`
`alt.politics.org`	`soc.senior.issues`
`alt.travel`	`soc.senior.health+fitness`
`misc.computers`	`soc.genealogy.misc`

Subscribing to Newsgroups

There are three primary activities involved in newsgroup participation: reading, posting, and replying.

In order to read messages or articles posted by others within newsgroups, you must first subscribe to a newsgroup. There is no charge for subscribing. Unlike magazine subscriptions which will begin sending you renewal notices before the first issue arrives, the word *subscribe* in newsgroup parlance simply means placing a selected newsgroup into a separate folder so it's segregated from the great unwashed mass of newsgroups. Placing subscribed newsgroups into a separate folder makes them easier to locate in the future, plus many newsreader programs permit you to attach special priorities or options to subscribed-to newsgroups.

Subscribing with Outlook Express

To subscribe to newsgroups with Outlook Express:

1. Click the news server and select **Tools** ➤ **Newsgroups**.

2. From the list presented, select the group or groups of interest to you, then click **Subscribe**. The **GoTo** button will start the downloading process.

During the downloading, you'll be retrieving article headers which contain the subject, date, and the name of the person posting the article. Having this information is very handy when you want to search for postings from a particular person or relating to a particular subject. You will also have the ability to sort these articles by subject, by date, or by author.

Articles sorted by subject are best sorted in *thread* order, which means in the sequence in which they were posted. Reading discussion group articles presented in this manner makes it much easier to follow a conversation between one or more individuals.

Once the headers have downloaded, clicking on an article will retrieve the body of the article, which you can then read in the preview pane or window.

If you retrieve a newsgroup, decide it's not for you, and have no interest in retrieving additional articles from the group in the future, you'll need to remove the group by selecting **Unsubscribe** from the **Tools** ➤ **Newsgroups** menu, or right-click your mouse and select it from the menu presented.

Subscribing with Netscape Collabra

Collabra (see Figure 7.2) is the newsreader bundled with Netscape Navigator. Could it be any more convenient? I think not.

The process of subscribing using Collabra is almost identical to Outlook Express, but I'm sure that's just a coincidence, a fluke of technology. What are the odds?

1. Select **Subscribe to Discussion Groups,** then open the folders and look through the groups listed until you find a group or groups of interest to you.

2. When you find something that looks interesting, intriguing, or perversely provocative, be sure to e-mail me. No, no, just kidding. When you find a newsgroup of interest, click **Subscribe,** and close the window.

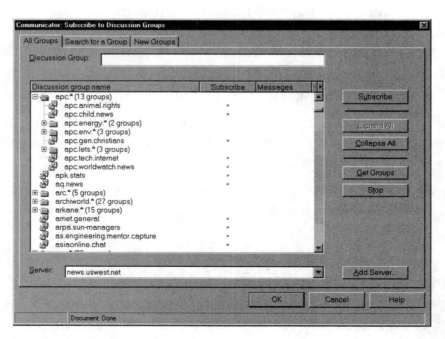

FIGURE 7.2: Netscape Collabra Newsreader

3. To begin retrieving article headers, highlight or select the specific group, then choose **Open Discussion Group** from the **File** menu or right-click your mouse and select it from the menu presented.

Now you can select any article to download the body of the message and display it in the preview pane. The unwritten rule associated with newsgroups is "no pane, no gain," so be adventuresome! Explore newsgroups and all the options available to you within your newsreader. You can't hurt anything, so why not have some fun?

To Lurk or Not to Lurk

Reading articles without contributing your own opinions or information is referred to as *lurking*. Though it sounds like a pejorative term, it's really not. Many people lurk. Some of my best friends are lurkers. But if you think of newsgroups as informational potluck suppers, if people only come to eat and never bring a dish, it won't take long before pickins are mighty slim. Just as a conversation is not a conversation if only one person is speaking, a newsgroup is only valuable if many people contribute information based on their own personal knowledge and experience.

Lurking is very appropriate when you first visit any newsgroup. It will afford you the opportunity to become comfortable with the ambiance of the group and develop an overall sense of the tone and tenor of the group. Just as you wouldn't walk into an ongoing meeting in the offline world and begin speaking immediately, the same rule applies to life online. Listen and observe before speaking. Participating members of the group will appreciate the courtesy, and above all, it will save you global embarrassment and humiliation.

Posting

Posting articles is very similar to sending e-mail. You can either start a new thread or topic, follow up by replying to an existing thread, or respond privately by e-mail.

When you start a new thread, you'll be prompted to enter a **Subject** that provides a hint to other readers regarding the topic of your underlying message. First, be sure you're in the most appropriate newsgroup for your posting. Don't post a question about the care and feeding of the Tasmanian aardvark in the `rec.bicycles` newsgroup. That will drive other participants crazy and you'll hear about it. Oh, boy, will you hear about it. Participants in most newsgroups expect you to respect the rules of the group.

Every newsgroup has one or more FAQ (Frequently Asked Questions) files which will describe the rules of the group, provide posting guidelines, and answers to—well, frequently asked questions. Before participating in any newsgroup, take a few minutes and read the FAQ associated with that group. Finding FAQ files is easy if you use the FAQ Finder Web site located at `http://faqfinder.ics.uci.edu:8001/`.

 MIT maintains an archive of most Usenet FAQ's at: `ftp://rtfm.mit.edu/pub/usenet-by-group/`.

Be sure to make your subject line meaningful and helpful to others. If your subject is too cryptic, other participants are not likely to read it.

To post a new thread using Outlook Express, enter the newsgroup, then click the **New Message** toolbar or select **Compose ➤ New Message**.

To post a new thread using Netscape's Collabra, select **Message ➤ New Message**.

Replying

Replying to articles is the original Internet no-brainer. The only choice you really have to make is whether to post your reply within the newsgroup itself, send it directly to the author of the article you're responding to, or both. If I'm replying to an article and just making general chitchat, I reply within the group. If I'm replying to a question posed by another participant, in the highly unlikely event that I actually know the answer, I'll reply *and* post meaning my response will be sent directly to the poster, and also appear in the newsgroup for others to see.

Testing, Testing, 1-2-3

When you first connect to a newsgroup, you'll feel like you entered an arena where everybody else knows what's going on and you're an intruder who is standing out like the proverbial sore thumb. If you're like most first-time newsgroupies, you'll be somewhere between clueless and moot, which are two small towns just outside of Yuma, Arizona, as I recall.

It's not a comfortable feeling to know that you could inadvertently stumble into a newsgroup and make a fool of yourself or initiate a FlameFest. A *flame* is a nasty or hostile message. If you participate in newsgroups, at some point you will be flamed. Some people

seemingly exist to flame others. Don't take it personally, and never, ever, respond.

So how can you get some firsthand, real-world newsgroup experience and avoid getting flamed in the process? There are several newsgroups created for testing purposes. These newsgroups are the perfect place to post articles in safety. You won't offend anybody, you can post as many articles as you wish, and you can see what articles and replies look like. You'll probably receive autogenerated responses and in some cases other participants who are also learning the newsgroup ropes may respond to you. Remember, everybody is just feeling his or her way along, so have fun, meet the other first-timers, and if you can help each other out, so much the better. That's the true spirit of the Internet in action.

Test newsgroups include `alt.test` and `misc.test`. Your Internet service provider may also host its own test newsgroup, so keep an eye out for that when reviewing that first download of newsgroups available to you.

When Is a Newsgroup Not a Newsgroup?

Within the Newsgroup family—let's call it a distant cousin twice removed—exists another means of communicating with many people in a discussion group format called a *mailing list* (or *mail list* among friends). Understanding the differences between a newsgroup and a mailing list can be challenging at first, though if I really work at this I can probably guarantee a lifetime of confusion.

Newsgroups and mailing lists are discussion groups devoted to specific subjects. The primary difference is this: When you post an article to a newsgroup, in order for anybody to read your words of wisdom they must go to the specific newsgroup where you posted your article. Not so with a mailing list. With a mailing list, any time you contribute a message, a copy of your message is sent to a subscriber's e-mail address.

So if you judge the quality of your life by the amount of e-mail you receive, and who doesn't, all you need to do is join a mailing list. Some mailing lists generate hundreds of e-mails every day; others generate very few. Either way, no cobwebs will be growing in your e-mail box once you subscribe to one or more mailing lists.

There are two categories of mailing lists, closed and open. A closed mailing list is a one-way list or what we refined, cultured types call the "shut-up-and-listen" type. These lists provide information to you, but you are not welcome to reply or offer your own comments. An open mailing list is more closely aligned with the newsgroup format in that the contributions of participants provide the content for the mailing list.

Mailing list terminology is similar to newsgroup terminology in several respects. To join a mailing list, you *subscribe* to a list, and to stop receiving e-mail from a particular list you *unsubscribe*. Subscribing is very easy and usually consists of nothing more than filling out a form on a Web site that requests your e-mail address. The first message you will receive from any mailing list, usually an autogenerated message within minutes, will be an administrative message and will contain important information about the list you have subscribed to, including information on how to unsubscribe. Unsubscribing is as easy as sending an e-mail to the administrative authority of any mailing list. LISTSERV and MajorDomo are two of the most popular automated mailing list systems administrators, hosting more than 250,000 mailing lists between them.

To Locate Mailing Lists of Interest to You, Visit Any of the Following Web Sites:

CataList, the Official Catalog of LISTSERV lists

Search more than 24,000 mailing lists

`http://www.lsoft.com/lists/listref.html`

listTool

Search more than 700 categories of mailing lists

`http://www.listtool.com`

Liszt, the Mailing List Directory

Search more than 90,000 mailing lists

`http://www.liszt.com`

Publicly Accessible Mailing Lists

Vivian's Mailing List Resources

`http://www.neosoft.com/internet/paml/indexes.html`

Newsgroup Netiquette

It's important to respect the Internet and newsgroup culture while participating. Long-standing rules and codes of conduct are referred to as *Netiquette*, short for "Internet Etiquette," in case you couldn't guess.

Unlike search engines, (see Chapter 10, "Internet Search Engines") which return results based upon your keyword queries, when you make an inquiry within a newsgroup, you're addressing your question(s) to other participants. Search engines don't become irritable or ill-tempered, and rarely lash out at others. Human foibles being what they are, on occasion you may ask a seemingly innocent and innocuous question and be flamed in response. How rude! But it happens, and when it does, just ignore it. Cybermorons are alive and well, but rest assured it's only a tiny minority of the Internet community that exhibits the social skills of a three-year-old.

In Chapter 13, "Effective Online Communication," I'll discuss the ten basic rules for writing on the Internet, in general. Limiting our focus to newsgroups for the moment, if you follow these few basic rules of Newsgroup Netiquette, you'll be well on your way to ensuring a positive newsgroup experience.

- Don't post articles USING ALL CAPS. This is a sure-fire way to spot a novice. Typing in all caps is the equivalent of shouting online and it's to be avoided at all times. Unless, of course, you intend to shout.

- Lurk n' smirk. Before you post an article, read a newsgroup for a period of time. The amount of time will vary, but just make sure it's long enough for you to develop some insight into the focus of the group, as well as the group's culture. Enjoy the process of lurking. It feels just like eavesdropping because it is eavesdropping. Reading posted articles for a period of time will help you understand what's appropriate for posting in the group and what's not.

- Read the FAQ. Most newsgroups have a FAQ file that will provide background information about the newsgroup as well as posting guidelines.

 A festival of Usenet FAQ's can be found at `ftp://rtfm.mit .edu/pub/usenet-by-group/`.

- If you post to a newsgroup, be sure your article contributes something to the discussion. Many people find it irritating to see articles that contribute nothing more than "I agree." When people become irritated in newsgroups, that's when its time to break out the asbestos fez because the flames won't be far behind.

- Quote back. If you reply to another article, include a pithy quote from the original article to provide readers some context for your comments. If the original article is long, delete as much of it as you can without losing the context of the original article or the portion to which you are responding.

- Check back. Once you've posted a question or comment, be sure to return to the newsgroup frequently to see if there are any responses or requests for clarifications. Check at least once each day.

Have Fun!

The Internet is many things to many people. For most of us comfortably ensconced in the 50 + generation, we've worked for many years, we've paid our dues, and it's our responsibility to make these the best years of our lives. Can that be accomplished alone? I suppose it can, but it will be infinitely more enjoyable if we interact with others along the way. Newsgroups afford each of us the opportunity to interact with individuals around the world and the results can be incredibly gratifying.

When I was growing up, it was a very big deal to receive a long-distance phone call in my household. The family would gather around the phone and shout into the receiver for no particular reason other than we knew the person on the other end was in a distant city. A long-distance call was a celebrated event.

Of course, times have changed and long-distance calls are an everyday occurrence. But communicating with other individuals around the corner or around the world from the comfort and convenience of your home computer through the Internet, whether it be by e-mail or Usenet newsgroup, is nothing short of a miracle. It's easy to get caught up in the technology and not really think about what's happening right in front of us or the power of the communications vehicle we have at our fingertips. So be sure to stop periodically along the way, step back, take a deep breath, and smell the modem.

Enjoy it, experience it, and most importantly, have fun with it.

What's Next?

I suppose at some point some digital doofus will come along and start predicting that one day we'll be using our televisions to access the Internet. On second thought, today we *can* access the Internet using a television, so stay tuned and don't touch that dial. In the next chapter we'll explore the new and exciting world of WebTV!

WebTV

Have you ever dreamed—dare I say fantasized—about
lounging in front of your television, comfy in your classic La-Z-Boy Dreamtime Reclina-Rocker, a profusion of
high-fat/low-nutrition snacks and beverages within arm's reach,
and simultaneously surfing the Internet? Me neither, but in this
chapter, you'll discover how Microsoft's WebTV and WebTV
Network Service are making those nondreams a virtual reality
for more than 700,000 subscribers in the United States, Canada,
and Japan.

With WebTV you can surf the World Wide Web using your television instead of a computer. You can also maintain up to six e-mail accounts and have access to thousands of discussion groups. In addition, you can monitor what your kids or grandkids are doing on the Web to make sure your 14-year-old doesn't wind up as a pen pal to somebody named Bubba at the state penitentiary.

Even if you know absolutely nothing about the Internet, computers, or the cost of microprocessor chips in Singapore, you can be accessing the Internet, receiving junk e-mail, get-rich-quick schemes, and virus hoaxes within minutes of using WebTV. Sounds like a dream come true, doesn't it?

WebTV is an excellent choice if you're not particularly interested in learning about computers. And if that's the way you feel, you're in very good company. But just because you may not be interested in computers doesn't mean you're out of the technological loop. Nor does it mean that you cannot communicate via e-mail with your children, grandchildren, friends, and former neighbors. The old neighborhood that physically may be thousands of miles away is always just around the corner on the Internet.

The process of setting up WebTV is as simple as plugging in the phone, hooking up the TV, and pressing the power button on the remote control unit. But first, you'll need to decide which WebTV service is right for you. Decisions, decisions, decisions.

Classic vs. Plus

WebTV is available in two popular flavors, WebTV Classic and WebTV Plus. WebTV Plus is a bit more expensive than WebTV Classic, but well worth the extra expense. Mr. Modem's rule of thumb when purchasing computers and related equipment is to purchase the best equipment—

meaning newest, fastest, most-current-but-will-not-be-obsolete-next-Thursday—that your budget will comfortably permit. The important word here is *comfortably*.

Let's pause for a combination philosophical moment and reality check. Face it. Despite all the hoopla, accessing the Internet isn't a necessity of life. If you're like me, you have lived a rich, full, rewarding life (it's my story, I can lie if I want to!) without the Internet. So let's be sure to keep this entire phenomenon in perspective. It's not worth taking out a second mortgage or selling the family kitty to obtain a computer or WebTV. In the overall scheme of things, it's just not that important. It's fun, it's convenient, it's wonderful, it's even kind of groovy, as we hipsters say, but it's not a necessity of life. Thus concludes today's Shermanette. Go in peace, my cyberfriend.

Okay, back to Classic versus Plus. Without going into mind-numbing detail, Plus is an upgrade from Classic—not that there's anything wrong with Classic—and the Plus user typically has a different focus from the Classic user. I used to have a different focus, too, but a good set of bifocals resolved that situation.

WebTV Classic offers everything you need to get started. If you think of the differences between Classic and Plus in terms of buying a car, WebTV Classic is your basic transportation. It will transport you from Point A to Point B in comfort and safety. But wouldn't it be nice to have power seats, quadraphonic sound, maybe a little sunroof or perhaps more horsepower so you can rev the engine and impress/annoy the neighbors? Of course it would! And that's why the good folks who offer WebTV include a number of upgrades in WebTV Plus.

Plus is really for those individuals who are interested in combining television and the Internet into what some might refer to as *Intervision*, or perhaps *Telenet*? *Intertele*? *TVNet*? *TubeNet*? *TeleTube*? Well, you get the idea. For example, Plus features scrolling TV listings, a little TV window so you can watch TV while on the Web, and actual links or connections between TV shows and Web sites, "yo, Vanna!" The Plus processor provides more horsepower than the Classic, it has more memory, the modem is faster, and there's a larger hard drive.

Author's Loophole

WebTV is continually evolving and improving, so be sure to check with your local consumer electronics store for the most current configurations available and/or additional differences between WebTV Classic and Plus. You can also visit http://www.webtv.com.

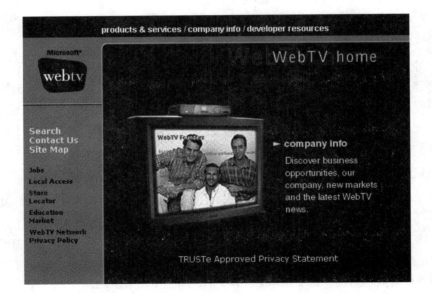

But if you can visit that Web site, that means you have access to the Internet, so perhaps you're just patronizing me by reading this chapter. Be honest, now. Are you reading this because you really want to or are you just doing it for me? Please, don't do it for me. I'll be fine. Go on, read ahead. Have fun. You have your whole book in front of you. I'll be fine. Really.

Equipment

WebTV-based Internet terminals and receivers are available from companies like Sony, Philips, and Mitsubishi at finer consumer electronics stores hither and yon, which is just a folksy way of saying "nationwide."

Only four pieces of equipment are needed to use WebTV: the WebTV terminal and remote control, a keyboard, and a few wires and cables so you can spend hours of quality time untangling them like most computer users do everyday. These cables, annoying as they may be, connect your WebTV terminal to your telephone line, your TV, and for you technical masochists, even your VCR. (You'll need WebTV Plus to be able to connect your VCR, though.)

When shopping for WebTV, you will learn that the keyboard is an optional item. Technically, it is an optional item, but trust me, it really isn't. You don't want to try to write e-mail using the on-screen keyboard. That would be like trying to drive with three wheels on your car. Can you do it? Sure, you can. You might even make the evening news. And wouldn't your family be proud? But it wouldn't be the most pleasurable driving experience of your life, so it would be best avoided if possible.

The Plus keyboard and the remote unit controls TV functions, which will permit you to perform the always-popular WebTV "flip" between the Web and regular TV. If channel surfing drives your spouse or housemate crazy, just wait until the added dimension of flipping between television channels and the Web is within your grasp! Rumor has it a future option may even offer a marriage-counseling component, though WebTV Syndrome will, of course, not be covered by most HMOs.

Cables, Wires, and Other Tangly Things

Let me state at the outset that I really don't like cables and wires. I'm always putting them in the wrong place or getting tangled up in them. It doesn't matter if the instructions suggest that "even a trained chimp can assemble this blindfolded," I never get it right the first time.

The good news is that connecting WebTV is about as foolproof as it gets. Rumor has it even the trained chimp was sending e-mail within minutes and is currently earning $5,000 every month stuffing envelopes from his cage.

There are only two types of cables and wires required: telephone and audio/video—or "A/V," as we who try in vain to impress our friends and neighbors call it. The telephone wire stretches from the WebTV terminal to the wall jack—or to the wall, Jack, as the case may be.

 Danger, geekspeak ahead!

To connect the WebTV system to your TV, your TV will need either an RCA jack (those are the round ones) or an S-Video input cable—the ones that have five or six pins. I love saying, "S-Video input cable." Go ahead and say it out loud. Doesn't it make you sound so knowledgeable and high-techie? Try to work it into a conversation with a loved one today, then enjoy the Nancy Reaganesque gaze of admiration that will be cast upon you. Feels good, doesn't it?

The colorful cables, red and white for audio, yellow for video, are used for moving audio and video from your WebTV terminal to your TV. If you have a VCR, you'll be running the audio and video to the VCR first, then from the VCR to the TV. Everybody sing, "The headbone's connected to the neck bone; the neck bone's connected to the collar bone...."

WebTV Plus has a few additional cables and wires because the Plus terminal has a TV tuner lurking within it. You can hook cable directly into the antenna coax input thingy (technical term), which is cable-ready. Your cable-converter box can also plug into the coax input.

All this cable and wiring stuff sounds a lot worse than it is. WebTV, Classic or Plus, is about as close to plug-and-play as nickels in a slot machine.

For Whom the Ma Bell Tolls

Hooking up your WebTV to the telephone is easy. You do not need to have another telephone jack installed, so when the door-to-door telephone jack salesman comes calling, don't be intimidated. All you need to do is use the little splitter device thoughtfully included with your WebTV system to plug into your existing telephone jack. Plug the phone into one side and your WebTV into the other. Voila!

The first time you power up and connect, your WebTV system will dial an 800 number to locate the closest access provider to your location. Configuring the system to use this number in the future is done automatically, so don't be concerned about it. For most folks, connecting to the Internet will be a local phone call. Documentation packaged with your WebTV will explain how to check first by using what's called the Phone Lookup Utility or PLU for TLA (Three-Letter Acronym) enthusiasts.

WebTV Networks also provide an optional service called OpenISP, which permits you to use the local or national Internet service provider (ISP) of your choice for access to the Internet. This comes in handy if Internet access would require a long-distance call using the access number provided by WebTV Networks. You don't want to be incurring long-distance charges every time you log on. The price of the OpenISP service is in addition to your ISP monthly charges.

Options and Accessories

It has often been said by those far wiser than Mr. Modem, that what distinguishes us humans from other members of the animal kingdom is our ability to accessorize (and the fact that we're not afraid of vacuum cleaners.) Nowhere is that truer than with WebTV. A plethora of accessories awaits your technology budget:

Wireless Keyboard   Though offered as an option, I would strongly recommend purchasing a WebTV-compatible wireless keyboard. The keyboard works by infrared, so you can hold it on your lap or use it just about anywhere without getting tangled up in cables. Additional benefit: Using the keyboard on your lap, if you place a slice of bread on each thigh, radiation emitted from the infrared keyboard will make toast in a jiffy. (Easy does it, WebTV lawyers; don't get your briefs in a knot. Mr. Modem is just yanking your cables.)

RF Adapter   An RF Adapter is available for WebTV Plus, which allows you to connect your WebTV Plus unit to older televisions without an RCA jack. An RCA jack is the type of jack found on most stereo speakers.

Printers   The WebTV Classic terminal requires a printer adapter which is only available for the Philips Magnavox system and is compatible with the Hewlett Packard DeskJet 400 and 600 Series. The receiver for WebTV Plus service has a built-in printer port which is compatible with Hewlett Packard DeskJet 400 and 600 series, and the Canon BJC-80, 200, 600, and 4000 Series BubbleJet printers. The HP670TV color printer is specially designed for WebTV.

The Price of Admission

WebTV is a very cost-effective method of joining your friends and family already frolicking in the Internet surf. But like all things in life, there is no free lunch, so you need to be aware of a few ongoing costs before deciding if WebTV is for you. The good news, however, is that WebTV is just a fraction of the price of a computer. A WebTV terminal is less than $200 and includes everything you need to cruise the Internet while sitting on your classic La-Z-Boy Dreamtime Reclina-Rocker.

WebTV Classic Pricing

Pricing (current at publication date) for WebTV Classic service is $19.95/month. WebTV Classic OpenISP service is an additional $9.95/month. This charge is in addition to your ISP monthly charge.

WebTV Plus Pricing

Pricing (current at publication date) for WebTV Plus service is $24.95/month. WebTV Plus OpenISP service is an additional $14.95/month. This charge is—let's say it together—in addition to your ISP monthly charge.

Billing

Every WebTV account requires a monthly subscription to WebTV Networks. A variety of subscriptions are available and average approximately $20/month. This service will be charged to a credit card—preferably your own—by the good folks at WebTV Networks. You will be requested to provide credit card information when setting up your WebTV equipment.

Once you're online, please visit `http://www.webtv.com` for more information.

What's Next?

If you place your ear close to this page as if you were listening to the sound of the ocean in a seashell, you may be able to hear a ring announcer in the background shouting, "Let's get ready to download!" Coming up next, while not exactly the "Thrilla in Manila," is our very own "Battle of the Browsers!" (And the crowd goes mild....)

The Battle of the Browsers

The browser war battle lines continue to be more clearly defined with each passing day, and we Web surfers are the ultimate beneficiaries of these cyber skirmishes.

In the glorious days of yesteryear, when 386 computers ruled the land and 9,600bps modems were squealing with delight, selecting a World Wide Web browser software program was easy. You could select Mosaic, or if you didn't like Mosaic, you could always try Mosaic. Mosaic was written by a student at the University of Illinois at Urbana named Marc Andreessen. Oh, sure, all the other geeks laughed and snapped their modem cables at him in the shower, but Marc's upstart program ultimately evolved into a less laughable, multibazillion-dollar program called Netscape Navigator. From October 1995 to April 1996, Netscape Navigator captured a staggering 85 percent of the World Wide Web browser market. When Netscape went public, profits from the initial public stock offering were so vast, it is rumored that his portion alone permitted Andreessen to make a hefty down payment toward the purchase of a new Yugo. Just another rags-to-riches tale from the 'Net.

During this same time, a young fellow by the name of Yates or Bates—something like that—from the Seattle area, had a vision. His vision started innocently enough and included, among other things, domination of all computerdom. When the World Wide Web exploded with growth, Mr. Gates—that's it, Gates—looked out upon the firmament known as the Internet, saw that it was good and proclaimed, "Let this be mine." Pledging a small portion of their petty cash, Bill Gates and his Microsoft Corporation began a crusade to develop a Web browser program that would ultimately dethrone the reigning champ, Netscape. The Microsoft browser came to be known as the Internet Explorer, or IE among friends.

As Netscape and Microsoft continue to battle, we lowly cyberslugs of the world are the ultimate beneficiaries. Development is fast and furious. A new version of Netscape Navigator is followed by a new version of Internet Explorer. An Internet Explorer update is followed by a new plug-in or add-on program from Netscape. Each successive update is better than the one before. It's like having Christmas all year long! *"Software hosting on an open line, Bill Gates nipping at the 'Net..."*

An unfortunate result of this evolutionary process has been confusion on the part of Internet enthusiasts. The question I am most frequently asked at my seminars—well, other than directions to the restroom—is, "What browser should I use?" There actually is no right or wrong answer. Netscape Navigator and Internet Explorer are pretty much running neck and neck, at the time of this writing, but check back in 30 minutes.

How Suite It Is

Before we meander deeper into the heart of browser territory, let's clear up a source of confusion surrounding the names associated with Netscape—the company and the software. The company that originally graced us with its fine software product is Netscape Communications Corporation, frequently referred to as Netscape, which has since been acquired by America Online—frequently referred to as AOL.

Its suite of software programs is Netscape Communicator, frequently referred to as Netscape. The six programs are all rolled into one luscious package designed to provide everything you need to get the most out of your new Internet lifestyle. Netscape Communicator includes:

Netscape Messenger for e-mail

Netscape Collabra for Newsgroups

Netscape Conference for real-time phone and chat

Netscsape Composer for designing Web pages

Netscape Navigator for browsing the Web; also frequently referred to as Netscape.

Throughout this chapter I'll be referring to Netscape Navigator when I refer to the browser software. And the next time anybody mentions Netscape in your presence, just grab them by the lapels and demand to know if they're talking about the company, the suite of software or the browser. Chances are they won't have clue, either.

Personally, I use both browsers, Internet Explorer and Netscape Navigator, just so I can stay current with both programs—or be hopelessly behind the curve with both programs, depending upon one's perspective. Trying to remain current with two or more rapidly evolving programs is an approach to technology that only a masochist could love.

Since browsers are just like any other piece of software, personal preference has to be the deciding factor. Netscape Navigator and Internet Explorer are free for the downloading, so my recommendation is to try them both, keeping in mind that you're not obligated to stick with one exclusively. Just use whatever you feel comfortable using. The Web is nothing if not democratic.

Installing Browsers

In the next sections, we'll take a look at installing both Netscape Navigator and Internet Explorer. Following the installation instructions, you'll find lots of user-friendly browser tips.

Both browsers have new versions and updates coming out fairly frequently, so don't hold off installing an update because something new is probably going to come along soon. The truth is that there's *always* something new coming along soon. You can easily upgrade your browser at any time by downloading the latest and the greatest version from the Web, as I'll soon explain in mind-numbing detail.

One suggestion before we begin: If you haven't upgraded to Windows 95 or 98, I would recommend you do that first. Using an older version of Windows such as 3.11 will limit your ability to experience some of the technological miracles emerging every day on the Internet.

Netscape Navigator

Netscape Navigator is one of the handiest tools available when it comes to finding your way around the World Wide Web. Using Netscape Navigator, you'll be able to locate Web sites of interest as well as bookmark those sites so you can return to them in the future. If you're not sure where to start your surfing adventures, Netscape Navigator thoughtfully includes a Personal Toolbar complete with a couple of navigational links (What's Cool and What's New) to help you get started. You'll find lots of flexibility throughout Netscape Navigator, so be creative and have fun as you create a customized toolbar with links to Web sites that you visit frequently. How? Stay tuned and after we walk through the easy installation process we'll take a look at some of the bells and whistles that make it easy to understand why Netscape Navigator is as popular as it is.

Installing Netscape Navigator

A commercial version of Netscape Navigator is available at finer software stores everywhere, but the program is also downloadable. The advantage of purchasing the commercial version is that it typically includes a lovely software manual that you can add to your collection of unread software manuals. If you are already on the Web and want to download the latest and greatest version of Netscape Navigator, point your browser to Netscape's home page (`http://www.netscape.com`), which will bring you to Netscape's NetCenter (shown in Figure 9.1).

Author's loophole: The following installation instructions were accurate as of the date of publication, but may not reflect installation instructions currently displayed on the Netscape Web site. Always utilize the most current information available on the Web site.

Click **Browsers**. The next page that presents itself will display the word *Download*. And as we all know, what good is a Web page without something to click on, so go right ahead and click **Download** and let the fun begin!

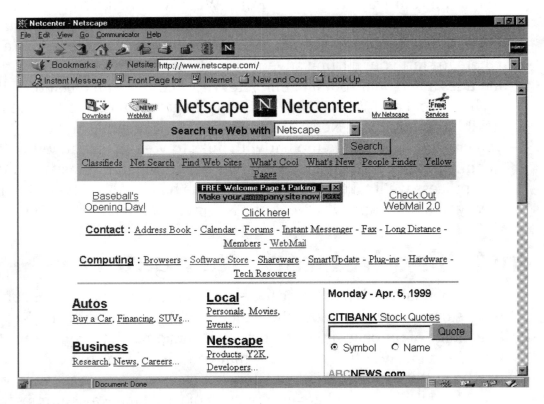

FIGURE 9.1: Netscape's Netcenter

Scroll down to **Full Download** or **Fast Update** (if you're updating from a previous version of Netscape). If you select **Full Download**, you'll be asked to select your platform—which is just a fancy way of asking you to identify what your computer is using for its operating system, Windows 95/98/NT or Mac PowerPC. Select the appropriate operating system to ensure that you download the correct version of Netscape Navigator. If you're using a Mac and you download a Windows 98 version of Netscape, massive global warming will result and you wouldn't want that on your conscience. So be sure to select the correct system.

If you're using Netscape 4.0, click the **SmartUpdate** link to get the latest Netscape (4.5 or higher) features without downloading the entire program.

After clicking the **Windows 95/98/NT** link, you'll be presented with the SmartDownload option. SmartDownload lets you pause, resume, and surf the web while you download. As the gratuitous hype exclaims, "Download with confidence using SmartDownload!" If you frequently lose your connection to the Internet when downloading, SmartDownload may be just what the doctor ordered.

A word to the wise: Before using the SmartDownload option, click the **Tell Me More About SmartDownload** link displayed. There are a few considerations and caveats you need to be aware of, so read this information carefully.

If you're a purist at heart, click **Download Communicator 4.5 Without Using SmartDownload** and let the games commence.

You will then see a Save As box that will ask you to identify a folder in which to save the Netscape download. Using Windows 95 or 98, I always download to my Desktop so I can install a program and then delete the icon from my Desktop, thus keeping my Desktop perpetually neat and tidy. If you prefer, you can put the file in a temp (temporary) folder on your hard drive. Be sure to write down the file's name if you put it in a location other than on your Desktop so you can find it later. Then click **Save** to download the file.

Netscape 4.5 is approximately 14.3MB in size, and the technical term for such files is *big honker*. At 28.8Kbps, this puppy will take about an hour and 15 minutes to download; at 56Kbps it will require about 35 minutes. If you are using a modem slower than 28.8, please stop reading immediately and if we ever meet, let's just pretend we don't know each other. It'll be better that way.

After the file has downloaded completely, you will have to launch the browser setup program. While you are still connected to the Internet, run the setup program by double-clicking the icon bearing the filename of the file you just downloaded (for example, cc32345.exe.). Please note that June 23 is National Netscape Day, so be sure to make plans to take your browser to launch.

The setup program itself will launch the Installation Wizard who will then escort you through the rest of the installation process.

Netscape Navigator 4 (and Higher) Tips

Here are three tips to speed up download times.

1. Turn Off the Graphics

Select **Edit** ➢ **Preferences** ➢ **Advanced**, then uncheck the **Automatically Load Images** box. To view any image or animation right-click the place-holder icon that appears on a Web page and select **Show Image.**

2. Deactivate Java

Select **Edit** ➢ **Preferences** ➢ **Advanced**. Uncheck **Enable Java** and **Enable JavaScript**.

3. Increase Cache Size

Select **Edit** ➢ **Preferences**. Click the symbol beside **Advanced**, then highlight **Cache**. Enter a new size value for your cache in the Disk Cache box. Recommended cache size: 15MB to 20MB, if you have room.

If you are a high-speed surfer careening from site to site and rarely return to the same site, you can speed up browsing by *decreasing* the size of your cache.

Revisiting Web Sites

To take a second look at a Web site you previously visited:

1. Right-click the **Back** or **Forward** buttons and a list of recently visited sites will pop up.

2. Review the list, select a page, and click on it to revisit.

or

1. Select **History** from the toolbar menu.

2. Highlight the site you wish to revisit. Sites can be sorted by name and date last visited.

> Using the Back or Forward button to revisit sites is not the same as using the History list. The History list displays all sites visited going back as many days as you have configured under **Edit ➤ Preferences ➤ Navigator**. The Back button displays the Web page you last visited. The Forward button returns you to your location at the time you clicked the Back button.

Speedy URL Address Entry

The autocomplete feature fills in a partially typed URL by comparing what you are entering to previously visited pages. If you enter **www.netsca**..., for example, and you have previously visited the Netscape Communications, Inc. Web site, the entire URL, `www.netscape.com`, will be completed for you.

Obtaining Netscape Navigator 4 Updates

To download updates, follow these simple steps. It's as easy as 1-2-3.

1. Select **Help ➤ Software Updates**.

2. Check any available updates needed.

3. Click the **Begin SmartUpdate** button at the bottom. Updated files are downloaded and automatically installed.

Stop Annoying Animation

Selecting **View** ➤ **Stop Animations** will freeze animations.

Select Your Own Startup Page

Choose **Edit** ➤ **Preferences** ➤ **Navigator**. In the Location field, type in the address of the Web page you would like to see each time you launch Netscape. Click **OK**.

Modify the Taskbar

Change the appearance and characteristics of the Taskbar by right-clicking its gray button and selecting items from the pop-up menu displayed.

Toolbar Tips

Toolbar tweaking may soon be an Olympic event, so here are a few of Mr. Modem's favorite tips and tweaks to incorporate into your training regimen.

- Expand, contract, or vaporize toolbars by clicking on the arrow appearing to the far left of each toolbar. When you see a hand icon replace the mouse pointer, click once.

- To create a Custom toolbar button for speedy access to a favorite Web site, go to the Web site, click the **Netsite** button, and drag it to the **Custom** toolbar.

- To edit the names of the Custom toolbar buttons created, click **Bookmarks QuickFile** ➤ **Edit Bookmarks**. Go to the Toolbar folder and highlight the bookmark you want to edit. Select Properties from the Item menu. In the Bookmark Properties dialog box displayed, edit the name of the custom button in the Name text box.

- Use the custom toolbar for your most frequently used bookmarks. Simply drag and drop URLs to the toolbar without going through the Bookmarks menu.

- Copy a folder of bookmarks into the Toolbar folder to create a button that will display a pop-up menu of bookmarks.

- To show or hide the Command, Location, or Custom toolbar, click **View** ➢ **Toolbars**, then select the toolbar.

- You can rearrange toolbar locations by clicking a non-functioning part of a toolbar and dragging it to a new location.

- You can change the Taskbar into a floating toolbar by opening the Window menu and selecting **Show Taskbar** or by clicking the grayed-out button at the left of the Taskbar. A larger version of the Taskbar will appear that you can drag to any location on your screen.

Want More Netscape 4 Browser Tips?

Click **Help** ➢ **Help Contents**. From the NetHelp Navigator, click the **Index** button for a complete list of browser tips.

Internet Explorer 5

Internet Explorer 5 has a number of significant improvements—what I'll characterize as neato features—over previous versions. It's actually not as large a program as its predecessors, so it loads faster than both Internet Explorer 4 and Netscape Navigator, plus it's easier to use. Since it looks so much like 4, the trauma of upgrading to a new program will probably be minimal for previous Internet Explorer users. Of course, that's easy for me to say. It may be the worst experience of your life. What do I know?

Some of its many new features include:

- New Cool tools! Well, cool toolbars would be more accurate. Follow the bouncing cursor to **View** ➢ **Toolbars** ➢ **Customize** to get to the new Customize Toolbar menu. You can add, remove, move, scramble—you really can make a mess of things if you put your mind to it. Try rearranging the buttons on your toolbars to personalize them or thoroughly confuse yourself. If you're sharing a computer with a loved one, don't miss this wonderful opportunity to rearrange their toolbars in the middle of the night. Then sit back and enjoy the hilarity that is sure to result just prior to the violence. Prankster Caveat: Remember the word *paybacks*. With that thought in mind, let your conscience be your guide and have fun.

- When you customize Explorer toolbars such as Favorites and History, Internet Explorer 5.0 will remember how you configured them. For your enhanced surfing pleasure, the last toolbar you had open prior to closing Internet Explorer will pop open the next time you launch your browser.

- The *Search Assistant* is a wizardish Search bar that lends a helping hand in searching for different Web sites, people, companies, graphics, etc. The wizard taps into one of several different types of search engines, depending on what you're searching for. You can choose which search engines you want to search, or search previous search results. This can be a real time-saver. You can also perform the same search with a different search engine.

- Speaking of searching, one feature I find particularly helpful is IE 5's ability to automatically highlight search terms contained within returned pages. Without this feature, the only option is to plow through each page looking for the word or phrase that triggered the search result. With automatic highlighting, it jumps right out at you. You can also save your most recent search questions so you don't have to reenter them.

- The *AutoInstall* feature really cuts down on dreaded plug-in anxiety. If you arrive on a Web page that requires additional Internet Explorer components, this feature will automatically download them and install them. Very painless, very smooth.

- The *AutoComplete Address* feature is very helpful because it doesn't just complete URLs, it segues into online forms to save you the trouble of having to fill out a form over and over again. For example, in my seminars I always use Yahoo! Maps (`http://maps.yahoo.com/py/maps.py`) to show how you can obtain driving directions on the Web. Once I fill in the starting address with IE 5, it remembers that address. So rather than having to reenter the street address and other information each time, I only have to start typing in the URL to bring up the site and my starting point information. You can also use this feature to save your username and password on some Web sites. Security buffs would have a conniption (or two, if they're small) over this, but if you're not too concerned about your username and password on certain sites, it really is a very handy way to log on easily.

- The *AutoCorrect* feature automatically correct typos that would otherwise prevent you from going directly to the page you want. For example, if you type **http:/**, the second forward slash will be added automatically; or if you mistakenly enter **ww** instead of **www**, that will receive a helpful nudge and be corrected for you.

- IE 5 users can import Netscape Bookmarks as Favorites, or export Favorites as Netscape Bookmarks. Something for everybody!

- With IE 5's *History Bar*, you can search previously visited Web sites by date, site name, most visited, least visited, most recently visited, most likely to visit again, least likely to visit again, most popular site in months when shellfish are in season, least popular sites during the vernal equinox, and on it goes. The options are seemingly endless. You can also view the history list next to links pages so you don't have to keep bouncing back and forth between the history list and the Web pages. In addition, you can review an alphabetized list of visited sites without the eye-glazing www prefix appearing before each listing.

- The new Favorites menu is one of my favori—well, let's just say it's very nice. Your Favorites file contains bookmarked Web sites so you can easily return to a Web site that you previously visited without having to remember its address. Right-click on any entry and you'll be presented with a menu that allows you to do the usual things such as rename, copy, send to, etc. A new option is *Make Available Offline*, which saves a Web site to your hard drive so you can view the site while not connected to the Internet.

- Probably the easiest way to manage your bookmarks is by using the Explorer Bar. Select **View ➤ Explorer Bars ➤ Favorites**. A bounty of buttons allow you to organize your Favorites, rename them, and generally get control over unruly Favorites.

- If you use Outlook Express as your e-mail program of choice, OE is now fully integrated as IE 5's e-mail program. You can manage multiple e-mail accounts, and a new Rules Wizard does a first-class job as a junk e-mail filter. The Start page includes separate sections for E-mail, Newsgroups, and the ever-popular Contacts feature, also known as an address book.

- The *Radio toolbar* is not a *must-have* feature, but it's awfully nice. It provides the ability to listen to radio stations anywhere in the world. You can review stations by category such as classical, country, adult contemporary music, talk, etc., and even add your favorite radio station to the play list.

- You can tell IE 5 which Web pages you want to view offline through a simple *Make Available Offline* feature. With offline browsing, you can create a schedule for updating Web sites of interest or downloading during off-peak hours.

- Use the *Parental Internet Content Selection (PICS) Rules* or *Content Advisor* to decide what your grandchildren can or can't access on the Web. You can also elect to follow the guidelines of one of several trusted organizational rating systems to determine which sites can or cannot be accessed. If you have specific sites you don't want the young 'uns in your household to have access to, you can insert your own list of URLs that become off limits.

- The *This Site Approval* feature serves the same purpose for a company's network administrator needing to restrict employees or other individuals from viewing any inappropriate Web sites while using the network.

- *Related links* is an intuitive feature that helps you find new sites related to the one you're viewing. You can view a list of related links as you continue surfing so you don't lose track of where you are.

I've only scratched the surface in mentioning the many new features incorporated within Internet Explorer 5. For a list long enough to cause your eyes to hemorrhage, please visit `http://www.microsoft.com/windows/ie/ie5/overview.asp`.

Installing Internet Explorer 5

To navigate directly to the Internet Explorer download page (see Figure 9.2), point your browser to: `http://www.microsoft.com/windows/ie/download/windows.htm`.

Return of the Loophole: The following installation instructions were accurate as of the date of publication, but may not be reflective of installation instructions currently displayed on the Microsoft Web site. Always utilize the most current information available from the Web site, `http://www.microsoft.com`. (Now, the lawyers are happy.)

You will first be asked to select your operating system: Windows 98, Windows 95 and NT 4.0; Windows NT, DEC Alpha, whatever that is; Windows 3.1, or Windows NT 3.51. Below each operating system category appears a listing of the products available for that system. Select **Internet Explorer 5** and **Internet Tools**.

Choose a language. English is the *default* (the normal, most typically used setting), and if that's acceptable, click the **Next** button. For a real hoot, select a nonEnglish version. Oh, the stories you'll be able to tell. Chinese (Traditional) is a personal favorite, but an hour after downloading, I've got a craving to download again.

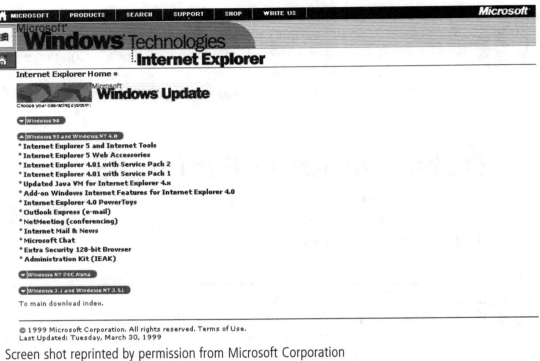

FIGURE 9.2: Internet Explorer download page

Select a download site appropriate for your location. USA is the default location. Read the instructions that tell you to Read these instructions. (Could it be any clearer?) Click the **Next** button.

You will then see a Save As box that will ask you to identify a folder in which to save the Internet Explorer download. Using Windows 95 or 98, I always download to my Desktop so I can install a program and then delete the icon from my Desktop, thus keeping my Desktop perpetually pristine. If you prefer, you can put the file in a temp (temporary) folder on your hard drive. Be sure to write down the file's name if you put it in a location other than on your Desktop so you can find it later. Then click **Save** to download the file.

After the file has downloaded completely, you will have to launch the browser setup program. While you are still connected to the Internet, run the setup program by double-clicking on the `ie5setup.exe` icon that you just downloaded, located on your Desktop or in the folder you selected.

The setup program itself will launch the Installation Wizard who will then escort you through the rest of the installation process. Just sit back, relax, and follow the prompts. It's fast, easy, and guaranteed to make you feel like a computer whiz!

As part of the custom installation process, you'll be presented with a list of more than 20 optional components you can install or not install, as you wish. But what's really neat is that the installer program sniffs around your hard drive and identifies what components you already have installed on your computer.

There are two installation options available under the Advanced button worth noting. The first option stops IE 5 from borrowing file associations. All this means is that if you have your system set up to open or launch certain files with certain other programs, you can preserve those associations rather than let IE 5 steal them away.

The next option is IE 5's Compatibility mode. This option lets you run IE 5 with IE 4. It won't overwrite 4 or elbow it out of the way. This is particularly helpful if you just want to try out 5 without making a commitment to it. Fear of commitment. It exists in the online world, too.

Sometimes there's just no escape, is there?

Okay, I lied. There's actually a third option that most of us will never use. If the spirit moves you, you can download only the setup files without installing them. Since most of us will never use this installation option, let me do my part for conservation and not kill any more trees by waxing expansive about something we'll probably all avoid. "Mr. Modem, CyberConservationist." It has a nice ring to it.

Internet Explorer 4 (and Higher) Tips

Here are three tips to speed up download times.

1. Turn Off Multimedia Features

Under **View** ➤ **Internet Options** ➤ **Advanced**, uncheck **Show Pictures**, **Play Animation**, **Play Videos**, **Play Sounds**, **Smart Image Dithering**. To view any image or animation, right-click the icon and select **Show Picture**. The Web is such a festival of sights and sounds, try to avoid turning off the multimedia features if possible so you don't miss out on the aural and visual funfest. If you have a slower connection to the Internet, try turning off the multimedia features while you're surfing, but once you find a site of interest, turn the features on, then click the **Refresh** button to reload the Web page.

2. Deactivate Java

Choose **View** ➤ **Internet Options** ➤ **Advanced**. Under Java VM, uncheck **Java JIT Compiler Enabled**. There is a downside to deactivating java—which is not the same as decaf, by the way. Java is a computer programming language that permits us to enjoy moving stock-tickers and rotating or scrolling images. We also use java when shopping online and for a number of other interactive activities. Because these features help create the Web ambiance that we've come to know and love, I would recommend deactivating java sparingly. It's not something you will want to continually have deactivated.

3. Increase Cache Size for Faster Page Viewing

If you typically view the same Web sites during an online session, increase your cache size to increase the chance that the page will be retrieved from your cache—a location on your hard drive where your browser stores Web pages you have previously visited. Choose **View ➢ Internet Options ➢ General ➢ Settings**.

Move the slider bar under Amount of Disk Space to Use to the right to increase cache size. Mr. Modem's recommended cache size: 15MB to 20MB, if you have room.

If you are a high-speed surfer careening from site to site and rarely return to the same site, you can speed up browsing by *decreasing* the size of your cache.

Revisiting Web Sites

1. Right-click the **Back** or **Forward** buttons, and a list of recently visited sites will pop up.

2. Review the list, select a page, and click on it to revisit.

or

1. Click the **History** button located on the toolbar. Internet Explorer will open up a frame on the left that shows where you have visited and when.

2. Double-click on a folder for a specific day or week.

3. Click on the page you want to revisit.

Changing How Long Sites Are Saved in History Folder

To adjust the length of time Web sites you have previously visited are retained, follow these steps:

1. Select **View** ➤ **Internet Options** ➤ **General**.
2. Under History, enter the number of days pages should be retained.

Clearing History Folder

Choose **View** ➤ **Internet Options** ➤ **General** ➤ **Clear History**.

Change the Default Start Page

Internet Explorer 4 is set to launch displaying the Microsoft Home Page, but you can configure 4 to start with any page your little modem desires.

To accomplish this, first go to the page you want to appear, then click **View** ➤ **Internet Options** ➤ **General**. Under Home Page, select **Use Current**.

High-Speed Web Page Addressing

The autocomplete feature fills in a partially typed URL by comparing what you are entering to previously visited pages. If you enter **www.micros**..., for example, and you have previously visited the Microsoft Corporation Web site, the entire URL, http://www.microsoft.com, will be completed for you.

Cutting to the URL Chase

If you know a URL starts with `http://www` and ends with `.com`, type in the main part (the web site name) and press CTRL + Enter. Internet Explorer 4 will complete the rest of the URL instantly, if not sooner.

Adding a Frequently Visited Page to the Links Bar

Drag the icon for the page appearing to the left of the Address (URL) field to the Links bar, or drag a link from a Web page to the Links bar.

Subscribing to Web Sites

The new term for offline browsing is *subscribing*. With Internet Explorer 4 you can specify which site to automatically retrieve and how much information should be preserved. To subscribe to a Web site, visit the site you want to subscribe to and follow these steps:

1. Select **Favorites** ➤ **Add to Favorites**.

2. Select the appropriate subscription option:

   Would you also like to subscribe to this page?

   A. No, just add the page to my favorites.

   B. Yes, but only tell me when this page is updated.

   C. Yes, notify me of updates and download the page for offline viewing.

3. Click **Customize** to specify your delivery schedule and notification options, including the ability to be notified via e-mail when updates occur.

Subscribing to a Channel

A *channel* is a Web site designed to deliver content from the Internet to your computer. I'm not a big fan of channels and prefer to retrieve information I might need rather than have it delivered to me. But it's a matter of personal preference, so give it a try and decide what's best for you.

1. On the toolbar, click the **Channels** button.
2. On the Explorer Bar, click the **Microsoft Active Channel Guide** and follow the instructions in the right pane.

Change Notifications

The Smart Favorites feature informs you when a page has changed since your last visit without having to actually visit the Web page.

1. Select **Favorites** ➢ **Organize Favorites**.
2. Right-click on a Web site or page and select **Properties**.
3. Click the **Subscription** tab, then click **Subscribe Now**.
4. Select whether to be notified only when the Web page is updated or to receive notification *and* request the updated page be downloaded.

Cookie Control

Cookies are small text files placed on your computer, generally to personalize or customize return visits to a site. Some folks prefer that cookies not be placed on their computer, which is easily accomplished.

1. Choose **View** ➢ **Internet Options** ➢ **Advanced**.
2. Scroll down to **Cookies**.

3. Click the desired option:

   A. Always accept cookies.

   B. Prompt before accepting cookies.

   C. Disable all cookie use.

4. After making a selection, click **Apply**, then **OK**.

Changing Fonts

Sometimes it's fun to change the appearance of the text on a page. To accomplish this, just kick up your heels and do the Font-Changin' Two-Step. Ready? And-a-one, and-a-two…

1. Choose **View** ➢ **Internet Options** ➢ **General**.

2. Click the **Fonts** button.

Adding/Removing Toolbars, Status Bar, Explorer Bar

Choose **View** ➢ **Toolbars** or **Status Bar** or **Explorer Bar**.

Blocking Access to Sites

A ratings system is being developed that can help you keep your grandchildren from viewing inappropriate material on the Web. To password protect the Content Advisor area, choose **View** ➢ **Internet Options** ➢ **Content** ➢ **Enable** and enter a password.

Want More IE 4 Browser Tips?

Choose **Help** ➢ **Contents** ➢ **Index**. Click the **Index** tab for a complete list of browser tips, or on the **Search** tab to locate a tip by keyword.

Browser Basics

A Mr. Modem truism: The best way to become familiar and comfortable with your browser is by using it. The Internet is an interactive medium, so the best thing you can do is to dive right in and start experimenting. You cannot hurt anything. Smoke will not come billowing out of your computer if you make a mistake along the way. That's precisely how most of us learn and how we learn best—so welcome to the club!

When it comes to your browser—and it doesn't matter if you're using Netscape Navigator, Internet Explorer or Big Bob's Browse-O-Matic—there are three areas you will need to get up close and personal with. All three areas are all located at the top of your browser, above the area where Web sites are displayed (see Figures 9.3 and 9.4). They are:

Navigational Toolbar Buttons   These are the big buttons that are labeled Back, Forward, Reload or Refresh, Home, etc. Try each one of these out and see what they do! You'll find the Back button returns you to the Web page you last visited. Armed with that information, it will probably come as no surprise then that the Forward button will return you to the page you went back from. The Reload or Refresh button (it's called Reload in Netscape Navigator but Refresh in Internet Explorer. Why? To confuse us, that's why!) redisplays the current page which can come in handy if you haven't visited a Web site in awhile and you want to be sure you're looking at the most current version of a Web page. The Home button will take you to the Home Page. Look in the Tips section to find out how to set your Home Page display.

The Address Field   This is the little area where you can type in Web site addresses. Depending on the browser software you're using it may be labeled as Address, Location or Netsite.

Bookmarks (Netscape Navigator) or Favorites (Internet Explorer)   Bookmarks permit you to memorialize the addresses of Web sites you have visited and intend to visit again in the future.

For more information on using Internet Explorer and Netscape Navigator to browse the web, check out *Internet: No Experience Required* by Christian Crumlish [Sybex, 1998] or *Internet Complete* [Sybex, 1998].

Bookmarks   Navigational toolbar   Address field

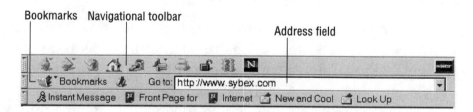

FIGURE 9.3: Netscape Navigator Toolbar

Navigational toolbar   Address field   Favorites

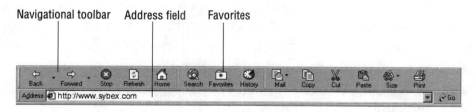

FIGURE 9.4: Internet Explorer Toolbar

Plugging Along with Plug-Ins

Plug-ins (sometimes referred to as *helper files*) are small computer programs that will enhance your enjoyment of the World Wide Web. Plug-ins are good things and are not to be avoided. These programs allow browsers to display multimedia files, including animation, audio, and video. Because new Web technologies are continually being developed, new programs are needed to play or launch these files. To use a simple television analogy, if you purchase a television, bring it home and plug it into the electrical outlet, you'll be able to receive a certain number of channels for your viewing pleasure by default. But if you want to use that same TV to enjoy additional programming only available on cable, your television is capable of displaying those channels, but not without a helping hand in the form of a cable box. (Yes, I know a subscription to cable service is also necessary, but would it kill you to work with me here?)

The same thing holds true for browsers. If you're using the no-frills, showroom version of Netscape Navigator or Internet Explorer, both programs will be able to launch a variety of Web-based programs it encounters while visiting Web sites. When new programs come along that aren't recognized by your browser, a plug-in lends a helping hand to your browser and keeps you teetering on the cutting edge.

The good news is that most plug-ins are free, provided to us out of the goodness of their developers' hearts. A Mr. Modem "hats off" salute to these developers. These good folks are continually experimenting and revising their files for our benefit. Plug-ins allow these files to be frequently revised without requiring us to download and install a new browser. All we need to do is replace the small plug-in file for the corresponding multimedia or other program.

Examples of plug-ins include the Acrobat Reader, NetShow Player, QuickTime Player, RealMedia Player, and Shockwave Plug-in. Don't be concerned about these names. If you need a plug-in, you'll receive a message on your computer screen advising you of your plug-in deficiency.

The message will also ask you, Get the Plug-In Now? and will provide a button or link to the appropriate Web site where you can then download the plug-in. Most are painlessly self-installing. You'll feel great after retrieving your first plug-in. You can't help but feel very high-tech afterwards, so be sure to bask in the glow of the moment.

Mr. Modem's Top Five Recommended Plug-Ins

Adobe Acrobat Reader: Reads documents in the very popular Adobe Acrobat format. These documents carry the .PDF extension.

> http://www.adobe.com

Quicktime Player: Plays and permits viewing of movies in digital format. Needed for viewing movie clip files with .mov, jpeg, gif, pict, mpeg, avi extensions, and AIFF Audio, AU Audio, SGI images, Sound designer.

> http://www.apple.com/quicktime

Realplayer: Needed in order to listen and view *streaming* audio and video files. Streaming files are files that play (video or audio) as they download onto your computer. In other words, you don't have to wait for an entire file to download before you can start enjoying its sites and sounds. These files carry an .RM or .RA extension.

> http://www.real.com

Shockwave: Allows you to view animation and interactive multimedia files.

> http://www.macromedia.com

Winzip: Compressed files carry a .ZIP extension. This plug-in lets you decompress or extract files as well as compress your own files before sending to others.

> http://www.winzip.com

Cookies: Friends or Monsters?

Debate and discussion abounds about cookies and whether they're a good thing or not. The verdict isn't in yet, but there are a few things to be aware of concerning cookie files which may be placed on your hard drive by Web sites. Nobody wants cookie crumbs in their computer, so being aware of what cookies are and what all the fuss is about is important in order to arrive at an informed decision.

First, the name *cookie* derives from absolutely nothing. It was a whimsical name selected because it sounds kind of cute, warm, and fuzzy. But names can be deceiving. Rumor has it Charles Manson's nickname was *Muffin* so let's not get all goopy over the cookie moniker.

A cookie is generally a tiny file placed on your hard drive, within Netscape Navigator or Internet Explorer and other browsers, that allows Web sites to store information about you or your most recent visit, for subsequent retrieval. Typically this information is used to personalize your next visit to the Web site, perhaps greeting you by name or remembering how you configured any available options on your previous visit. The file theoretically can be up to 1.2 megabytes big—the size of a medium-sized computer program, but in actuality most are very, very small.

Cookies first appeared on the Internet scene several years ago, but have only recently garnered much media attention because of the uneasy feeling computer users have knowing that foreign files may be placed on their computers. While cookies certainly do have many legitimate uses, improper or inappropriate usage has the potential of raising questions involving privacy, intrusiveness, Big Brotherism, and stuff that can cause you to toss and turn at night. An inappropriate use would be a Web site selling to third parties information you provided about your personal interests. For example, if you had the ability to personalize a Web site and receive weather reports from Gstaad, and the Web site then provided that information to the GCC (Gstaad Chamber of Commerce) and you started receiving e-mail solicitations or advertisements from Gstaad-based merchants, realtors, insurance agents, etc., that would be inappropriate.

Due to the way you connect to the Internet, cookies will not tell a Web site your name, address, or what green furry things reside in the vegetable bin of your refrigerator. Instead, cookies can advise a Web site that you have visited the site before, along with whatever other information it is programmed to collect. The use of cookies, even to this extent, poses two concerns because it compromises certain assumptions computer users may have about the Internet, and as a result gives many users the heebie-jeebies.

The first assumption is that exploring the World Wide Web is a confidential and anonymous experience that leaves no record. The other is that users' hard disk drives are off limits and shouldn't be invaded without an owner's knowledge and approval.

Both Netscape and Internet Explorer contain three cookie-related options for users: To refuse all cookies; to accept all cookies; or to be notified before accepting a cookie—in other words, having the ability to decide whether to accept a cookie or not. Some discretion is in order when deciding whether to accept a cookie or not. My mother always told me never to accept cookies from strangers, and that's still good advice. If I'm surfing the Web and I accidentally encounter Big Ralphie's Filth-O-Rama Web site, I'm going to decline a cookie invitation. I don't know Big Ralphie from a hole in the ozone layer, so I don't want him *or* his cookie in my computer.

On the other hand, if I visit the Microsoft site or a professional association's site—a site of unquestionable repute—and I am offered a cookie, I always accept it. I have yet to hear about or read about a single user ever being injured by accepting a cookie. That doesn't mean it won't happen, but using a little bit of good, common sense can go a long way toward avoiding problems.

There are currently more than 320 million Web pages.

Source: AltaVista, http://www.altavista.com

The original intention of using cookies was to enable sites to personalize content offerings to individuals on subsequent visits by remembering their personal preferences gleaned as a result of tracking their previous site excursions. Offline, this would be the equivalent of going to a shopping mall and having your travels within the mall documented. The next time you arrive at the mall you would be advised about specials or other semi-interesting items that may have been added within those stores or departments since your last visit. Is that good or bad? It's truly a matter of personal preference.

Personally, because I'm perpetually grumpy, I like to be left alone when I shop so I don't want people noting my mall movements. Besides, I have been known to cast a furtive glance into the window of Victoria's Secret on occasion and that could cause a host of problems at home if I suddenly started receiving Christmas cards from Victoria. "Mr. Modem, you've got a lot of 'splainin' to do!"

A very good and constructive use of cookies is, for example, keeping track of areas you have visited on a Web site that have not changed since your last visit. Armed with that information, you can avoid revisiting unchanged areas thus making your Web surfing more efficient. And of course, that's the ultimate objective of all surfing. Heaven forbid anybody waste any time while surfing.

Another positive cookie application—or *cookie app*, as groovy computers dudes say—would remember your username and password on a site and permit you to revisit password-protected areas without having to reenter your password and username each visit. A friendly, personalized greeting is also accomplished through the use of a cookie, and it's always nice to be greeted by name.

The only conclusion I can reach at this juncture is that there are many legitimate applications associated with cookies and it's too early in the technological development and use of cookies to come to any definitive, concrete opinion that all cookies are good or all cookies are bad.

Personally, I accept all cookies because I never met a cookie I didn't like. I also tend to stay out of the darker, danker areas of the Internet. Any technology can be used inappropriately by irresponsible individuals, but the alternative is to stifle the advancement of technology, and that is simply not a viable option, in my opinion.

The final decision is up to you. Accept all cookies, reject all cookies, or request notification before permitting a cookie to be placed on your computer. If you're not sure what to do, you can't go wrong requesting notification so you can dither about it at a later date. When in doubt, procrastinate. It works like a charm.

Opera: The Little Browser That Could

Though Netscape and Internet Explorer continue to be the two primary players in the wild and wacky world of Web browsers, they're not the only game in town. Not by a long shot.

The newest kid in town—born and raised in Norway, I might add—is a browser called Opera—not to be confused with Oprah—and it's garnering a lot of attention for a very good reason: Opera, shown in Figure 9.5, is a lean, mean, browsing machine. Netscape and Internet Explorer are powerhouse programs, but they're bloated space hogs. Sure, they're laden with features, but many of us only use a fraction of the features available, and many more of us don't have a clue what buried features are present that we're not using.

So if you're looking for a streamlined program that takes a low-key approach to browsing, requires a minimal amount of hard drive space, and won't tax your computer's resources to the max, by all means take a look at Opera, from Opera Software. It's well worth trying, particularly if you're using an older computer or disk space is in short supply.

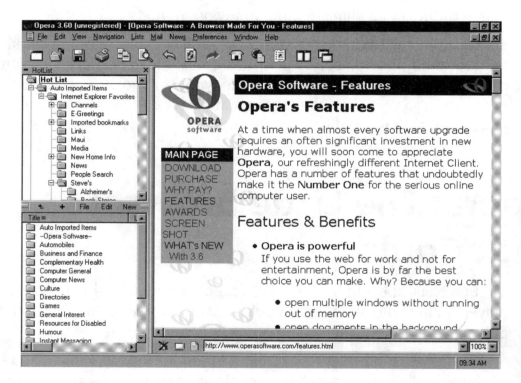

FIGURE 9.5: Opera Web browser main screen

The current version of Opera is less than 2MB, which is just a fraction of the size of Netscape Navigator or Internet Explorer. Using a 28.8Kbps modem, Opera will download in little more than six minutes; a little less than three minutes at 56Kbps; and with cable access or other high-speed Internet access, faster than you can say—well, you'd already have down-loaded it by now.

Opera's diminutive physical attributes means that it can run on an older 386SX with 8MB of RAM. But if you are using an ancient 286 computer, don't even think about the Internet. Trust me, it won't be a good experience.

Even though Opera is a pip-squeak in size, it contains several features also found in Netscape Navigator and Internet Explorer such as the ability to open multiple windows. By holding down the Shift key when you click a link—or *clink*, in shorthand—you can open a new window for a new Web page. Why would you want to do this? If you want to visit a number of Web pages from a list of search results, for example, by keeping the window with the list of links open, you won't have to click back, back, back, etc., to get to the next site. Also, if one page is loading sluggishly, you can select another Web page to visit, open another window, and while the first page is oozing into the first window, you can be surfing the second page. Opera's Turbo mode can also kick your downloads into high gear.

Opera can also display your bookmark file in its very own frame. The pages appear on the left of the window(s) displaying the actual Web pages. Opera allows you to import your Netscape Navigator Bookmarks or Internet Explorer Favorites file, so you won't have to start compiling a new bookmarks list from scratch. Perish the thought!

Most major Web site features such as JavaScript and frames, as well as lots of graphic and multimedia formats are supported. Popular plug-ins work with Opera as well, so if you visit sites that use Quicktime, Shockwave, RealAudio, Adobe Acrobat, and others, you can enjoy their features with Opera, too.

One thing Opera does that Netscape and Internet Explorer do not is allow you to resize a page. Netscape and Internet Explorer permit you to enlarge or reduce font size to make text more legible, but Opera resizes everything, including graphics. Click the dropdown box in the lower-right corner that contains a percentage numeral, and simply change the number. You can resize the page from 20 percent to 1,000 percent of its original size. Since Mr. Modem is a member of the bifocal generation, this is particularly useful. Prior to this, I had to get up and move to a position four or five feet from the monitor to bring screen images into focus. Though very time consuming, these computaerobics did wonders for my cardiovascular system.

You can also customize and personalize Opera, set your preferences for colors and fonts, and choose to hide or display various components such as Opera's menu, the status bar, and other items. The good folks at Opera Software will even alter their underlying programming code to meet your specifications, but they do charge by the hour for that service. For most of us, there's more than enough flexibility in Opera to keep us content for many happy downloads.

In addition, Opera includes newsgroup and e-mail readers, supports file uploading, and also offers free e-mail accounts to its users.

Additional information is available on the Opera Web site located at http://www.operasoftware.com. Opera is available for both Windows 3.1 and Windows 95. You can download a free 30-day evaluation copy from their Web site. The purchase price is $35.

I've used Opera for several months. During that time I've discovered that Web pages load faster using Opera than if I were to load the same pages using Netscape or Internet Explorer.

The battle of the browsers continues to rage, and while Netscape and Internet Explorer continue to duke it out, keep your eye on Opera. It's the little browser that seemingly came out of nowhere, but it's making even the big boys sit up and take notice.

What's Next?

Now that we're browser savvy, let's put our browsers to work ferreting out some of the invaluable information that you've heard resides on the Internet. So how do we find what we're looking for? In the next chapter we'll dive into Internet Search Engines and learn all about it.

Internet Search Engines

The World Wide Web need not be a tangled web. Information appears at first glance to exist in a seemingly elusive yet chaotic world of data. In reality, every bit and piece of information has its own unique address, based on no particular geographic location. When these bits of data are located and presented as a search result, they can appear on a computer screen anywhere in the world. It's amazing to me that the whole thing even works.

Accessing the Web is easy. Okay, "So much for his credibility," you may be muttering, but let's stop and think about it for a moment. All connections to the Web transport you to a screen within your Web browser software (usually Netscape or Internet Explorer). Each browser provides you with a blank field in which to type a Web address or URL. Once you enter your first URL, the world is at your fingertips and life will never be the same.

Okay, that's all fine and dandy, but what if you don't know the URL or address of a particular Web page or Web site? How in the world do you find anything on the Web? First, stop whining. Nobody likes a whiner. Fortunately, the Web comes equipped with many specialty sites called search engines that are designed to help you find the information you're seeking. Bet you're feeling better already, aren't you?

Most search engines prompt you to input keywords or words related in some way to the topic about which you are seeking information. When you enter a keyword, the search engine examines its database and presents to you a listing of sites that, in theory, match your search criteria.

The most common search technique deployed by millions of Internet users is the Single Keyword Search, or SKS for members of Acronyms Anonymous. This type of search casts a very wide net and will return lots of meaningless, irrelevant results. With a wee bit more sophistication, deploying a double keyword search with a "plus" sign (+) between the words will significantly improve your search results. The plus sign ties the two search terms together—for example, **tuna + melt**. Without the plus sign, a search engine would search for the word *tuna* and the word *melt* but not necessarily the scrumptious combination together.

Surrounding search terms with quotations marks (**"tuna melt"**) will also result in search results that are an exact match. See "Boolean Searches" later in this chapter for a more in-depth look at the scintillating science of searching.

Search engines work best when you have a particular topic in mind that can be expressed in specific terms. But the downside to broad, keyword searches is that you'll sometimes be faced with hundreds or thousands of search results, referred to as *hits*, 90 percent of which will be meaningless for your purposes. The search results that contain your keywords are likely to be grouped at the top, and chances are you'll find what you're looking for among the first 25 to 50 hits returned.

There are actually hundreds of search engines residing on the Web and new ones make their cyber debut weekly. So how do you select a search engine? Many people ask me what my favorite search engine is and my answer is usually, "I'm using XYZ search engine right now, but check back with me in an hour." I continually experiment with and explore new search engines; my favorite at any given moment is the one that produced the most satisfactory results the last few times. If I use a particular search engine and the results aren't what I'm looking for, I'll usually try another one.

I would recommend creating a "Search Engines" Bookmarks or Favorites folder that contains an assortment of search engines so they're always just a mouse-click away. As you discover new search engines or lose interest in others that aren't particularly useful to you, add them or remove them from this folder. Bear in mind, however, that search engines reinvent themselves periodically, so a search engine that's a dud today may be the latest and greatest six months from now. It's worth revisiting the duds periodically. Ultimately, you'll find two or three search engines that feel comfortable, are easy to use, and sticking with those few will probably serve your purposes beautifully.

The Internet experiences a rush hour just like the average freeway. Peak hours of usage are from 7:00 to 11:00 P.M., local time.

Source: StatMarket, Inc., http://www.statmarket.com

No matter what search engine you prefer, be sure to take the time to familiarize yourself with that program's capabilities. Most search engines include annoyingly detailed search tips documentation. It's time well spent getting up close and personal with a search engine's strengths, weaknesses and search tip recommendations. You'll not only improve your short-term results, but you'll become a more skilled and sophisticated Web searcher in the process.

Types of Search Engines

There are three types of search programs: indexers or crawlers, directories, and metasearches or metacrawlers.

Indexers

These search engines use an automated or robotic method of collecting information. Sometimes they're referred to as *crawlers* because these programs crawl through the Internet 24 hours a day cataloging or indexing Web sites. It's best to use indexers when you want to cast a wide search net. An indexer will return lots of worthless sites and information, but once you separate the wheat from the chaff you may find some real gems— or perhaps some mixed metaphors. To further confuse things, some of these search programs straddle categories, and you know how uncomfortable that can be if it's not done correctly. Excite, for example, is both an indexer and a directory. My best advice: Try as many search programs as you wish, as frequently as you like. Nobody says you have to pledge undying loyalty to just one or two search engines.

Examples of Indexers:

Alta Vista: `http://www.altavista.com`

Excite: `http://www.excite.com`

HotBot: `http://www.hotbot.com`

Magellan: `http://www.magellan.excite.com`

WebCrawler: `http://www.webcrawler.com`

Directories

A close encounter of the directory kind will reveal a search engine that relies on living, breathing human beings to catalog Web sites that are often submitted by Internet users. Due to the human factor, these search engines tend to have a higher degree of accuracy, but generally return fewer hits. They are also typically updated less frequently. Think of directories as the card catalog of the Web.

Examples of Directories:

AskJeeves—technically an answer service, but definitely worth taking a look at: `http://www.askjeeves.com`

Galaxy: `http://www.galaxy.com`

LookSmart: `http://www.looksmart.com`

Lycos: `http://www.lycos.com`

Yahoo!: `http://www.yahoo.com`

Metacrawlers

Operating on the theory that if using one search engine is good, using multiple search programs at one time is even better, metacrawlers scour the databases of multiple search engines and deliver the results as one listing. Think of it as one-stop searching on the Web.

Examples of metacrawlers:

DogPile: `http://www.dogpile.com`

Go2Net (formerly MetaCrawler): `http://www.go2net.com`

Highway 61: `http://www.highway61.com`

Inference Find: `http://ifind.com`

Boolean Searches

If your web searches are not returning the kind of information you're looking for, try not to take it personally, but it's probably the way you're conducting your searches. Refine your search query using special keywords called Boolean (pronounced "BOO-lee-an") operators. These nifty little words can narrow your search and reduce the amount of irrelevant material (referred to in geekspeak as *crappola*) that comes up as a result of overly broad searches. I don't like to brag, but when it comes to crappola, millions of people worldwide think first of Mr. Modem. I sincerely hope you're one of them.

The technical definition of Boolean is "of or relating to a logical combinatorial system treating variables, such as propositions and computer logic elements, through the operators AND, OR, NOT, IF, THEN and EXCEPT." Try tossing that gem out at the next garden club meeting and you're likely to be beaten to death with a shovel.

continued ➡

Boolean Searches (*continued*)

In simple Mr. ModemSpeak, Boolean searches include the words AND, OR, NOT, and NEAR. When used in conjunction with your search keywords, these operators help narrow or refine your searches.

- Use the word AND to search for information containing more than one keyword. For example, if you type **Internet AND legislation**, your query will give you only information containing both of these keywords.

- Use the word OR to search for results containing at least one of the keywords. For example: **munchkins OR leprechauns** would return any document that contained either of the words.

- The word NOT tells the search engine to look for results that do not contain the keyword, for example: **pets NOT anaconda**.

- The word NEAR shows results that contain the keywords only when they appear within approximately ten words of each other, for example: **Nixon NEAR resigned**.

A Boolean search can achieve better results faster and will save you time, NOT add to your frustration.

As a quasi-interesting side note, the word Boolean derives from George Boole, a British mathematician, 1815–1864, who, legend has it, kept misplacing his car keys. Under the influence of Mogen David wine, he developed a calculus of symbolic logic that permitted him to retrace his steps and find his keys through his unique form of logic: "I don't have my keys. Where do I last remember having them? I had them at the health club, NOT in the golf cart. I thought I had them in my Bermuda shorts EXCEPT today I was wearing my Dockers." Through this fascinating process of elimination and search refinement, Boolean logic emerged. Remarkably unchanged since the passing of Mr. Boole in 1864, Boolean logic is still in use today, which explains why most of us can't find anything on the Internet.

continued ➡

Boolean Searches (*continued*)

All seriousness aside, if you spend a lot of time utilizing the Internet—and who doesn't—it's in your best interest to master the art of conducting efficient and effective searches. Understanding which search engine to use is the key to achieving the best results from your search queries. Toss in a few Boolean search operators to refine your searches and you'll soon be pestered unmercifully by friends and family members everywhere to find information for them on the Internet.

Mr. Modem's Top 31* Search Engines

Millions of readers—well, maybe five or six people—have inquired why the top *31* search engines? Admittedly, it is an unusual number. Two reasons: First, every big-shot author uses an asterisk somewhere in his or her work to draw the reader's attention to a note or clarification of profound importance. I knew that *profound* and *importance* weren't adjectives likely to be associated with this book, so I seized upon this cheesy opportunity to include an asterisk. I could explain further, but inevitably I'd end up bursting into a chorus of *I Gotta Be Me*, and I wouldn't wish that on anybody. Some things are simply better left unsung.

Secondly, I began with the intention of writing "Mr. Modem's Top 10 Search Engines," but clearly lost my bearings somewhere along the way. There are just too darned many noteworthy search engines, so I expanded the Top 10 list to the Top 20, then the Top 25. Finally, demonstrating not even the slightest measure of self-control, I expanded it to 30. Done. Fini. I then remembered ZenSearch. So that's it, 31. No more, no less. At least so I thought. I then discovered that 31 search engines were too many for this book if I had any hopes of complying with the Surgeon General's recommendation that paperback books not exceed 47 pounds.

Because Mr. Modem is a law-abiding citizen, some adjustment was clearly in order. Accordingly, on the following pages you will find my top ten favorite search engines. And that's just for starters!

In keeping with the great and wonderful spirit of cyberspace, I have added an Internet dimension to this book that is available to you right now, as you read these very words! Just point your browser to my Web site located at `http://www.mrmodem.net` and you will find more than 20 additional search engines profiled, along with hundreds of other links to my favorite Web sites, all frequently updated for your surfing pleasure!

What better opportunity to hone the skills you've been learning? So please stop by at your convenience, and be sure to use the e-mail link to say hello!

Name That Tuna!

Mr. Modem's patented-yet-worthless TM testing protocol was utilized in order to assign a numeric value to the following search engines, where applicable. This rigorous testing involved searching for the term *tuna melt*. Depending upon the search engine used, the search query was launched using **"tuna melt"** (the search term surrounded by quotation marks) or **tuna + melt**. The Results notation reflects the number of hits each search engine returned.

Testing was conducted by an Internet professional in a controlled, laboratory environment with technical supervision. Trained medical personnel were standing by at all times. Do not attempt this testing protocol at home! Results under similar circumstances may vary.

No animals were harmed during search engine testing, though the test administrator experienced inexplicable, episodic cravings for tuna. He was fed, treated, and released without further incident or complication.

So without further ado, here are Mr. Modem's Top 31 Search Engines (presented in alphabetical order)....

1. AltaVista

More than 150 million indexed Web pages. AltaVista, shown in Figure 10.1, made its Web debut in December 1995, so its staying power is a tribute to its usefulness and popularity. It is modestly self-proclaimed as "The most useful and powerful guide to the Internet." The Simple Search permits you to input your keywords. A separate field invites you to Enter Boolean Expression. Not particularly helpful if you don't have a clue what a Boolean expression is. I had two years of high school Boolean and still have trouble speaking the language. The Advanced Search permits you to enter a question or use keywords. Comprehensive help is available, though it's more fun to fumble around searching than it is reading help pages. Results: 1,297.

```
http://www.altavista.digital.com
```

2. Ask Jeeves

A relative newcomer to the search scene, Ask Jeeves invites you to type a question in plain English and click the **Ask!** button. For example, instead of using one or two search terms, Jeeves welcomes conversational questions such as "How do I make a tuna melt?" Ever the thoughtful host, Jeeves inquires if you would like to check your spelling before submitting

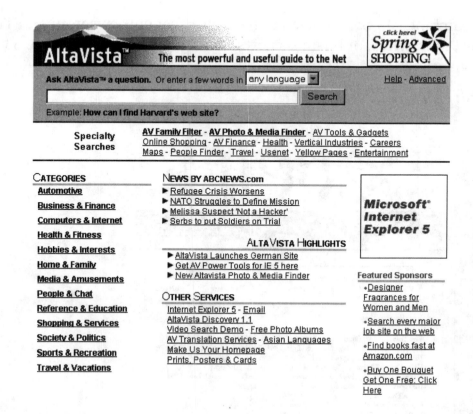

FIGURE 10.1: AltaVista

your query. Jeeves, in true metasearch-engine format, displays results by search engine: 10 matches by AltaVista; 9 matches by InfoSeek, etc. The What People are Asking feature is similar to Webcrawler's Search Ticker and displays other ongoing searches in real time. Results: 37.

```
http://www.askjeeves.com
```

3. DogPile

One of my favorite metasearch engines. DogPile (see Figure 10.2) is fast and easy to use, just the way I like 'em. Type in your search term, click the **Fetch** button, and results will be presented by search engine, ten at a time. Searching can be restricted to the Web, Usenet (newsgroups), FTP archives, newswires, or business news resources. Results: the Web: 639; Usenet newsgroups: 3,302.

```
http://www.dogpile.com
```

FIGURE 10.2: DogPile

4. Excite

Is it just me, or are search engines trying to cram too much information on one page? Excite is a wonderfully robust search engine, but it's just too busy for my tastes. Call me a purist or just call me cranky.

Searching is straightforward and easy to use: Type in a keyword. When search results appear, so does a Search Again button along with a variety of related search terms that you can select to further refine your search; a very nice feature. Additional search terms presented after the initial search for **tuna + melt** included casserole, grilled, tablespoons, lettuce, salad, brine, grated, and wenzel. Results: 44,933. And what the heck is a wenzel?

`http://www.excite.com`

5. Google

A newcomer on the search scene, and a model of simplicity. Enter a keyword and press either the **Google Search** or **I'm Feeling Lucky** button. Conducting a Google Search permits you to select 10, 30, or 100 search results. An I'm Feeling Lucky search returns one result, assuming you are, indeed, lucky. A red bar along with a percentage rating appears with each Google Search result. This reflects the PageRank, which is described as the "importance of a page; a result has high PageRank if lots of other pages with high PageRank point to it." There you have it. So have a giggle and try the Google. Results: 2,965.

`http://www.google.com`

6. GoTo

When it comes to searching, there is no simpler search tool on the Web. In fact, GoTo's tag line is "Search made simple." Even their tag line is simple. Type in a keyword, click the **Find It!** button, and you're done. No screaming banners, no weather reports, no stock tickers, horoscopes, farm reports, lottery numbers, or any of the other hoopla/clutter that adorns other search engines. Clean, crisp GoTo (see Figure 10.3) is one of the few search sites that doesn't appear to be suffering an identity crisis. It knows what it does, and it does it very well. Results: 240.

`http://www.goto.com`

FIGURE 10.3: GoTo

7. Magellan

The Magellan Internet Guide is a refreshingly quiet search engine. No screaming headlines, no sensory overstimulation. If you're searching for sites that are appropriate for impressionable minds, select the Green

Light Sites Only box. **Tuna + melt** returned 1,748 results from a generalized Web search, but only five from a Green Light sites search. So not only are children being protected from X-rated material, they're also being protected from fatty foods. Hats off to Magellan! Search results are presented ranked by relevance. As explained in the Search Tips and Hints section, "Relevance ratings are automatically generated by our search engine, which compares the information in the site against the information in your query." Makes sense to me. If you're searching for a simple yet comprehensive search engine, be sure to give Magellan a try.

```
http://magellan.excite.com
```

8. Webcrawler

I'm not ashamed to admit it: I like Webcrawler. Oh, sure, it's not the most sophisticated search engine ever to appear on the Web, but as its tag line says, "It's that simple." It truly is. Webcrawler is one of the original Web search engines, and maybe because I'm one of the original Web inhabitants, perhaps we share a common bond.

Webcrawler, shown in Figure 10.4, is a model of simplicity and functionality. As soon as the site appears on your monitor, you will instantly observe a field for entering your search term(s) and a **Search** button. No dizzying array of animated figures, no happy little tunes. Just a **Search** button. It's that simple.

Critics of Webcrawler suggest that it returns too many results because it casts too wide a net. My **tuna + melt** query returned 2,333 results in the form of Web site titles. Using one of the oldest search techniques in the book and surrounding **tuna melt** in quotation marks—which restricts a search to precisely the search terms entered—returned 20 results. Try the old put-it-in-quotes trick next time you receive four million search results. After retrieving your results, click **Show Summaries for These Results** and review more descriptive information about each search result.

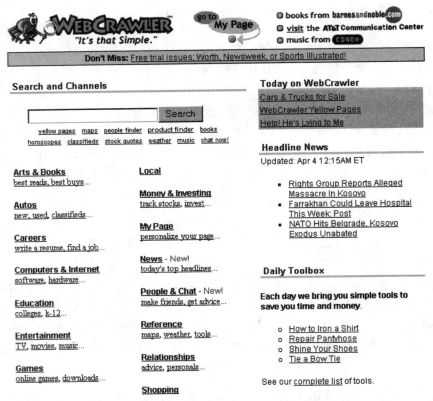

WebCrawler is a trademark of Excite, Inc. and may be registered in various jurisdictions. WebCrawler screen display copyright ©1994-1999 Excite, Inc.

FIGURE 10.4: Webcrawler

A fun feature for the little curious person that resides in each of us is the WebCrawler Search Voyeur. As other users type in searches, their text scrolls across your screen in ticker-tape fashion. Click on any of the scrolling search terms and you'll see the search results. Caution: The Webcrawler Search Voyeur is not for the easily offended. See the Webcrawler Search Voyeur at `http://webcrawler.com/SearchTicker.html`.

`http://www.webcrawler.com`

9. Yahoo!

Yahoo! is not technically a search engine. Instead of searching the Web at large, it searches its own database. But that's not to suggest that Yahoo! is limited! Au contraire, data dudes and dudettes. Yahoo! covers everything from heavy-duty technical and scientific research sites to health, news, sports and entertainment. When it comes to searching, Yahoo! is the granddaddy of all search engines. Think "search," think Yahoo! (see Figure 10.5).

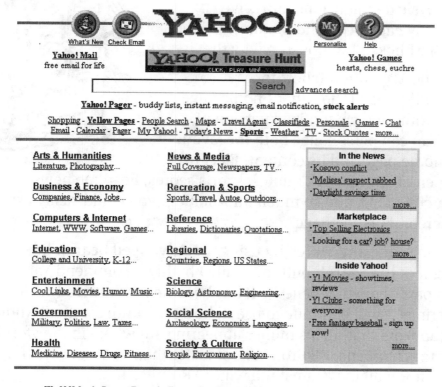

FIGURE 10.5: Yahoo!

Yahoo! has also created a number of handy geographical indices (World Yahoo!s and Yahoo! Get Local) that make it much easier to locate Internet resources with a local or international focus. There's also Yahooligans for the kiddos featuring a playground full of sites with a particular focus on the junior surfer.

Yahoo!'s People Search is legendary for its ability to help locate friends, relatives, colleagues, and people who owe you money. You can search by first name, last name, e-mail domain, hair color, eye color, birthmarks, physical dimensions, intrusive thoughts (by category), and proximity to the nearest Starbuck's. I'm not sure why that is.

Click the **My** button (short for My Yahoo!) at the top of the Yahoo! home page to create your own customized version of Yahoo!. You can personalize both the layout of your home page and its content. Elect to receive personalized stock quotes, sports scores, headline news, weather, city maps, and so much information, you could easily experience a cerebral hemorrhage.

You can refine any search by using the **Advanced Search** link located to the right of the **Search** button. While I highly recommend Yahoo!, there's a part of me that believes it has become too cluttered with lots of side offerings. I will continue to use it, however, until a Yahoo! Mime Locator appears that tracks mimes appearing anywhere in the world. The day that happens, I'll drop Yahoo! faster than you can say, "Look! It's an author walking against the wind!" Results: 467.

`http://www.yahoo.com`

10. ZenSearch

One of Mr. Modem's favorites because ZenSearch doesn't return 100,000 search results. Its focus is quality as opposed to quantity—a rare commodity, indeed. Sites presented are evaluated based on content, appearance and usability. Those that don't cut the mustard are not included in ZenSearch's searchable database. Sure, it's subjective, but these folks know what they're doing. I trust 'em. Results: None. Finally, a search engine that's gently suggesting to me that I'm wasting my time searching for **tuna + melt**. It's a nice way of saying, "Get a life, Mr. Modem!" Thanks, ZenSearch. I needed that.

`http://www.zensearch.com`

What's Next?

Time to sit back, relax and let the grand adventure begin! In the next chapter, "Mr. Modem's Web Sites for Seniors," I'll share with you my favorite Web sites that were carefully, painstakingly, dare I say lovingly collected over many years of involuntary confinement. But that's another story altogether....

Mr. Modem's Web Sites for Seniors

When I first ventured into cyberspace, long before there was a World Wide Web, the Internet was a dark, disturbing primordial digital soup. It was kind of spooky, actually. To this day, I wake up in a cold sweat at night screaming "archie," "veronica," "gopher," speaking in strange Unix-based tongues or inexplicably humming Gregorian chants.

In those lazy, hazy, crazy days of hummer, the World Wide Web was so new and there was so little content, it was relatively easy to stay current with newly arriving Web sites. The debut of a new site of substance was a big event and word-of-modem spread the news like virtual wildfire.

As the Internet's growth exploded and the amount of content on the Web increased exponentially, casting a wide search net using any of the popular search engines (see Chapter 10, "Internet Search Engines") would frequently result in tens of thousands of *hits*. Only a very small percentage of returned results would be even remotely useful. As increasing numbers of search engines appeared on the cyber scene, it became apparent, not without a smidge of irony, that you could literally spend days searching for a search engine.

In January 1994, I set aside the 12-foot ball of string I had been collecting since childhood. I began collecting and cataloging Web site addresses by topic, proving definitively that if it were not for a shallow and meaningless life, I would have no life at all. Gratuitous hyperbole notwithstanding, site collecting wasn't a particularly extraordinary feat in and of itself at the time, but as millions of sites began to appear on the Web, updating, refining, and maintaining an ever-growing list of relevant Web site resources became increasingly challenging. The key words here are *relevant* and *challenging*. Relevant, meaning useful; challenging meaning a royal pain in the ASCII.

I am not suggesting that this chapter contains every site on the Web that might possibly be relevant to seniors. Rather, this chapter is a partial collection of the most informative, useful, entertaining or fascinatingly strange sites I have encountered during my daily excursions into the cyber cosmos through the years. Think of it as a starting point for your own exploration.

On the following pages you'll be introduced to a few of my favorite sites in each of 14 categories. But in the words of the immortal Al Jolson, "You ain't seen nothing yet!" Visit me on my Web site at `http://www.mrmodem.net` and you'll find hundreds of additional sites, all neatly categorized, all with semi-helpful descriptions, and all easy to get to by clicking on each site's respective link. Could Mr. Modem make it any easier for you? I think not!

As you visit the sites on the following pages and on my Web site, make sure to bookmark ones of particular interest so you can easily return to them in the future or share them with your friends. Many of the sites presented contain links to thousands of other related Web sites, so be selective when creating your own bookmarks; otherwise, you'll need a search engine to find anything within your own bookmarks. Think *quality*, not *quantity*.

The World Wide Web is a continually evolving resource with more than 100,000 Web pages arriving, departing or changing addresses each month. Today there are an estimated 320 million Web pages on the Internet and that number is expected to double within the next two years.

Since the Internet is such a fluid, transitory medium, it is possible that on occasion a Web site address may not function properly. This situation may be the result of a change of site address, the discontinuation of a particular site, or simply a temporary situation—what we refer to technically as "One of those Internet thangs."

To Err Is Human; to Understand Is a Miracle

Error messages can easily ruin any cyberspace outing, but they're not impossible to overcome. In fact, you can avoid many error messages by using a few simple techniques—and when it comes to simple, who else are you going to turn to but Mr. Simple himself? Thank you. I'm truly honored and deeply moved.

Sooner or later you will encounter one or more Internet error messages. It's part and parcel of that grand adventure known as the Internet experience. Even though coming face-to-face with an error message can be a bit frightening at first, just think of it as learning the Internet by trial and terror. It worked for me; it will work for you.

To help you understand pesky Internet error messages, a bonus chapter entitled, "To Err is Human; to Understand is a Miracle: A Compendium of Internet Error Messages," awaits you on the Internet! That's right, *on the Internet!* You didn't think you were going to be able to read this book without practicing what I'm preaching, did you? Heck no! Mr. Modem wants to see some power surfing!

So at your convenience, point your browser to my Web site located at `http://www.mrmodem.net`. On the site, we'll examine some of the most common Internet and World Wide Web error messages. Also provided are semi-practical solutions that may prevent you from indulging in delightful Internet user activities such as teeth-gnashing, primal screaming, or the ever-popular aortic embolism stretch. See you on the Web!

If you cannot access a particular site referenced, try it again later or even the following day. If you are repeatedly unable to access a given site contained within this chapter or receive a message on your screen that the site no longer exists, please notify me by e-mail so I can investigate further and remove the site from future editions of this book.

Setting Your Sights on Sites

The Web sites I share with you in this chapter are segregated into subject categories and presented in alphabetical order for ease of reference. Some sites may appear in multiple categories. For example, a currency converter may appear in the "Investment and Finance" category as well as "Travel."

A few additional words of wisdom before you dive into the Web surf: Web site addresses *are* case sensitive, so when you are manually copying addresses into your browser's address field, be sure to copy and enter them *exactly* as they appear. The letter "l" (as in loopy) and the numeral "1" (as in 1 in a million) are often difficult to distinguish in Web addresses. If you try an address that contains either character and the site fails to appear, try the other character instead. All it takes is one character out of place to prevent access.

All addresses presented are publicly-accessible sites located on the World Wide Web. Inclusion of any site does not constitute an endorsement by the author or publisher. (Just another attempt to keep the lawyers happy.)

If you have a favorite site, your contribution is welcome! Please e-mail the URL to me at MrModem@home.com or fax it to 602-808-7773. All sites submitted will be reviewed for appropriateness before inclusion. Decision of the judge is final. You must be 18 years of age or older to play, and no wagering, please.

Happy surfing!

Stet centering the tilde

Arts, Music, Literature

A treasure trove of museums, galleries, audio files for audiophiles, and more great literature than you can shake a primer at!

Classical MIDI Archives   More than 7,000 classical music files in MIDI format from more than 500 composers. An integrated search engine makes for fugue-finding with finesse.

> http://www.prs.net/midi.html

Classics at the Online Literature Library   The full texts of everything from Aesop to Voltaire. Nothing from Mr. Modem...yet.

> http://www.literature.org/Works

Dancescape   Everything you could possibly want to know about the sport of competitive ballroom dancing.

> http://www.dancescape.com/info

History of Art Virtual Library   Links to sites of interest for people with a general interest in art history, as well as for students and scholars. Comprehensive listing of links to collections, exhibitions, museums, universities, online teaching resources, art history organizations and online publications.

> http://www.hart.bbk.ac.uk/VirtualLibrary.html

Jazz Online   Created in 1991, Jazz Online was the world's first commercial interactive network devoted to jazz. All styles of jazz are covered. Jazz Online's mission statement has remained the same since the beginning, "Everybody needs a little jazz in their life and Jazz Online is the place to find it!"

> http://www.jazzonln.com

Literary Links   While not exhaustive, this site certainly provides more than enough information to give any reasonable person a headache. Included are many of the best literary links on the Web and connections to other major online lists.

```
http://www.ualberta.ca/~amactavi/litlinks.htm
```

Louvre, The   Take a virtual tour by clicking on the Treasures of the Louvre link.

```
http://www.paris.org/Musees/Louvre
```

Museum of Bad Art   "Art too bad to be ignored" is the featured attraction at this museum. The Museum of Bad Art is a private institution dedicated to the collection, preservation, exhibition and celebration of bad art in all its forms and in all its glory.

```
http://www.glyphs.com/moba
```

Past Perfect   The Sounds of the 20s, 30s and 40s all digitally remastered and available on CD-ROM. Lots of sound samples and photos in the Photo Archive section.

```
http://www.pastperfect.com
```

Rock and Roll Hall of Fame   See it, hear it, experience it. It's the Hall of Fame, cyber-style. Tour exhibits, inductee speeches, news and information.

```
http://www.rockhall.com/media/index.html
```

Shakespeare, The Complete Works of William   Searchable; includes a discussion forum, a chronological and alphabetical listing of his works, quotations and a glossary. "Therefore my age is as a lusty winter, Frosty, but kindly"—*As You Like It*. "These are my lawyers. All Harvard men"—*Some Like It Hot*.

```
http://www-tech.mit.edu/Shakespeare/works.html
```

Worldwide Arts Resources   An interactive gateway to all exemplars of qualitative arts information and culture on the Internet. Artists, museums, galleries, art history, art education, antiques, dance, opera, classified ads, resume postings, arts chat, and discussion forums.

http://wwar.com

Bonus feature! Think of this as the chapter that never ends. For your surfing pleasure, I will be maintaining a regularly updated list of Web site discoveries online, so please stop by, say hello and enjoy Mr. Modem's updated Web sites list at http://www.mrmodem.net

Computers, Technology, and the Internet

Gigabytes of the greatest gadget and gizmo Web sites from the wild and wacky world of technology.

BrowserWatch   The leading site for information about browsers, plug-ins, and ActiveX controls. The New Room section provides the latest news stories and rumors about browsers and developers.

http://www.browserwatch.internet.com

Calculators Online   More than 8,000 calculators. For some real fun, challenge the Pulsar Distance Calculator with your slide rule. Calculators. Bah, humbug.

http://www-sci.lib.uci.edu/HSG/RefCalculators.html

Catch Up   A free service that searches for the newest versions of many popular Windows software applications and hardware drivers. With the click of a button, Catch Up generates a list of updates and upgrades to your computer's software, including links to download sites.

http://www.manageable.com/catchup.html

Donate Used Computers   Share the Technology, a nonprofit organization that donates used computers and matches up donors with local organizations in need of computers.

http://www.libertynet.org/share

Download Calculator   Enter the size of the file to be downloaded, select your modem speed, and determine whether you have time to order a pizza during the download process.

http://www-sci.lib.uci.edu/HSG/AATimeCalc.html

Eudora   Qualcomm's Eudora Place for news and information about Eudora e-mail programs. Download programs and updates.

http://www.eudora.com

Internet Software   The full name of this site is actually Stroud's Consummate Winsock Applications. That's quite a modemful, but the site contains hundreds of software programs you can download. This site focuses on software for use with the Internet, such as browsers, plug-ins, and add-ons.

http://cws.internet.com

ISPCheck   A search engine for web hosting and Internet access services. If you need to find the best service provider with the best price, this is the place!

http://www.ispcheck.com

McAfee Network Security   One of the premium virus-checking programs. Download a trial version, or update for registered users. Visit Virus Information to learn about the latest virus craze sweeping the Internet. Be sure to also visit the Virus Hoax Library next time you receive an e-mail proclaiming the end of the digital world. Many times these reports are hoaxes. Check it out before warning all your friends.

    http://www.mcafee.com

Opera Web Browser   Not free, but a viable alternative Web browser for older or slower computers. Just a fraction of the size of Netscape or IE, yet laden with features. Take it for a free test drive! (See "Opera: The Little Browser That Could" in Chapter 10.)

    http://www.operasoftware.com

QuickTime   Download the free QuickTime Player for enhanced control of online movie playback.

    http://www.quicktime.com

Reviewfinder   More than 5,700 categories with links to thousands of product reviews.

    http://www.reviewfinder.com

Virus Myths and Hoaxes   Learn about the myths, the hoaxes, the urban legends, and the implications of computer virus myths.

    http://kumite.com/myths

Bonus feature! Think of this as the chapter that never ends. For your surfing pleasure, I will be maintaining a regularly updated list of Web site discoveries online, so please stop by, say hello and enjoy Mr. Modem's updated Web sites list at http://www.mrmodem.net

Finding Friends and Family

A collection of people-finding sites so comprehensive that veteran private investigators have been observed weeping openly while reading this section.

Bigfoot.com   "The Web's most powerful, accurate and fast search engine for finding people." Locate e-mail addresses and, if registered, real-world street addresses. Sources of listings include voluntary submissions and public information.

> http://www.bigfoot.com

Classmates Online   Great for finding old high school friends and acquaintances.

> http://www.classmates.com

Database America   A national telephone directory offering a reverse look-up feature. Type in a phone number and you'll get back a name and address.

> http://www.databaseamerica.com/html/index.htm

Geneaology Gateway   A gateway to more than 42,000 resources. Get started by clicking the Beginner Help and Information link. Other sections let you search by surname, check out Ancestral Homepages, or post a link to your own family Web page.

> http://www.gengateway.com

GTE SuperPages

> http://superpages.com

People Finder   "One of the best people locators on the Web." People Finder uses the power of the Web to present your search to millions of people. It doesn't matter if the person you are looking for is on the Web or not, maybe someone who is will recognize them.

    http://www.peoplesite.com

Stars and Stripes   Locate long-lost comrades-in-arms.

    http://www.stripes.com/Looking.html

Webgator   A directory of public records information. Includes everything from unclaimed property lists to medical examiner records. Some site links take you to sites that ultimately charge you for information. But the site is a great place to get started if you're searching for people.

    http://www.inil.com/users/dguss/wgator.htm

WhoWhere   A broad offering of look-up services, including personal phone numbers, addresses, e-mail addresses, business directories, toll-free numbers and difficult-to-find government offices.

    http://www.whowhere.com

Wired Cybrarian - People Finder   A metasearch engine for finding people and e-mail addresses. Sponsored by Wired Magazine.

    http://www.wired.com/cybrarian

World E-mail Directory   Access to more than 18 million e-mail addresses and 140 million business addresses and phone numbers.

    http://www.worldemail.com

Yahoo! People Search   Search by name or e-mail address.

    http://people.yahoo.com

Bonus feature! Think of this as the chapter that never ends. For your surfing pleasure, I will be maintaining a regularly updated list of Web site discoveries online, so please stop by, say hello and enjoy Mr. Modem's updated Web sites list at `http://www.mrmodem.net`

General References

A warehouse of Web sites covering everything from aphorisms to ZIP codes.

Area Code Decoder   Very useful when trying to figure out what those long-distance calls are on your telephone bill. Enter an area code and retrieve the city or vice versa.

> `http://decoder.americom.com`

Business Tools, Forms, Letters   Sample letters, forms, contracts, spreadsheets and checklists.

> `http://www.toolkit.cch.com/tools/tools.stm`

Consumers Digest Online   The magazine we've come to know and trust through the years, now online!

> `http://www.consumersdigest.com`

Date and Time Gateway   Provides local time for every major city and region around the world.

> `http://www.bsdi.com/date`

Kelley Blue Book of New and Used Car Pricing   Includes names, manufacturers, models, options.

```
http://www.kbb.com/index.html
```

Measurement Conversion Calculator   Extremely useful Web site the next time you need to convert kilderkins to vedros. Let's see, are there 5.538 vedros in a kilderkin or is it 1.125 firkins to the reaumur? Perhaps I'm just preaching to the quire.

```
http://calc.entisoft.com/scripts/unitscgi.exe
```

Newstand, Ecola   A handy resource for locating newspapers and magazines online. This site lists more than 6,100 newspapers and magazines. A search engine is available to quickly locate the news source you seek.

```
http://www.ecola.com
```

One-Look Dictionaries   Over 147 dictionaries and glossaries in one location.

```
http://www.onelook.com
```

RefDesk   A compendium of proven news, information, entertainment, and weather sites. Beautifully organized, this site houses hundreds of excellent links. Makes a great start page for your browser. The site's host is Bob Drudge, Matt Drudge's (The Drudge Report, `http://drudgereport.com`) father. Small world, this Internet.

```
http://www.refdesk.com
```

State Government Link Access   Links to all known state government Web sites. Maintained by the Indiana University School of Law.

```
http://www.law.indiana.edu/law/v-lib/states.html
```

Universal Translator   Enter a word in any language and it will be translated into many other languages.

```
http://www.itools.com/research-it/research-it
.html#Translator
```

Virtual Reference Desk   If I could only bookmark one site on the Web, this would be it. Categorized links to thousands of useful Web sites and resources. Don't miss this site!

```
http://www.refdesk.com/fastfact.html
```

Bonus feature! Think of this as the chapter that never ends. For your surfing pleasure, I will be maintaining a regularly updated list of Web site discoveries online, so please stop by, say hello and enjoy Mr. Modem's updated Web sites list at `http://www.mrmodem.net`

Government

One person's "Big Brother" is another person's repository of invaluable information. If it's Government related, you'll find it here!

Census Bureau, U.S.   Resources and statistics focusing on social, demographic, and economic information about the United States. Enough charts to make you choke. Click alphabetically listed categories or use the search engine to search by word, place or map.

```
http://www.census.gov
```

Drudge Report, The   Part news, part gossip, part rumor, but entirely interesting!

http://drudgereport.com

FedWorld Information Network   A comprehensive central access point for searching, locating, ordering and acquiring government and business information. An agency of the U.S. Dept. of Commerce.

http://www.fedworld.gov

GovBot   A search engine for U.S. Government Web sites. Contains more than 500,000 Web pages, which is slightly less than the average U.S. tax return.

http://www.business.gov/Search_Online.html

House of Representatives, U.S.   In addition to phone, mail and e-mail links to members' sites, you can keep current with bills and resolutions being considered in Congress.

http://www.house.gov

National Archives   A treasure-trove of historical information, documents and photographs.

http://www.nara.gov

National Library of Medicine   Includes links to searchable Medline and MedlinePlus information, as well as a host of related medical databases. Enough information to make you queasy.

http://www.nlm.nih.gov

National Weather Service   Provides weather and flood warnings, public forecasts and advisories for all of the United States, its territories, adjacent waters and ocean areas, primarily for the protection of life and property.

http://www.nws.noaa.gov

Postal Service, U.S.   Who among us hasn't yearned to know what's happening today at the post office? Visit the "Unforgettable Letters" area to "explore the power, humor and drama of the written word." Includes "Dear Santa," President letters and love letters from famous people in history.

`http://www.usps.gov`

Senate, U.S.   Phone, mail, and e-mail addresses or links to senators and various Senate committees.

`http://www.senate.gov`

State Government Link Access   Links to all known state government Web sites. Maintained by the Indiana University School of Law.

`http://www.law.indiana.edu/law/v-lib/states.html`

White House, The   All sorts of government information, including access to Social Security, student aid, small business assistance, as well as a tour of the White House.

`http://www.whitehouse.gov`

Bonus feature! Think of this as the chapter that never ends. For your surfing pleasure, I will be maintaining a regularly updated list of Web site discoveries online, so please stop by, say hello and enjoy Mr. Modem's updated Web sites list at `http://www.mrmodem.net`

Health and Medicine

Paging all coughers, wheezers, sneezers and snifflers! Where else can you find a doctor who makes house calls, and who can schedule an appointment with less than six months notice, where you can always find a parking spot at the office, and where there is never a surly receptionist? Right here on the Web, of course!

About Living   A gathering place for people who want to live a holistic life. Leave your wieners on the grill, this feel-good site addresses such topics as mind and spirit, health and body, and personal growth.

    http://www.aboutliving.com

AMA Online Doctor Finder   Information on virtually every licensed physician in the United States and its possessions, including more than 650,000 doctors of medicine (MD) and doctors of osteopathy or osteopathic medicine (DO).

    http://www.ama-assn.org/aps/amahg.htm

Ask Dr. Weil   Each day Dr. Andrew Weil posts a new alternative medicine topic dealing with everything from AIDS, cancer, and arthritis, to the common cold, skin conditions and headaches.

    http://www.drweil.com

Ask the Dietitian   Sound nutritional advice by Joanne Larsen, MS, RD, LD.

    http://www.dietitian.com

Doctors, Best in America   For over a decade, Best Doctors has been at work building the largest, most comprehensive database of "best" doctors currently available to medical consumers today. Representing virtually every medical specialty in over 1,600 communities throughout the United

States and more than 150 countries worldwide, each physician was chosen by a peer review process.

http://www.bestdoctors.com

Drug Index, The Internet   http://www.rxlist.com

Drugstore.com   An online drugstore, the Amazon.com of off-the-shelf drugs, personal care products, and cosmetics. It even offers to deliver prescription drugs to your door.

http://www.drugstore.com

Health A to Z   Developed by health care professionals, this site includes a directory of more than 50,000 professionally-reviewed Internet resources, supportive online communities, and the Health A to Z Calendar.

http://www.healthatoz.com

Managed Health Care   Practical, timely online information about health-care costs and quality managed care.

http://www.modernmedicine.com/mhc

Mother Nature's General Store   Features alternative medicine products, including aromatherapy, hair and skin care, vitamins, homeopathy, and herbal products.

http://www.mothernature.com

QuackWatch   The focus of this site is to provide accurate information on health-care fraud and quackery, so you can make intelligent health care decisions.

http://www.quackwatch.com

Virtual Medical Center, The   100 percent dedicated to the needs of individuals with medium- and long-term medical conditions. One of the fastest-growing medical sites on the Web.

http://www.mediconsult.com

Bonus feature! Think of this as the chapter that never ends. For your surfing pleasure, I will be maintaining a regularly updated list of Web site discoveries online, so please stop by, say hello and enjoy Mr. Modem's updated Web sites list at http://www.mrmodem.net

Investments and Finance

Have I got a deal for you! A virtual vault of Web sites for everyone from the novice investor to those previously indicted and who are now logging on from the prison library.

American Association of Individual Investors   The stated purpose of the AAII is "to arm individual investors with knowledge that will help them manage their own assets more effectively."

http://www.aaii.org

Big Charts   Comprehensive and easy-to-use online charting and investment research. Provides access to interactive charts, quotes, reports and indicators on more than 50,000 stocks, mutual funds and market indexes.

http://www.bigcharts.com

Bloomberg Personal   News and information for online investors.

`http://www.bloomberg.com`

CD Rate Scanner   Compare interest rates for CD's from over 3,000 financial institutions. You can also purchase a CD directly through this site.

`http://bankcd.com`

Cheapskate Monthly   Dedicated to helping those who are struggling to live within their means find practical and realistic solutions for their financial problems.

`http://www.cheapskatemonthly.com`

Company Sleuth   Scours the Internet for free, legal, inside information on the companies you select.

`http://www.companysleuth.com`

CNNfn-Quote Search Service   Utilizing the vast resources of CNN, this site offers instant quotes of any stock, mutual fund, or money market fund regardless of which exchange they're traded on.

`http://cnnfn.com/markets/quotes.html`

Market Player   Investment tools and games. Participate in online competitions and see if you can corner the market!

`http://www.marketplayer.com`

Morningstar   Everything you always wanted to know about mutual funds.

`http://www.morningstar.net`

Motley Fool   The Motley Fool has risen from relative obscurity to become the most-consulted financial forum in the online world. If you haven't visited "The Fool," be sure to stop in and you'll soon understand why.

```
http://www.fool.com
```

Retire Early   A financial site with a sense of humor. How to get the most out of your retirement years.

```
http://home.earthlink.net/~intercst/reindex.html
```

Wall Street Research Net   Includes over 500,000 links to assist professional and private investors research actively traded companies, mutual funds, and other important economic data.

```
http://www.wsrn.com
```

Bonus feature! Think of this as the chapter that never ends. For your surfing pleasure, I will be maintaining a regularly updated list of Web site discoveries online, so please stop by, say hello and enjoy Mr. Modem's updated Web sites list at `http://www.mrmodem.net`

Lifestyles, Recreation, and Hobbies

Just when you thought life couldn't get any better, along comes this campground full of Web sites. Arts, crafts, camping, gardening, pets, games, golf and more are now only a mouse-click away!

Baby Boomers Home Page   A must-see for any baby boomer. A collection of current boomer obsessions, lifestyle quirks, and lots of boomer humor.

    http://www.netwalk.com/~duchapl

CampNet America   The best places to camp, how to get there, what to do once you get there. Includes RV parks and the Campground Locator, a complete listing of National and Public Parks, camping and outdoor suppliers, log cabin rentals, travel clubs and associations.

    http://www.kiz.com/campnet/html/campnet.htm

Cookbooks Online   Register for free access to over one million recipes located in the searchable recipe database.

    http://www.cookbooks.com

Garden.com   Sponsored by "Garden Escape" magazine, this site is blooming with information about hundreds of flowers, vegetables, and herbs, as well as planting, gardening, and landscaping tips.

    http://www.garden.com

InterLotto   A one-stop source for Lottery information. So do you feel lucky?

    http://www.interlotto.com

Mr. Cranky's Movie Reviews   His name alone captures perfectly the style of these entertaining movie reviews.

http://internet-plaza.net/zone/mrcranky

Pet Channel, The   A one-stop pet site for dogs, cats, horses, animals large and small.

http://www.thepetchannel.com

Rate Your Risk   Three very focused questionnaires that will help you determine your risk of robbery, assault, burglary, and murder. Sponsored by the Nashville Police Department.

http://www.Nashville.Net/~police/risk

Suddenly Single   Dedicated to men and women over 50 who would like to meet somebody new.

http://www.suddenlysingle.com

The 19th Hole   Tips from the golf practice tee, lots of jokes to share with your golfing buddies, PGA tournament updates, and a newsstand that includes statistics, previews, reviews, and observations from Sandy Bunker.

http://www.19thHole.com

Virtual Vineyards   Hundreds of wine and food selections to tempt you. Let Proprietor and Head Cork Dork Peter Granoff answer your wine questions or help you select the perfect wine for any occasion.

http://www.virtualvin.com

Volunteer Match   Helping individuals nationwide find volunteer opportunities posted by local nonprofit and public sector organizations. Search thousands of one-time and ongoing opportunities by zip code, category, and date.

http://www.volunteermatch.com

Bonus feature! Think of this as the chapter that never ends. For your surfing pleasure, I will be maintaining a regularly updated list of Web site discoveries online, so please stop by, say hello and enjoy Mr. Modem's updated Web sites list at `http://www.mrmodem.net`

Memory Lane

The good old days are alive and well in Mr. Modem's malt shop on the Web. Join me for a stroll down memory lane as we wax nostalgic, remember days gone by and think about the way we were.

50 Best Commercials from Advertising Age   This site recalls classic commercials spanning 50 years, 1946 to 1996.

`http://www.adage.com/news_and_features/special_reports/commercials`

Biography   A&E's award-winning television program on the Web. More than 20,000 biographies and 1,200 videos.

`http://www.biography.com`

Burma Shave Slogans

If you remember…
With all your might…
The Burma-Shave signs…
You must see this site.

`http://www.iea.com/%7Edgookin/burma.htm`

Early America   Historic documents from eighteenth century America.

`http://www.earlyamerica.com`

Fifties Web, The   If you can remember sock hops, poodle skirts, circle pins, Dick Clark's "American Bandstand," and the Mouseketeers, stroll on over to this site.

http://www.fiftiesweb.com

Hippy Land   Slip into your Birks and groove on over to the site where you can find everything from astral travel to Zeppelin.

http://www.hippy.com

History Net, The   An extraordinarily comprehensive site laden with historical information, personality profiles, eyewitness accounts, interviews, photographs, and more.

http://www.thehistorynet.com

Nostalgia Central   A trip back to the sixties, seventies and eighties via TV, music, movies, toys & pop culture.

http://www.geocities.com/SoHo/Atrium/3451

Reflections on Aging   Don't miss this one! A time of innocence lives on, on the Internet.

http://members.aol.com/penny2849/aging.html

Remember When   A stroll back in time when the music, drive-in movies, three tv stations, hot rods, the malt shop, and sock hops were the keenest!

http://www.erols.com/mlbl

Retro Active   Retro is an online magazine that celebrates classic popular culture from 1900 through 1975. Includes articles on vintage personalities, politics, music, media & entertainment, fashion, design, decorating and more.

http://www.retroactive.com

This Day in History

`http://www.historychannel.com`

Yesterdayland   A nostalgic recap of television shows from the Golden Age of television. They're all here, from *Captain Video* (the favorite show of *The Honeymooners* Ed Norton) to *The World of Sid and Marty Kroft*, creators of H.R. Pufnstuf and other adults in ridiculous costumes.

`http://www.yesterdayland.com`

Bonus feature! Think of this as the chapter that never ends. For your surfing pleasure, I will be maintaining a regularly updated list of Web site discoveries online, so please stop by, say hello and enjoy Mr. Modem's updated Web sites list at `http://www.mrmodem.net`

Mr. Modem's DME's (Don't Miss 'Ems!)

Mr. Modem's personal, eclectic collection of sites from the wilder, wackier, weirder side of the Web.

Annals of Improbable Research   Reports of unusual research and improbable happenings.

`http://www.improb.com`

Apology Note Generator, Mark's   Fill in the blanks from the drop-down menus and generate the perfect apology for any occasion. I'm sorry. I'm really sorry...

    http://net.indra.com/~karma/formletter.html

Chia Pet Zoo   Don't miss this one! And they say there is no culture...

    http://www.accessone.com/~jonathin/pets.htm

CRAYON - CreAte Your Own Newspaper
    http://crayon.net

How to Keep an Idiot Busy   A classic!

    http://junior.apk.net/~jbarta/idiot/idiot.html

International Collection of Tongue Twisters   None of your ordinary tongue twisters like "Which witch wished which wicked wish?" Child's play! Over 400 tongue twisters in 39 languages! And you haven't heard a tongue twister until you've heard a Farsi tongue twister: "Ruye rune marde Lore mu dore." I've been guffawing for days over that one!

    http://info.uibk.ac.at/c/c7/c704/qo/people/_mr/twister/
    index.html

MyFamily.com   Create a free, private, online gathering place for your entire family. E-mail, chat, a family events calendar, photo album, bulletin board, and more.

    http://www.myfamily.com

PhoNETic   Converts a telephone number into all combinations of the associated letters on the phone keypad, and vice versa. Call me at 1-800-GETALIFE.

    http://www.soc.qc.edu/phonetic

Political Babble Generator, The

A must-see for political junkies. Mix three-word phrases together from actual political speeches and output a new "creation" every ten minutes. See if you can tell the synthetic product from the real thing.

`http://www.webcorp.com/polibabble.htm`

Puzzle Depot

This site is devoted to puzzles, board and logic games, skill contests and trivia, as well as related books and software for recreation and K-12 education. You'll find crosswords, riddles, word puzzles, logic and strategy, as well as board games.

`http://www.puzzledepot.com/index.html`

Smoking Gun

Did Martha Stewart try to run down her neighbor's gardener in a car? Did Elvis label the Beatles as "nefarious liberal Hollywood influences?" What sort of bizarre demands does Michael Bolton make on his roadies? The answers to these life-altering questions and more can be found at this site.

`http://www.thesmokinggun.com`

U.S. Speed Traps

Searchable by state. "One Adam-12...One Adam-12..."

`http://www.speedtrap.com/speedtrap/us-traps.html`

Bonus feature! Think of this as the chapter that never ends. For your surfing pleasure, I will be maintaining a regularly updated list of Web site discoveries online, so please stop by, say hello and enjoy Mr. Modem's updated Web sites list at `http://www.mrmodem.net`

Specifically for Seniors

In this section we'll explore an assortment of Web sites for, by and about our 50+ generation. So if you're over 50, pull up a chair and come sit by Mr. Modem!

AARP WebPlace   The nation's leading organization for people 50 and older. Includes information about Modern Maturity and the AARP Bulletin.

> http://www.aarp.org

Age of Reason   Over 5,000 Links to sites of interest to the over 50 age group.

> http://www.ageofreason.com

Elderhostel   A nonprofit organization providing educational adventures all over the world to adults aged 55 and over. Elderhostel is for people on the move who believe learning is a lifelong process.

> http://www.elderhostel.org

Geezer Brigade, The   "Empowerment through humor." Don't miss this site!

> http://www.thegeezerbrigade.com

Grand Times Magazine Online   A unique weekly magazine published for active older adults. Controversial, entertaining and informative, this magazine celebrates life's opportunities and examines life's challenges.

> http://www.grandtimes.com

Microsoft's Seniors & Technology   The web site of the Microsoft Senior Initiative, "a worldwide program enhancing community, creativity and employability via the use of computer and Internet technologies."

http://www.microsoft.com/seniors/default.asp

SeniorCom   An online community providing products, services, information, and entertainment to the 50+ market.

http://www.senior.com

Senior Friendly Products   An independent research and product certification company specializing in identifying "easier-to-use" technology-based products for people age 50 and over.

http://www.seniorfriendly.com

SeniorWorld Online   A wonderful source of daily news on topics of interest to adults over 50. More than 400 columns, features and news stories organized in eight major categories and 40 subject areas.

http://www.seniorworld.com

Sex and Senior Citizens   News and bulletins on sex for and by seniors. You must be 18 or older to enter this site. This is *not* an x-rated nor a prurient Web site.

http://seniors-site.com/sex

ThirdAge   A Web-based community started by ThirdAge Media, Inc. where ThirdAgers can voice their opinions, recount experiences, and share advice with new friends through interactive technologies such as chat rooms and discussion boards.

http://www.thirdage.com

WidowNet   An information and self-help resource for and by widows and widowers.

http://www.fortnet.org/~goshorn

Bonus feature! Think of this as the chapter that never ends. For your surfing pleasure, I will be maintaining a regularly updated list of Web site discoveries online, so please stop by, say hello and enjoy Mr. Modem's updated Web sites list at `http://www.mrmodem.net`

Travel, Destinations, and Maps

A steamer trunk full of Web sites with a focus on travel. No reservations or deposits required, so please sit back, relax and enjoy the journey!

Airline Toll-Free 800 Numbers

`http://www.princeton.edu/Main/air800.html`

Amtrak   Browse the travel planner for a railroad vacation package perfect for you. You can also use the Trakrouter to map out your own rail travel plans. All aboard!

`http://www.amtrak.com`

Bed & Breakfast Encyclopedia Online   More than 12,000 bed & breakfast listings for the United States and Canada.

`http://homearts.com/affil/ahi/main/ahihome.htm`

Currency Converter   Want to know how many Zloties to the Markka or want to change your Renmimbis into Rupiahs? Just type in a dollar amount and receive the conversion rate. Impress your friends!

`http://www.xe.net/currency`

MapQuest!   Great for planning destination routes. Click TripQuest and enter your starting and destination points with an address and city. Receive detailed best routes and streets to travel.

http://www.mapquest.com

Netcruise   Nine of the 10 most popular cruise lines, including Princess Cruises, Royal Caribbean, Carnival Cruise Line, and Norwegian Cruise Line, call this site home port. Visitors to this site can virtually walk onto each ship and review deck maps, read cabin descriptions, sample onboard activities, and browse the lists of cruise destinations.

http://www.netcruise.com

Park Search by L.L. Bean   The great outdoors now at your fingertips! Search the nation's parks and forests by state, region, name or service. This site includes more than 1,500 recreation areas. Be sure to wear your tough, waterproof-yet-breathable three-layer Gore-Tex, all-conditions parka with optional fleece lining, when surfing the Web in colder climates.

http://www.llbean.com/parksearch

Priceline.com   A very popular buying service that lets you name your price for airline tickets, hotel rooms, home financing services and automobiles. Post the amount you're willing to spend and guarantee your offer with a credit card. Priceline then tries to find a seller.

http://www.priceline.com

Time Zone Converter   Can't remember if Lubumbashi is 16 hours ahead or 9 hours behind? Or is it tomorrow morning in Kiritimati or yesterday afternoon? If you're among the chronologically challenged, this site is for you. Find out what time it is anywhere in the world with a click of the mouse.

http://www.timezoneconverter.com

TrafficSpy   Pick the city/state of interest and receive your personal briefing on traffic reports and road construction and travel information. Many sites have real-time traffic reports, some even have live cams.

`http://www.trafficspy.com`

Travelocity   Offers schedules for more than 700 airlines, reservations and ticketing for more than 400 airlines, and reservations for more than 34,000 hotels and 50 car rental companies.

`http://www.travelocity.com`

WeatherPost   Weather information for 3,600 cities worldwide.

`http://www.weatherpost.com`

Bonus feature! Think of this as the chapter that never ends. For your surfing pleasure, I will be maintaining a regularly updated list of Web site discoveries online, so please stop by, say hello and enjoy Mr. Modem's updated Web sites list at `http://www.mrmodem.net`

Web TV

In this section, WebTV aficionados will find a cornucopia of resources just for them!

Alan's WebTV Guide   Lots of useful Internet resources for WebTV users and others.

`http://www2.cybernex.net/~ajy/index.html`

Andreson Family WebTV Special Interest Group (SIG) An online discussion group focusing on WebTV.

http://www.webtvsig.com/splash2.htm

Bill's Games Free WebTV-compatible games for the whole family.

http://www.billsgames.com

Club WebTV An electronic newsletter published by WebTV Networks.

http://webtv.net/corp/clubwebtv/newsletter

Haven, WebTV Tips, tricks, links, and fun!

http://www.geocities.com/Yosemite/Gorge/5991/webtv/index.html

Helpful Hints for WebTV Users The name of this site says it all.

http://www.expage.com/page/helpfulhintsforwebtv

Home Page Building Helpers Utilities, graphics, animation, clip art, icons, buttons, bells and whistles galore.

http://www.geocities.com/MadisonAvenue/9386/build.html

Hot 50 WebTV Sites

http://www.webtvsearch.com/hot50.html

Planet WebTV, Jim and Dee's Excellent resource. Includes tips, tricks, links, RealAudio, page construction utilities, and more.

http://members.tripod.com/~webhed4net/index.html

Ray's WebTV World WebTV help and information.

http://members.tripod.com/~nytak/wtv.html

Ultimate WebTV Search   A search engine made specifically for WebTV users.

http://www.webtvsearch.com

WebTV, Microsoft's   News and information about products, services, company information, developer resources.

http://www.webtv.com

Shopping online is becoming more popular with each passing day, but is it really safe? In the next chapter we'll sidle up to the cash registers and take a close look at the phenomenon known as e-commerce.

Bonus feature! Think of this as the chapter that never ends. For your surfing pleasure, I will be maintaining a regularly updated list of Web site discoveries online, so please stop by, say hello and enjoy Mr. Modem's updated Web sites list at http://www.mrmodem.net

E-Commerce: Shopping Online

Purchasing goods, services and tchotchkes online is a growth industry. According to the experts at `http://emarketer.com`, $3.7 billion was spent on consumer goods purchased online in 1998; $6.1 billion in 1999; and a budget-bustin' $10 billion will be spent in 2000. Why do you think that is? Can't we spend our money fast enough offline? And what happens if your credit card gets stuck in the floppy drive when attempting to make a purchase via computer? In this chapter, we'll explore the phenomenon of online shopping from the consumer's perspective—your side of the credit card. Not only do you need to know it's safe, but you also need to know what you can do to protect yourself from the e-slime who are just waiting to tap into your hard-earned dollars.

First, let's understand what the term *e-commerce* means. E-commerce is simply a high falutin, high-tech way of saying "buying things online." E-words are very popular on the Internet. Too popular, if you ask me. So any time you see e-something, be sure to roll your eyes and know in your heart that it's the result of another marketer's less-than-fertile e-magination at work.

Few thoughts strike more terror into the hearts of Internetters than the notion of purchasing something online using a credit card. While common sense is never out of style and always appropriate, the reality is that it's generally very safe to use a credit card—preferably your own—online. But if you have a concern about transmitting your credit card information via the Internet, relax, take a deep breath, and know that you're not alone.

Truth: There is not a single, documented case of a credit card ever having been stolen or misappropriated while being transmitted over the Internet. If you know of one such incident that is, indeed, documented and authenti- cated by the credit card com- pany or a law enforcement agency, please e-mail me at MrModem@home.com. In the following sections we'll explore why and how some people have developed the perception that using a credit card online is unsafe. If we can understand the basis of these fears, we'll be well on our way toward eliminating any unfounded anxiety—and we'll do it all without Prozac. (Mr. Modem…Nobel Peace Prize…it's all com- ing together.)

To Fear or Not to Fear?

Let's begin by thinking about how we use our credit cards in the offline world. How many of us wouldn't think twice about using a credit card in a restaurant? After presenting our credit card to a person we don't know, we sign the charge slip, remove our copy of the receipt, leave the other copies on the table, and walk away. Let's pause for a dramatic moment and reflect: *We leave the other copies on the table and walk away.* Hello? What's wrong with this picture?

Does it make any sense at all to leave your credit card information on the table, unattended, unsupervised, unmonitored, and walk away? Of course not. In theory, anybody could pick up the receipt and have access to your name, credit card number, and expiration date. And armed with that information, at least for a short period of time, that person has access to more fabulous merchandise than what awaits behind Door Number 2.

Yet somehow, in some strange and amazingly complacent way, we don't worry about things like that because we're comfortable using a credit card in this manner. It's the norm for most of us. We just assume the credit card will be processed in an appropriate manner and the charge will appear on our monthly statement. How that happens is a mystery to most of us, but our history and experience tells us that it works, so why be concerned?

The 50+ age group leads the way when it comes to online spending, according to a study conducted by Zona Research, Inc. of Redwood City, California (`http://www.zonaresearch.com`). More than 1,000 Internet users were surveyed after the 1998 holiday buying season.

- Results show online holiday spending by Internet users rose from an average of $216 in 1997 to $629 in 1998, nearly a 200 percent increase.

- Spending for respondents age 50 to 54 grew 545 percent, while spending by those 55-plus rose 547 percent. Online holiday shopping spending by the under-25 set grew by just 36 percent, compared to the previous year.

- More than half the sample said their primary reason for shopping online was to save time or money.

Source: Arizona/Nevada Senior World Newsletter, Feb, 1999. `http://www.seniormedia.com`

So why the fears about using a credit card online? Several reasons. First, fear of the unknown is a basic human characteristic. For many individuals, using a credit card online is a new and therefore unfamiliar experience. It may even be a little intimidating, just like using a credit card, debit card, fax machine, microwave oven, cell phone, computer, or CD-ROM for the first time.

Confronting Our Fears

The perception of risk about credit cards being stolen online originates with the media. But this is one time when it's really not the media's fault. We listen to stories, we hear the buzzwords and then we often form our own inaccurate conclusions.

For example, on occasion *hackers* (CyberScoundrels who break into computer databases) have gained unauthorized access to credit card databases at large banking institutions. These break-ins result in the breaker-inners having access to millions of credit card numbers and related information. So these criminals used the Internet as their vehicle for breaking into the databases, but what they had access to was your credit card information, my credit card information, and the card information of millions of other individuals who may or may not have used their credit cards online. Oh, the irony of it all. These modem marauders may or may not have used the purloined credit card information to make purchases from respectable merchants.

When stories like these are presented by the media, the public is generally left with buzzword impressions. These buzzwords include: *Internet, hacker, credit cards,* and *purchases.* Misperceptions arise when we blur these terms together and come to the erroneous conclusion that using credit cards online is very dangerous. The truth is, it is not.

The hackers in our example did not steal credit card information from good folks like you and me while we were transmitting our credit card information over the Internet. Reaching that conclusion is as appropriate as believing that because you can fly to Las Vegas and lose all your money, that airplanes are therefore dangerous to your financial health. In these instances, both the Internet and the airplane are simply vehicles. Some people use vehicles for good purposes, others don't.

Hysterical Precedent

For many years, whenever you presented your credit card to a retail merchant, it was swiped through a little terminal. You then waited anxiously for authorization or approval from somebody unknown. Now comes the big surprise: That data transfer and authorization, in most instances, occurred via the Internet. So for many of us, our credit card information has been careening around cyberspace for digital eons, yet we've never really known about it. How do you like them apples? Who says ignorance isn't bliss?

Also, as opposed to perceived risk, consider your actual risk. If, and it's a big IF, your credit card information is the first in Internet history to be stolen while being transmitted, your liability is generally limited to $50. It's been my experience that if you notify the credit card company as soon as you discover an unauthorized charge, chances are excellent that you won't even have to pay the $50. The bottom line is that it's simply worth the convenience to use a credit card for online purchases, software registrations, and a host of other financial transactions.

Faxing and Phoning Credit Card Information

Through the years I have encountered individuals who, while having the desire to purchase something online, expressed concern about using a credit card. They chose to fax their credit card information to an Internet-based merchant instead of transmitting it online. Faxing information is frequently viewed as an acceptable alternative, but lets talk about that. Exactly how safe is it?

When you fax information, you typically have no idea who is on the receiving end—and that's assuming you dial the fax number correctly. Unlike an online, form-based financial transaction that is routed to one specific e-mail address, a faxed document usually winds up in hard-copy format, languishing in the tray of a distant fax machine. It will remain in that location, accessible by anybody with access to the fax machine, until somebody comes along, removes the document and processes the information in an appropriate manner—you hope.

Faxing credit card information is a risky process at best, yet most people are comfortable with the concept of faxing, so it is not perceived as being particularly insecure. Many of the same people who refuse to transmit credit card information online are infinitely more receptive to the idea of transmitting that same information by fax. I have no idea why, other than it's comfortable and familiar.

The same thing holds true when providing credit card information by telephone. Think about the process: You're providing your credit card information to somebody you don't know, in an unknown location, and if you call the same number back immediately, it's highly unlikely that you'll ever reach the same person again. There's no paper trail, it's all verbal, and chances are you won't even know the name of the person you're speaking with. If you do obtain the name of the person you're speaking with, which is always a good idea, it's going to be Jennifer, Heather, or Jason. It's always Jennifer, Heather, or Jason.

E-mail addresses used for the online routing of credit card and other personal information are typically embedded hyperlinks within a Web page or order form. That means you need only click the link to retrieve a form, enter your information, and transmit it to a predetermined e-mail address. The chances of entering an incorrect address are minimal, and certainly far less likely than manually dialing a 10 + digit fax number. Transpose two digits of a fax number and you'll be sending your credit card or other personal information to a complete stranger. And unless you're Blanche DuBois relying on the kindnesses of strangers, you're not likely to know you faxed your information to an incorrect location. Talk about anxiety!

Bank's cost to process an in-person transaction: $1.07
Bank's cost to process an Internet-based transaction: $0.01

Source: Wells Fargo Bank, http://www.wellsfargo.com cited in ComputerWorld, http://www.computerworld.com

A Calculated Risk

So what is the risk or danger associated with using your credit card online? Reality check: Insurance experts tell us that you're more likely to have your credit card stolen offline than have your information misappropriated on the Internet. Okay, maybe not insurance experts, but I do have a neighbor who has an insurance policy and that's what he thinks. As increasing numbers of people use the Internet (some 600,000 new users every month), the probability of your credit card information being intercepted during transmission decreases from nil to what we in the biz call *IAGH* or "It ain't gonna happen."

Is it possible for somebody to intercept the transmission of your credit card information over the Internet? Technically, yes, it is. But let's not toss common sense out the window here. Ask yourself why anyone with the level of skill necessary to intercept the transmission of your credit card information would want to go to all the trouble? Wouldn't it make more sense for that person to simply get a job as a clerk in a store and have access to credit card information all day long? If one really wants to have access to credit card information, there are infinitely more opportunities, that require a heck of a lot less computing skill and knowledge, than waiting for you to decide to purchase something online.

12 Steps to Safe Online Shopping

E-commerce and shopping online are here to stay. As we discussed in this chapter, transmitting credit card information on the Internet is at least as safe, if not safer, than telephoning or faxing the same information. When considering purchasing anything online, there are a few things you should keep in mind at all times. Follow Mr. Modem's 12 Steps to Safe Online Shopping and you'll be well on your way toward ensuring that your online shopping experiences will be both enjoyable and safe.

1. Start Conservatively

If you have never shopped online before, start by purchasing a small, inexpensive item just to get a feel for the process. Many people fear online shopping because it's unknown to them. Online shopping is a wonderful convenience, but like anything new, it may take a few times before your comfort level reaches the point where it's—er, um, well, comfortable. Remember the first time you pulled into a self-service gas station and had to pump your own gas? I sure do. It was very intimidating to me to be pumping ethyl right out there in front of everybody. But once I became familiar with the process, it was no big deal and I quickly mastered the art of spilling gas on my car just like the pros do.

2. Be Patient

Shopping online will require you to fill out one or more forms to process your order. On occasion your connection to the Internet may be slow or the site you're visiting may be very busy, and it may take a few minutes for information you provide to be processed. Be patient. Don't provide your credit card information, then throw a hissy fit about waiting for a few extra minutes. No matter how long it takes to process your order online, it's still infinitely faster than driving to a store (in the case of software) or waiting for a mail order to arrive. Just think back to the days when *online ordering* meant calling Sears on the telephone line. You would provide a product number from their 400 pound catalog, then wait three weeks. (Good news: The Sears catalog is also online at `http://www.sears.com`.)

3. Comparison Shop

Just because you're comfortable with the price of an item found at one site doesn't mean there aren't better values available elsewhere on the Web. Prices vary widely on the Internet, just as they do in the offline world, so be a savvy shopper and do some comparison shopping. And while you're comparison shopping, don't compromise on quality, size, color, or model. If you can't find exactly what you want at one site, just keep looking. The world is at your fingertips. Comparison shopping is only effective when it's applied apples-to-apples, tchotchke-to-tchotchke.

4. Don't Forget Shipping and Handling Charges

Many online merchants don't tell you how much the shipping and handling charges will be until you're almost finished checking out. If the shipping is too high, don't complete your order just because you're in the checkout line. Simply click the Cancel or Reset Form button to bail out. Sometimes the default shipping method is a more expensive overnight or second-day shipping service. Always select a slower and less expensive method of shipping, if possible.

5. Check Out the Company

One of the highest and best uses of the Internet is its ability to place vast amounts of information at your fingertips. Use this ability to do a little investigating on your own about the company or merchant with whom you're doing business. Several e-commerce e-sources are presented at the end of this chapter.

6. Look for Additional Contact Information

Try to shop with merchants who include a toll-free number on their Web site so you can place a customer service call if you have a problem or question. Sometimes just knowing that there is another way to contact a merchant can be comforting. It wouldn't hurt to look for a street address, as well. Who knows? They might be located right down the street. If that's the case, just get up and walk there. The exercise will be good for you.

7. Understand the Offer

Read all the information presented about the item you're contemplating purchasing. If you would like more information, request it by e-mail. If you don't receive a response, you have your answer about dealing with that company. Make sure you know and understand what you're purchasing, the total price, the delivery date, the return and cancellation policy, and the terms of any guarantee. Merchandise purchased must be delivered by the promised time or, if none was noted, within 30 days.

8. Protect Your Personal Information

Some sites sell the personal information they collect from shoppers, which usually results in junk e-mail or even junk snail-mail cluttering up your mailbox. If you're not comfortable with that—and many people are not—look for a privacy policy statement posted on the Web site of any company with whom you're considering doing business. If you're not satisfied with the policy as posted, don't make any purchases.

9. Pay by Credit Card

As we discussed earlier in this chapter, nothing is more misunderstood in the wild and wacky world of e-commerce than using a credit card to make purchases. Purchasing by credit card is the safest method of shopping online. Not only do you have all safeguards and protections afforded by the credit card company, but you can often earn frequent flyer miles or bonus points towards the purchase of aluminum siding for your house, as well. If you don't have a credit card or the thought of using a credit card online makes you drop before you shop, try to find a seller who will place your money in escrow until the merchandise arrives in satisfactory condition. Due to the increasing popularity of online shopping, third-party escrow services are popping up on the Internet to perform this very service. Service availability will be noted by participating merchants.

10. Use a Secure Web Site

Look for a message on screen that informs you that your transaction is being transferred to a secure server or system. A *secure server* is one that encrypts or scrambles your personal information during transmission over the Internet. A secure site will display a little key icon, a picture of a closed padlock, or a Web address that begins with https (see Figure 12.1). For more information about encryption, visit http://www.mrmodem.net.

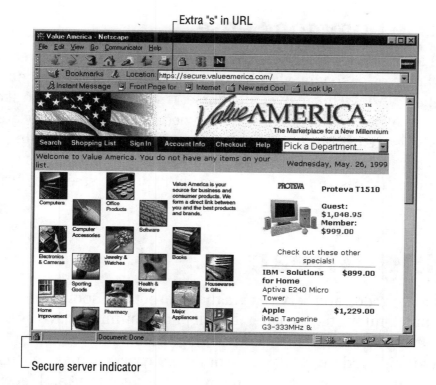

FIGURE 12.1: Secure Server Indicators

11. Stay Informed

Information about shopping online abounds on the Web, so do your homework! See the "Additional E-Commerce Resources" box at the end of this chapter for a list of Web sites that provide helpful online consumer protection information. The more you know and understand about shopping online, the more comfortable you will be with the process. Stay informed and stay safe.

12. Use Common Sense

You've accumulated a lifetime of common sense and use it every day in the offline world, so why should you set that aside when functioning in the online world? The answer, of course, is you should not. Be skeptical of offers that sound too good to be true because they probably are. Listen to the voice of your inner modem. If that little voice is telling you to be on your guard about a certain merchant, don't do business with that company. Chances are that little voice isn't going to steer you wrong.

Looking Ahead

Purchasing goods and services via the Internet will soon be as commonplace and comfortable as using the telephone or microwave oven. Today, students register for classes and purchase their books online; parents register their children for day care online; physicians make virtual house calls by e-mail; and you can even pay your taxes online and receive your refund (we can dream, can't we?) electronically by direct deposit.

As technology continues to evolve and further integrates with society, and as our collective comfort level with the Internet grows, we will continue to see online communication and commerce converge to the point where they will simply be a part of our everyday e-life.

Additional E-Commerce Resources

Better Business Bureau Online—News alerts, searchable business report databases.

```
http://www.bbb.org
```

Better Web Business Bureau—Free consumer access to the BWBB complaint and history database.

```
http://brbc.net/www.bwbb.com
```

Consumer Reports Online

```
http://www.consumerreports.com
```

Internet Scambusters—Mr. Modem's favorite!

```
http://www.scambusters.org
```

U.S. Consumer Gateway—A one-stop link to federal information about online scams and fraud.

```
http://www.consumer.gov/Tech.htm
```

What's Next?

Now that I've gone out on a limb and predicted the convergence of online communication and e-commerce, in the next chapter we'll explore what we can do to ensure that our online communications are effective.

Effective Online Communication

Through the years I have conducted hundreds of seminar presentations focusing on mastering, or at least understanding, online communications. In this chapter, I will share with you some techniques that will significantly enhance and facilitate your ability to communicate electronically, and help you recognize and understand two universal yet very different styles of communication.

Accompanying the ever increasing integration of electronic communications within our society are many issues regarding your ability to communicate online. It's a good news/bad news proposition. The bad news is this: Just because you can write a letter or stick a Post-It on your refrigerator does not mean you necessarily possess the requisite skills to communicate effectively online. The good news is that these skills are relatively easy to learn.

Always keep in mind that your audience is infinitely larger when communicating within an Internet-based discussion group, chat room, forum or newsgroup, than any audience you have likely encountered in the past. Remember, too, that e-mail never dies. You never know how many other people will receive copies of your e-mail or where it will eventually wind up. One classic example of an e-mail that made the rounds was an e-mail sent from one surgical nurse to another. The message said, "Did you see what Dr. (name deleted) did today? If that patient manages to survive, it will be a miracle." The surgeon was not amused when that e-mail later surfaced during a malpractice action.

Thousands upon thousands of individuals around the world may read and place their own interpretations on the words you choose. It makes good sense, therefore, to have some working knowledge of the medium and some level of comfort with your own online communication skills before diving in.

Assertive vs. Aggressive Communication Styles

To effectively communicate with others, your focus must initially be on yourself as you formulate your thoughts and compose your messages and e-mail. Then your attention must shift to your intended audience, the recipient of your messages.

There are two primary styles of communication—assertive and aggressive. The differences between these styles sets the standard for what is acceptable, appropriate and productive communication and what is not.

An assertive communication style is acceptable and welcome; it's more inviting, more compelling, and more conducive to creating an environment where people can freely exchange ideas, information and discuss differences of opinion.

An aggressive style of communication discourages discussion and limits the free-flowing exchange that is so important in any healthy dialogue.

The ratio of male-to-female Internet users reached 50/50 in 1999, contrasted with a 82/18 male-to-female disparity three years earlier.

Source: Media Metrix, http://www.mediamextrix.com.

Your ability to communicate will be infinitely more effective if you embrace an assertive communication style and at the same time become exquisitely sensitive to those who display an aggressive online style.

Assertive and aggressive communication styles exist offline as well as online, but our focus here will be intentionally narrow and limited to online communication. I can't resolve communication problems in the offline world, either. Even Mr. Modem has his limits.

Applying the Mr. Modem Assertive versus Aggressive Acceptability Standard (patent pending) to any communications platform, an assertive communication style is always well received by others, which results in greater participation. The aggressive communicator, however, instantly erects a barrier that has a chilling effect on what could otherwise be a productive, informative, friendly discussion. Understanding and recognizing the differences between these communication styles can be tricky, but there are several easy-to-spot indicators.

Watch for the Signs

An aggressive communicator focuses on others rather than on self and employs many "you" statements. "*You* should," "*You're* wrong," "If *you* can't take it, that's *your* problem." "If *you* don't like what I'm saying, don't read my messages."

An assertive communicator uses "I" statements: "*I* feel," "*I* think," "*I* believe," "*I* would like." It's as subtle as the distinction between "*You* are wrong," and "*I* disagree." The thrust of both statements is the same; there's a disagreement about something. An assertive communicator ("I disagree") takes responsibility for his or her own statements; the aggressive communicator ("You're wrong") attempts to shift responsibility to the recipient of his or her message.

The assertive communicator, by stating, "I disagree," hasn't erected any barriers and is keeping the conversational doors wide open. This person is saying, "Look, I disagree, but let's talk about it."

The aggressive communicator, by stating, "You're wrong," immediately places the other party to the conversation on the defensive. If two people are having a conversation and disagree about something, one person doesn't have to be wrong. Both can feel strongly about their respective positions and simply agree to disagree. The important thing is that both people *respect* each other's opinions. The aggressive communicator who states, "You're wrong," is saying "I don't respect your opinion. There is no validity to your position." It's very concrete, very black-and-white, and does nothing to promote ongoing discussion.

Your Words; Your Responsibility

When you compose a message, whether it's in a discussion group, chat room, or as part of a mailing list, you are responsible for the appropriateness of that message and its possible results.

Bear in mind, also, when venturing out into cyberspace, that the laws of libel and slander are not waived simply because your communication occurs online. When I'm in a tizzy about something somebody said in an online discussion group or newsgroup and I'm about to fire off a SCUD (Silly, Controversial, or Uncharacteristically Dopey) missive, I've discovered that softly chanting the words *libel* and *slander* have a wonderfully soothing effect. Ahhhhh… I think of them as my digital mantra, and I am happy to share them with you.

Taking our example one step further, let's say I disagree with you and I fire off an e-mail or a publicly posted message containing hostility, nastiness or any of a number of verbal barbs that will likely upset or hurt you—called a *flame*.

That is inappropriate, unacceptable, and grotesquely inconsiderate. There are no excuses for communicating in this manner. We're not children, we needn't throw online temper tantrums. It's up to us to behave like responsible, intelligent adults and appreciate the fact that each one of us is an instrumental part of our global Internet community. If we're having a bad day, we need to be careful not to ruin it for others.

And if you see others engaging in an inappropriate manner or if you are on the receiving end of a flame (the *flamee*), remember that some people are nasty just to be provocative in hopes of getting a rise out of others. Don't be the tinder that permits the flame to continue to burn.

The Aggressive Communicator

The aggressive communicator may not consciously recognize his or her own deficient communication style and may attempt to subconsciously rationalize or justify it with, "I always tell it like it is." If you find yourself on the receiving end of such a statement, let it serve as a red flag placing you on notice that what the person is really saying is, "I am completely lacking in communication skills, therefore I'll just blurt out anything I feel like saying and assume no responsibility for the consequences of my words." It's the not-so-charming adult version of "kids say the darndest things."

Not taking responsibility for one's own words does not foster productive communication online or off. To the contrary, it can actually result in the message recipient *not* responding, thus having a chilling effect on what could otherwise be a productive, informative discussion. Aggressive communicators stifle productive discussion by creating an unpleasant environment for others. And when good communicators choose to stop communicating rather than having to endure the rantings of even one inappropriate individual, the entire discussion suffers.

The First Amendment

It is also important for all participants in any online community to understand that the First Amendment of the Constitution (Freedom of Speech) protects against *government* censorship. This is often misunderstood within the context of online venues. I have created a number of online discussion groups, and every now and then a CyberBozo arrives and insults other members of the group. When taken aside for a private review of the community's standards, he or she will often launch into a passionate, yet ill-conceived monologue about their *right* under the First Amendment, to say whatever they wish.

If that's your perception, let me break it to you gently: It ain't necessarily so.

If you want to stand on a street corner and shout your innermost thoughts to the world or espouse the gospel according to you, the Government is prohibited under the First Amendment from silencing you. Let me repeat that in order to pay homage to the god of redundancy: *Government* is prohibited under the First Amendment from silencing you.

To test this theory—though it's not nice to challenge Mr. Modem— try shouting your personal philosophy, reciting poetry, or yodeling your favorite Slim Whitman love song in the lobby of a privately owned building and you will likely be escorted to the exit. Quickly. For even more Constitutional high jinks, try writing an article and demanding that the *New York Times* publish it. Call me a cynic, but chances are it's not going to happen.

It is every private (non-government) online venue's right and responsibility to delete any message or revoke the access of any member failing to comply with its operating rules. It is not a birthright to belong to or to participate in such communities.

Membership in online communities often requires registration, and in order to register, you must agree to abide by a few basic rules that explain what is and what is not appropriate and acceptable. These few basic rules form the basis of any online community's standard. If you don't agree with the standards applicable to all members of the community, don't become a member. It is truly as simple as that. Fortunately, the rules are generally based on common sense and generally accepted courtesy tenets. They are extremely easy to embrace by most individuals.

Many public venues such as newsgroups often indulge an *anything goes* philosophy when it comes to interactive, online communication. While this inexplicably appeals to many individuals, unfortunately it also brings out the worst in some people. This phenomenon may be referred to as the Jerry Springer Syndrome. Those who disagree with this characterization are welcome to smack each other around, exchange four-letter epithets, and pause occasionally for a commercial message.

If you visit Internet newsgroups, keep your eyes peeled for the aggressive communicators. Once you understand the difference between aggressive and assertive communication styles, you'll be able to spot an aggressive communicator in a heartbeat. When you observe one—and it won't take long—sit back and enjoy the show. It won't be long before some unenlightened individual responds to the provocateur and they'll be off and running.

Self-Awareness

If you're planning to participate in online discussion groups, you need to be aware of your own feelings, your own emotions, and how those feelings and emotions are expressed online. Make sure passion is not confused with anger, or hostility, or that it attempts to masquerade itself as *caustic wit*. There needn't be any victims of verbiage, online or offline.

Incorporating some of these communication concepts and techniques can be challenging, but they are tried and true, and work beautifully. Once the differences between "I" statements and "you" statements, and assertive and aggressive communication styles are understood, a new and exciting world of improved communications will emerge.

And that, beloved readers, is the primary objective of online communications.

Mr. Modem's Rules for Writing on the Internet

Since first venturing onto the Internet in the Year of our Modem 1988, I have participated in thousands of online discussion groups, written or received more than a million e-mail messages, and generally squandered the best years of my life. Regrets? I've had a few, but then again, too few to mention….No, wait. That's Frank Sinatra, not Mr. Modem. As a result of more than a decade of daily online interaction, in-depth personal research, extensive reader feedback from my newspaper columns, and occasional late-night, nacho-induced hallucinations, I present to you the following keys to successful online communication, "Mr. Modem's Rules for Writing on the Internet."

1. Quote back. If you are replying to an e-mail or message you receive, your e-mail program will automatically incorporate the *parent* message within your Reply window. Don't delete it; though editing it is appropriate. As you exchange an increasing volume of e-mail, it is often helpful to be able to read what transpired previously in order to frame a response within the

proper context. Your response should appear *above* any quoted material so the recipient of your response does not have to wade through one or more previous messages in the conversation (called a *thread*) in order to view your reply.

2. Obtain Permission. If you receive an e-mail and want to forward it to other individuals, request the author's permission to do so. Many times e-mail and messages posted within a particular discussion group are intended for a specific audience or to be read within a specific context. "Do unto others…" translates very well into the Internet environment.

3. DON'T SHOUT! When you use all capital letters, it is the online equivalent of shouting. Sometimes you may wish to RAISE YOUR VOICE and that's fine…in small doses.

4. No sale! Don't try to sell something in a chat room. Chat rooms are intended to be conversational areas, not flea markets—or flee markets as is the case when sales people appear. There are many venues available on the Internet where you can sell goods and services. Public chat rooms, unless so designated, are not an appropriate venue.

5. Use asterisks for emphasis if you *really* want to emphasize a word or phrase.

6. Don't overuse punctuation!!!!!!!!!!!!!

7. Don't use profanity in public venues. Remember that the Internet is a global platform and people of diverse cultures may read your words. What may be perfectly acceptable within one society may be patently offensive to someone in another culture. Children have access to the Internet, as well, so let's try and set a good example. Appealing to the lowest common denominator is all too common today. When you communicate online, you should

strive to communicate in an intelligent manner. Let's try to raise the standard of communication and celebrate our language.

8. Know and use acronyms, IYKWIM (see Appendix B, "FUIA: Frequently Used Internet Acronyms").

9. Don't be kute! Cutesy phonetic spellings get old in a big hurry, so don't overuse them. Examples: *kewl*, *windoze*, enuf already! Same with intercapitalizations. Reading text in this fOrMaT is aNnoYiNg. When communicating online, just relax and be yourself.

10. Use emoticons. Inflection does not translate well into text, so in the online world we have ways to work around that. To indicate jokes, sarcasm, or other such feelings, you can use sideways faces made with ASCII characters. These range from smile :) to frown :(and beyond (see Appendix C, "An Extravaganza of Emoticons").

11. Make the subject line of your e-mail and posted messages meaningful to others. Rather than using "Need help!" use "Help with WordPerfect" so people with knowledge about your specific area of inquiry can immediately respond.

12. Keep your signature line short. Most popular e-mail programs permit you to automatically append one or more signature lines or messages to all or selected e-mail and newsgroup postings. Limit your signature to four or five lines of text. Many times people attach quasi-amusing sayings or what are referred to as *tag lines*—not unlike the little one- or two-line messages received in fortune cookies (see Appendix D, "Mr. Modem's All Time Favorite Signature Tag Lines").

13. Watch for the red flags. Some people who inhabit public chat rooms attempt to be provocative just because they can be. Don't

fall for the bait. If you encounter a CyberJerk, just ignore the person, or use the Ignore button. Provocateurs get no enjoyment out of being ignored.

14. Apply the 12-hour rule. For better or worse, the Internet provides a means of firing off an e-mail or other message in the heat of the moment. If you're angry or upset about something, compose your message or e-mail, vent your spleen, articulate your thoughts, and let the words fly—*but don't send it!* Wait 12 hours. Sleep on it. After 12 hours, read what you wrote. If you're still comfortable with the tone and tenor of the message, go ahead and send it. Chances are you'll be relieved that you didn't. You cannot unring the bell when it comes to e-mail, so think before you act.

15. Be a class act. Nobody is grading or correcting messages for grammar and punctuation, but try to spell correctly. If you participate in many general public chat rooms or newsgroups, you will probably be appalled at the level of grammar and spelling. We need not pander to the lowest common denominator when communicating online. If you have an above average vocabulary and good command of the English language, use it! Be proud of it. Other participants may learn a thing or two just by observing your postings.

16. Be nice! The relative anonymity of the Internet brings out the worst in some people. If you encounter an angry or nasty person online, you are under no obligation to respond. Be polite, be courteous, and never let somebody else's e-mail or message dictate the tone of your message. You control your own words. Respect for others is never out of style.

Try a Little Kindness: The Benefits of Global Warming

Recently, I started to calculate the number of times that I've sent an e-mail to a Web site's Webmaster, a customer service representative, a technical support person, or used a Comments button to simply say "Thank you." The total number of occurrences from 1988, when I first embraced the online lifestyle, to the present, ranges between zero and never. Yet the Internet is the greatest informational resource that's come along since Uncle Rudy won a set of encyclopedias at the Grange raffle back in '56. So why shouldn't I say "thanks" periodically? And don't just sit there looking at me, what about you?

A simple "thank you" can go a long way toward brightening some-body else's day, and it takes what, maybe a minute to write and send an e-mail? So why don't we do it more frequently?

Just imagine if even one person every day sent you an e-mail, wrote you a note or left a voicemail containing an appreciative word. You would probably be smiling from dawn 'til dusk. And you would likely continue the pattern by offering a kind word or appreciative comment to others. That's how it spreads, like a kinder, gentler virus.

Think about the trickle-down effect. How would this type of positive reinforcement affect your business, your friends, your family, your dis-position? You won't know if you don't try, so why not take a chance? You have nothing to lose other than the risk of brightening somebody else's day.

The Internet is our community. It belongs to you, it belongs to me, and it belongs to every other user. All it takes is a kind word along the way and, as invaluable as the Internet is today, the best is surely yet to come.

Courtesy as a Technical Issue

When we're on eternal hold or clawing our way through layers of voice-mail menus on our never-ending journey to tech support nirvana, it's easy to become irritated and annoyed. Particularly when the ingratiating voicemail recording assures us that our call is very important—but evidently not important enough to warrant a live body answering the phone. We've all heard it:

Press 1 to be thanked again.

Press 2 for a heartfelt message of appreciation for your business.

Press 3 to provide payment information before we place you on hold for 37 minutes and then disconnect you. Have a nice day.

Yes, that whole voice-menu routine is irritating. But let's face it, we computer users aren't more fun than a barrel of modems to technical support personnel. I've had the dubious pleasure of providing technical support in the past. It's no walk in the park. In support of the technical folks at the other end of the phone, it takes a tremendous amount of self-restraint to keep from lobbing a few verbal barbs in the direction of callers, as well.

In fact, when it comes to stressful jobs, being on the receiving end of a technical support line is right up there with air traffic controllers, neurosurgeons and authors of Internet books who are forced to sit at home, day after day, wearing big, fuzzy slippers and sipping hot cocoa. It's grueling…grueling I tell you!

In a survey released by Concord Communications, Inc., (`http://www.concord.com`) tech support and help-desk managers were asked about the most difficult aspect of their job. A staggering 84 percent said dealing with computer users—that's you and me—who engage in abusive and even violent behavior. Yes, some of us have even resorted to smashing monitors, shattering keyboards or trying to score a field goal with our mini-towers.

Why is that? It's not that we're bad people, is it? Of course not. Our irritability and anger is borne of frustration. Frustration because many of us simply lack basic, fundamental knowledge about our own computers. That's nothing to be ashamed of, but we do need to understand why we feel as we do. Further, we need to be sure we're not projecting our feelings onto others and expressing our frustrations by speaking angrily or discourteously. See how nicely this all fits together?

Of course, trying to communicate with a technical support person who may be struggling with the English language doesn't help the situation. But that's precisely when we need tolerance. We need to understand that the average tech support person is doing the best he or she can, and whatever we can do to help the situation is what we need to do. Becoming frustrated, angry or irritable is too easy. Remaining calm, speaking slowly and providing as much detailed information as requested is the challenge.

I've discovered one truism regarding technical support. If you're experiencing a hardware problem, the tech support person will blame your software; if you're experiencing a software problem, the tech support person will blame your hardware. When you encounter this diagnosis, as you inevitably will, just view it as a rite of passage on your way to technical support nirvana.

Having been beaten into mental submission by years of computer-induced frustration, I now begrudgingly accept the fact that most of that frustration is a result of not knowing how to do something or not entering the right commands or following the correct protocol. Two loathsome words capture the essence of this phenomenon perfectly: *User error*.

In short, the overwhelming majority of the time, my frustration is a result of my own inability to accomplish a particular computer-based task. Sure, better instructions or a more intuitive software interface would help, but the bottom line is that it's up to me to figure something out, and when I can't, that's when I depend on tech support.

For a glimpse into what the good folks of tech support endure from us, please visit `http://www.mrmodem.net`.

Your Global Community Awaits

As we have seen, the keys to effective online communication include tolerance and understanding, as well as respect and kindness extended to others. As computer users, we need to be patient with ourselves and understand that some measure of frustration simply goes with the territory.

If you feel yourself becoming frustrated or antsy with something you're trying to accomplish with your computer, or if a Web site isn't downloading quickly enough, or if you lose your connection in the middle of a file download, try not to become angry or frustrated. Instead, just stop, walk away for a while and return to it at a later time when you're in a better place emotionally.

As members of the global Internet community, we need to be tolerant of others and respect each other's cultures. The Internet is a virtual melting pot, full of challenges, but equally full of rewards for those who take the time and invest the energy to be a responsible member of this worldwide neighborhood.

Lastly, be nice and have tolerance for the technical support person, friend, neighbor, and of course, Mr. Modem. We're simply trying to help you. For some it's a job; for others it's a lifestyle.

What's Next?

Are you ready for a sneak peek into the future? Now that I've hosed off the crystal ball, in the next chapter we'll put it to good use as we take a look at what the Internet has in store for us. One thing is for certain, as you'll see in the next chapter, "The Best Is Yet to Come!"

The Best Is Yet to Come:

A Fast-Forward Look into the Future of the Internet

The Internet will become increasingly important and meaningful to all of us in the future. In this chapter, we'll take a look at the profound impact this remarkable technology will have upon all of us. Indeed, the best is yet to come.

It's not always easy being a visionary when it comes to computer technology as evidenced by the following notable quotables:

> "I think there is a world market for maybe five computers."
> —Thomas Watson, Chairman of IBM, 1943

> "640K ought to be enough memory for anybody."
> —Bill Gates, 1981

> "I have traveled the length and breadth of this country, talked with the best people, and I can assure you that data processing is a fad that won't last out the year."
> —The editor in charge of business publications for Prentice Hall, 1957

It is thus with some historical precedence and in the presence of some very prominent individuals that I offer my quasi-visionary musings in this *The World According to Mr. Modem* chapter.

The future for online seniors has never been brighter. If you are not yet online you haven't missed the boat, but now is the time to make it happen. And the Internet *is* happening. Whether your gateway is America Online, CompuServe, Prodigy, the Microsoft Network, or your local Internet service provider, all roads are converging on the Internet. The Internet will become increasingly important and meaningful to you in the future, and time will reveal the profound impact it can have on you, your family, your friends, and your colleagues. It is unavoidable and it is here to stay.

Historically, seniors often become isolated for a variety of reasons. That's not good, nor is it healthy. But today's technology and our growing online community has empowered us all to put an end to isolation. As our children and extended families embrace online communications, our sense of community continues to expand, to become more global. Lines of communication that may have ceased to exist years ago within families and between friends residing in distant communities are being reestablished every day through the miracle of online communication.

Most new residential construction today includes wiring for Internet connectivity. Using this virtual backyard fence, neighbors are beginning to know their neighbors again, as a sense of the physical community that has eroded over time is once again on the upswing.

A new phenomenon known as the *Generation Lap* is also in full swing, courtesy of the Internet. Grandparents are establishing an electronic connection with grandchildren. E-mail is as common in grade schools today as slide rules and manual typewriters were for our generation. And many seniors are the recipients of *hand-me-up* computers, which become available when children upgrade or replace computers with newer, faster, shinier models. What to do with the old computer has never been an easier decision. "Give it to Mom and Dad," is rapidly becoming today's technological mantra.

There is much for us—members of the 50 + generation—to learn. But have no fear, Mr. Modem is here to help you sort through the glut of information. After reading this book; (your only required homework from Mr. Modem) if you have questions about the Internet or online communications, you are welcome to e-mail me at MrModem@home.com. But by the time you have a few hours of firsthand experience online, you probably won't even need Mr. Modem anymore. Sniffle, sniffle.

In addition, you will have unlimited access to countless other individuals within newsgroups, other discussion areas and millions of Internet-based informational resources. It all exists today, and as exciting as that is, the *really* exciting news is that the best is yet to come!

Among Internet Users Over 50...

- 90 percent go online for news
- 86 percent are under the age of 64
- 83 percent go online daily
- 83 percent go online for product information
- 76 percent go online for travel information
- 74 percent go online for medical information
- 69 percent are male (versus 58 percent for all users)
- 68 percent are employed
- 50 percent completed college
- 25 percent are retired

Source: Excite and Third Age, `http://www.excite`; `http://www.thirdage.com`.

The explosive growth of the Internet will continue for years, fueled by the arrival of novice computer users, more families, more children and more seniors. This phenomenon translates to an even greater emphasis on high-speed connectivity, more affordable pricing structures, more technical support, easier navigation, and more creative *daily life* applications.

Social changes will abound, as well. The texture of our online society will be influenced as much by politics and parenting as by technological developments. Many organizations and task forces exist to help parents and children steer clear of the darker side of the Internet, while at the same time struggling to tread the very fine line that exists between censorship and freedom of expression.

The Internet and its attendant digital revolution will bring about societal changes as profound as the creation of movable type, the industrial revolution and space exploration.

A Look to the Past for a Glimpse of the Future

In order to look to the future, it is sometimes helpful to look to the past. And when it comes to the Internet, we need only take a quick glimpse at the history of radio and the telephone in order to observe some striking similarities.

When first conceived, both were feared and viewed with suspicion. Both radio and television were perceived to be within the province of the techies with shades of the military thrown in for good measure. As we learned in Chapter 2, "A Musical History of the Internet," at least in the early years, the Internet wasn't envisioned as an entertainment medium at all. Neither was radio.

Critics of radio published dire predictions, such as the following, more than 75 years ago: "This new technology could bring about the downfall of democracy. The free-for-all of unedited information requires serious regulation. It might replace real sex with artificial interaction." These predictions could be applied to the Internet and be just as current, just as relevant, and just as inaccurate today.

The commercialization of the Internet is a controversial topic today. As annoying on-screen banner ads become either a force to reckon with or a helpful shopping assistant for consumers, depending upon one's perspective, history tells us this is not unique to the Internet. In a 1924 speech, then–Secretary of Commerce Herbert Hoover said,

> *I believe that the quickest way to kill broadcasting would be to use it for direct advertising. The reader of the newspaper has an option whether he will read an ad or not, but if a speech by the president is to be used as the meat in a sandwich of two patent medicine advertisements, there will be no radio left.*

Tell it like it is, Brother Herbert! With total disregard to his opinion, radio blossomed, as did radio advertising.

In the early days of the telephone, critics warned that female operators would lure husbands and businessmen away from their wives and families. And, of course, the movies—well, they were proclaimed "dangerous dens of darkness" where youngsters would be tempted into all kinds of unacceptable behavior. These critics should have spent some time with me in high school. Movie theaters or drive-ins, it didn't matter. I was always the one who ended up watching the movie.

For as many people who extol the virtues of technological advancements, there will always be the gloom-and-doomers. But technology will prevail. And the Internet is leading the charge.

Internet 2

As powerful and as vast as the Internet is today, there is actually a new Internet heading in our direction. You probably haven't heard much about Internet 2 or the *Next Generation* Internet, but this term refers to massive university and government driven efforts to upgrade the current Internet. What we know as today's Internet is a *best-effort* information delivery system that slices and dices information into tiny data packets, slaps a destination address on each packet, and blasts them into cyberspace. The data packets travel independently via any of a number of routes and then reassemble at their final destination. Today, the transmission of these packets of data is frequently slowed to a crawl due to traffic jams caused by the staggering number of Internet users—or the number of staggering Internet users, as the case may be. This is a problem that didn't exist five years ago.

Internet 2 to the rescue! Representatives from more than 100 universities met in Chicago recently to master plan a faster, more advanced method of data transmission and communication. By the summer of 1998, some of the first high-speed connections made their debut at the University of Minnesota. Initially, these faster links—or *flinks*, if you say it in shorthand—will form a high-speed communications network connecting universities and government labs nationwide. After the college crowd and the men and women in uniform have their fun with it, access will become available to the private and commercial sectors, as is Internet 1, today's Internet.

Planners estimate it will take three to five years for the paint to dry on Internet 2, but the results will benefit all of us. Researchers estimate connections to the Internet will be 1,000 times faster than are available today. Of course, talk's cheap and who's going to remember these claims three to five years from now? In addition, Internet 2 technology will be able to distinguish between different types of load (traffic) demands, supplying the necessary power and bandwidth to accommodate them. Without question, the best is yet to come.

Utilizing Internet 2 technology and other high-speed access via fiber optic cable and satellite, we will be able to tap into huge virtual libraries, classrooms, doctors' offices, and the fun-loving folks at the Motor Vehicles Department. Capabilities will include smooth, real-time video conferencing with digital sound. Video conferencing via the Internet will be an everyday occurrence. Digital television is also on the way, and by 2006, consumers will have to replace or convert their existing analog TV sets to receive movie-quality television. Since digital TVs can operate as computers, Microsoft, Compaq, RCA, Sony, Phillips, and other technology giants are forming new alliances to take advantage of this golden opportunity to merge digital TV with computers and the Internet. The initial result: WebTV (see Chapter 8, "WebTV").

The Internet will continue to converge mass media and personal interactivity. Our challenge, as a society, is to learn how to work within this new global framework. During the next decade the Internet will become as normal a part of our everyday lives as the telephone and television are today.

A Hint of Things to Come

Today, my new toy—excuse me, my wristwatch—is a wearable computer (available from www.beepwear.com). Throughout the day, news headlines, sports scores, and weather reports are received, stored in the watch's memory, and displayed as scrolling text across its face. It is also a pager. Anybody wishing to page me can either dial a toll-free number and leave a message with a living, breathing operator or visit www.beepwear.com, enter my number, and type in a message on a Web page. A quick click of the Send Message button and within seconds my watch will beep, darn near sending me into cardiac arrest. But by the time I regain consciousness, the message will be displayed on my watch.

No matter where I travel, the watch adjusts to the correct time zone. In some mysterious way, the watch knows where I am at all times. Wonderful technology for paroled fugitives, if you ask me.

The ability for Internet Access Devices (IAD) to know where you are at all times will become more commonplace in the future. Fugitives notwithstanding, this really is a good thing for the rest of us, as well. What will evolve are highly customized informational *feeds* accessible to all who use the Internet. These geographically based Internet channels will be automatically recognized by your Internet access device. You won't have to do a thing.

When connecting to the Internet, your point of access will be instantly identified and information related to your location will be immediately available. For example, if I'm in Paris attending the annual Croissant Festival, information about local bistros, brasseries, and other things I know nothing about and cannot pronounce will be available to me. A much more probable futuristic scenario will find me schlepping through a supermarket, my Internet Access Device interacting with the store's Web-based inventory database, showcasing sale items, and announcing special pricing. So sophisticated and powerful will these devices become that programming a device in advance to include other stores in your area will permit you to comparison shop and obtain prices for similar items at other locations.

Physically traveling to a store to shop will be a choice, not a necessity. In the future, instead of firing up the old Buick and heading to the mall, your Internet Access Device, with 24-hour Internet connectivity, will transport you to a clothing store, for example. There you will be able to view clothes modeled by virtual models, your measurements taken— "Watch that inseam, Buster!"—your order processed, and the garment delivered within 24 hours.

Speaking of the old Buick, for digital movers and cyber shakers on the go, the Mercedes E420 Web Car is equipped to provide driver and passengers full access to the World Wide Web. And you thought cell phones were a distraction to drivers? Think again, Wolfgang! Interactive maps, roadside assistance, emergency services, restaurant reservations, and directions, as well as available parking spaces will all be accessible from your vehicle. Where this technological revolution will stop is anybody's guess. It seems like only yesterday I was in my car, singing my little heart out to the concert-hall quality sounds of *Abba's Greatest Hits* via the miracle of 8-track technology. Come to think of it, it *was* only yesterday. Though only available for demonstration purposes at this point, Mercedes says commercial applications of Web Car technology are only five years away.

We'll also see a trend away from hard-wired connectivity. Today, most Internet users connect via telephone line. Wireless data transmission will enable us to send and receive e-mail anywhere, at any time— the benefit of true global connectivity. Forget about Rolex watches and Louis Vuitton luggage; *the* status symbol for all conspicuous consumption enthusiasts will be full-time, high-speed, wireless access to the Internet. It gives me goose bumps just thinking about it.

Social *classes* of Internet users will emerge based on access speed. Pricing structures will emerge providing the online equivalent of first-class and coach-class service—and you just wouldn't want to be caught surfing coach.

Oh, the shame of it all!

Percentage of retail stock trades now taking place on the Internet: 25.

Source: *Wall Street Journal*, Jan. 1999, http://www.wsj.com

For those of you who fear that all this connectivity may result in your inability to ever escape and get away from it all, I will now share with you a tip—dare I say a covenant, so powerful, so life-altering, so frightening in its power, and that up until now has been a closely guarded secret, never before revealed to the public. Mr. Modem's key to mankind's eternal dominance over technology is this: the *off* switch. Use it! Just remember that no matter how high-tech the device, it will always have an *off* switch. Just because you have the technology doesn't mean you have to use it 24 hours a day, anymore than the fact that you have a car means you have to be driving day and night. The Internet and its related technologies are simply tools to be utilized at your discretion. Embracing technology does not mean giving up control over your life.

Changes in Technology

As traditional libraries continue to evolve into digital libraries, you will no longer have to travel to a library to obtain information. Simply connect from your home computer and access whatever information you need. This means there is theoretically no limit to the number of people who can 'borrow' the same book once the book exists in electronic format. Better still, no penalties for overdue books!

Hard drives will go the way of wax cylinders, wire recorders, and 8-track tapes. Stored data and information will reside in your personal cyberspace *vault*—an unlimited storage area on the Internet that will permit access to your information at any time, from any location, using any device that affords access to the Internet.

High-speed, full-time connections will be the norm in the future. Remember the early days of television when there wasn't 24-hour programming and black-and-white picture quality wasn't very good? If you think of the development of the Internet in terms of that early era of television, that's where we are today.

Today, we think in terms of information being located on a floppy disk, on our hard drive, or on the Internet. In the years ahead, we won't be concerned about the location of any particular piece of information. All we'll need to know is how to obtain the information we seek, and that will be easily accomplished through the use of intelligent search wizards. These programs will understand conversational search requests. Through the use of voice recognition technology, the question, "What's the weather like in Djibouti?" will result in an instant weather report and real-time video of current weather conditions, pollen count, local holidays, events, and the number of people in line at the Djibouti McDonald's.

The telephone will communicate wirelessly with your desktop Internet Access Device and continually synchronize itself so files and data are always current. Update your telephone directory on your cell phone and your desktop computer's directory will be simultaneously updated, as well.

Viewing a news story or other information and issuing the voice command, "Save that," will preserve the information for super-fast access in the future. No file names will be required. Everything will be keyword searchable by voice command.

More affordable devices will permit widespread Internet access. And as you use your $250 Internet Access Device —formerly known as a computer—to visit an informational resource—formerly known as a Web site—any software or programming needed to interact with the site will be instantly downloaded. The process of downloading, installing, and virus-checking will be invisible to you, as you forage for information.

Your IAD will also learn from you—learn what kinds of things you do online, what types of information you seek, how many times you log on to your refrigerator to check for snack availability. By monitoring, analyzing, and developing its own profile of your preferences, it will become more intuitive. The more you use it, the more responsive it will be to your likes, dislikes, and personal peccadilloes. Of course, some day your Internet Access Device might wind up testifying against you in a court of law, so be careful.

Use of the words *computer*, *Internet*, and *the Web* will vanish from our vocabularies. Just as we don't say, "I'm going to drive to the mall in the car," neither will we say, "I'm going to get a traffic report on the Internet." It will be presumed that the Internet is the informational resource to which everybody turns to obtain information.

ApplianceNet

In the months and years ahead we will see a convergence of cellular phones with Personal Data Assistants (PDAs), combining the ability to store thousands of phone numbers and personal calendar entries with the ability to retrieve e-mail. Every e-mail sent or received will be retained, your personal calendar will stretch to infinity, and a single contact manager will last a lifetime. Better still, the system will be so simple that it will be mastered in five or ten minutes. The accompanying manual will, of course, be incomprehensible. The more things change, the more they stay the same. It's enough to make your head hurt!

Today we speak in terms of computer networks exchanging data and information. In the years ahead we will see the emergence of appliance networks, as well. Who says your refrigerator isn't talking to your microwave late at night?

Some day, when you purchase a new refrigerator, television, VCR, or dishwasher and plug it into a power outlet, it will automatically connect, and via satellite, log into its own network. Then, as technological improvements and upgrades become available, programming will be automatically installed into the appliance.

Sure, the Internet is cool, but think how much cooler it will be in the future when your refrigerator is online! Yes, some day in the not too distant future, microprocessors in refrigerators will monitor when food supplies are low, when the milk is about to turn sour, or when UFTs (Unidentified Fuzzy Things) are growing in last summer's onion dip.

And if you're like Mr. Modem and enjoy a therapeutic dish of Pralines & Prozac ice cream before bed, you'll be able to put your Internet Access Device to its highest and best use ever by actually logging in and connecting to your freezer. Once connected, you'll be able to adjust a temperature setting specifically for your freezer's ICCA (Ice Cream Containment Area). As a result of this Internet-based control, the temperature will elevate slightly at a predetermined hour every day to ensure softer, scoopier ice cream. (Finally, a lip-smackin' technology Mr. Modem can use!)

In the future, microchips embedded in your home's walls will monitor and adjust room temperatures 24 hours a day and be an ever vigilant smoke detector and burglar alarm.

Microprocessor chips embedded in streets and highways will monitor traffic and road conditions. A quick visit to a Department of Transportation or Highway Department Web site will reveal traffic and road conditions around the corner or around the world.

While some of these developments are years off, others are being utilized today. In Japan, for instance, more than 800,000 Coca-Cola machines have microchips in them, creating what we might call ColaNet. Maybe not. The microchips track sales and inventories and provide instant data for Coke's marketing and merchandising departments.

In Sweden, a manufacturer of hotel uniforms sews a radio-broadcast microprocessor into every uniform. The chip records the name of the person to whom the uniform has been assigned, the hotel location, the frequency with which the uniform is washed, and how long it has been worn between washings. Holy soup stain! The cost is just 80 cents per chip.

Are these truly technological advances or merely glimpses of a frightening era of Big Brotherism that lie ahead? Probably a little bit of both. Let me state for the record that I, Mr. Modem, being of sound mind—well, so much for credibility—am unalterably opposed to any kind of intrusive application of the Internet or its related technologies. Now, if you wouldn't mind, please raise this book to eye level and squeeze the cover once so I can get a good look at you. Thank you.

Everyday Life

Voter registration and even casting your vote via the Internet will be the norm. Corporate America has already embraced the power of the Internet and shareholder voting is now a daily occurrence on the Internet thanks to www.proxyvote.com.

The ability to pay your taxes, renew your car's registration, renew your driver's license, send flowers, check on a doctor's prescription, obtain traffic and weather reports, and shop for groceries are an online reality today.

And speaking of voting—they don't call me the Prince of Segues for nothing—we will also see political candidates attempt to reach us directly through e-mail, chat, virtual "Town Halls," and other interactive media. The problem for candidates will be the loss of the all-precious wiggle room. Real-time transcripts of speeches will be searchable and contrasted with previous statements that may or may not prove consistent. Okay, who am I kidding? Of course they will reveal conflicting statements. The big difference is that voters will know about these inconsistencies and will be able to use the Internet to perform their own analyses, as well as review political commentary of all the top political reporters.

Virtual reality will provide graphical depictions of the result of voting for a particular highway-building bond issue, for example. Drawing upon a database of demographic information, you'll be able to enjoy a virtual view of traffic gridlock if a particular highway isn't constructed or a surface street widened.

Professional services such as medical consultations and conferences with attorneys and accountants will gain a foothold on the Internet. A hospital room camera connected to the Internet will permit friends and family members to visit with loved ones. Births, weddings, and funerals will also find a home on the Web, permitting others to participate in events and ceremonies from great distances, at no expense.

As traffic continues to clog streets and air travel becomes increasingly inconvenient and costly for the business traveler, the Internet will become more popular as a virtual conference room. Groups of individuals will be able to meet more conveniently and more cost-effectively. An English-speaking person in New York will be able to converse with a German-speaking person in Dusseldorf, with Internet-based software providing the real-time translation between the parties.

Though making its debut in the corporate world, this technology will quickly be embraced by smaller businesses, associations, organizations, and ultimately small private groups. Clubs, families, and virtual pen pals will routinely meet face-to-face and monitor-to-monitor.

Many companies have invested millions of dollars developing a Web presence. The verdict isn't in yet if they're making any money from that investment. That remains to be seen. Some will and some won't. However, the need to generate profits will result in a trend for Web site content providers to charge a fraction of a cent for viewing specific content.

The two-way communication aspect of maintaining an Internet presence will keep companies involved and tightly integrated with the Internet. The ability to obtain immediate feedback from users of products will shape future product development as well as advertising campaigns.

Banner advertising, pop-up ads, and a host of other intrusive devices will appear to wring every advertising dollar possible out of the Internet. The backlash to this continued commercialization of the Web will be the emergence of increasingly sophisticated *ad-blocking* filters—software programs which will permit users to eliminate or significantly reduce the number of advertisements seen. For a sneak peek at some of the products blazing a trail in this area, visit AtGuard (`http://www.atguard.com`), InterMute (`http://www.intermute.com`), and Web Washer (`http://www.siemens.de/servers/wwash/wwash_us.htm`).

Television will continue to be a popular source for news and entertainment, but the decline of newspapers will continue. Newspapers are costly and environmentally irresponsible—though nothing beats a Sunday morning with the newspaper, a hot cup of coffee, and a 32 ounce glass of Tang. It's not quite the same to sit down in front of the computer and read an online newspaper. However, most media companies have already staked their respective claims on the Internet, and we'll continue to see a convergence of print and electronic news.

Web page construction and site hosting will become easier. The result will be huge numbers of individuals becoming Web publishers, even if they don't have anything of value to say. Some will actually have the nerve to write Internet books. Go figure.

The Internet in Education

For a glimpse into what the Internet has in store for us, we need only to look to colleges as a model for how our communities and society will be affected.

Colleges with populations mirroring those of cities and towns are more efficient and the communication is more intimate among students and administrators by virtue of the Internet. Today most college students receive an e-mail address as part of their registration process. More than half of all the schools in the United States have Internet access, and within five years that number will rise to 100 percent.

Over the past two years, long distance learning has become an invaluable teaching tool in universities throughout the world. College recruiters are now marketing to older individuals such as working professionals who have experienced the adverse impact of corporate reengineering and downsizing. Educational institutions realize that students no longer finish their education at age 22. Universities understand that the job market will continue to change and people will have an ongoing need and desire to be reeducated.

Recognizing the need to develop Internet-based courses for older students, Arizona State University, for example, developed a Long Distance Learning program in 1996. These online courses make higher education available to those who wish to learn from home or whose career demands prevent them from attending scheduled campus classes. To observe distance learning in action, visit Arizona State University Online at `http://www.asuonline.asu.edu`.

According to the Student Monitor Computer & Internet Study, of the approximately 5.3 million full-time students in four-year colleges in the U.S., 90 percent use the Internet, and half are on the Web daily or more frequently.

Preschoolers, on the other hand, receive their first exposure to the Internet in day care centers or while sitting on a parent's lap. Grade schools and secondary schools, already connected to the Internet, have students e-mailing homework assignments. Snow days may be a thing of the past as students connect with teachers and classmates on the Internet during inclement weather. (I never said all this technology was a good thing!) Parents receive permission slips and notices of PTA meetings via e-mail, and report cards are also e-mailed or available on the Web. A child's entire educational history will reside in one password-protected location—a Web page created when the child starts kindergarten. Every memo, every grade, every evaluation will be in that record. And that can extend through college, post-graduate education and into the work place, as well. Creepy, isn't it?

Legal and Moral Issues

Concerns over copyright infringement and pornography issues will escalate, without resolution. Copyright issues will be particularly contentious regarding the recording and movie industry. The ability to distribute bootlegged copies of music and movies via the Internet will continue to be a major problem. Radio play lists will be meaningless as increasing numbers of individuals tune into Internet-based radio stations that aren't stations at all but are instead music distributors. A user will be able to select their preferred music and artists and create a playing sequence. Through *streaming* video technology, full-length motion pictures will be accessible at any time via the Internet, causing a major shake-up in the video rental industry.

State and national legislative bodies continually debate legislation in an attempt to resolve copyright infringement, online gambling, pornography, and other issues, but meaningful enforcement will be all but impossible.

Top Ten Predictions

I was recently invited to participate in an Internet think tank sponsored by a consortium of Internet service providers. (They must have been desperate for participants.) Our mission was to formulate our top ten predictions for the future of the Internet. The experience provided an intensive, intellectually stimulating, sometimes heated discussion and an occasional slap fight. This went on for the better part of a day. One concept was immediately agreed upon by every participant: When it comes to the Internet and online communication, the best is yet to come.

1. A Web shakeout, as tens of thousands of sites shut down. Among the first to disappear will be *vanity* sites and stand-alone home pages that offer little in the way of interactivity or updated content. Cyber ghost towns will appear in the form of hundreds of thousands of abandoned Web sites, originally constructed for free or as part of an Internet service provider's package. As the Web becomes an everyday appliance with as much sizzle as a toaster oven, hobbyist Web sites and sites devoted to digital photos of Uncle Ralphie's surgical incisions will be adrift and unattended in cyberspace.

2. Over the next two years we'll begin to see a meeting of the minds between attorneys and clients, physicians and patients, associations and members, and other provider-client relationships. Business, professional, service, and support communities will increasingly understand and embrace the value of online communication, e-mail, and interactive discussion group platforms.

   Example: A live Internet connection in the surgical suite or physician's office provides access to unlimited current clinical information and interaction with experts worldwide—all at the fingertips of the local physician. Will HMOs cover this type of global consultation capability? Probably not—unless one uses an approved Internet access provider.

3. Information is available online at any time, whenever it's needed. However, interpretation of that information will remain within the province of human beings. Artificial intelligence will make advances but will support, not replace, the human decision-making process.

4. Internet-based educational programs will continue to develop and become a cornerstone of the educational process at all levels, from kindergarten through postgraduate education.

5. Private, online *gated* (secured) communities will proliferate to meet the needs of groups of individuals sharing a minimum of one common attribute or interest (seniors, for instance). Member citizens will enjoy private discussion areas, as well as discounts from merchants and vendors with a particular interest in the group. Discussion within these online communities will be translated, in real time, into Spanish, French, and other languages.

6. There will be a convergence of the personal digital assistant, pager, and cellular phone into one unit capable of Internet-based voice, video, paging, and faxing. This new personal digital assistant will provide wireless access to the Internet from anywhere in the world.

7. Immediate access to information will be the norm. This phenomenon will be triggered by an integration of notification services through e-mail, pagers, and fax. Personal notification services will provide immediate delivery of customized news, legislative updates, appointment reminders, as well as requested product and service information, all without charge to recipients.

8. With the distribution of Internet telephone-related technology, individuals will soon be able to send voice messages via the Internet and return calls for a fraction of the cost of standard telephone communications. While the cost of an average telephone call is 22 to 24 cents, the cost of an average Web interaction is only three or four cents.

9. The term *Internet user* will become an irrelevant, meaningless description. Rapid changes in technology and its integration into everyday life will mean that the Internet is simply "the way we do things." Functions will blend together as users

access a variety of Internet-enabled appliances, from the television and telephone to the wristwatch and computer.

10. The most difficult components of electronic commerce, the three A's—authentication, authorization, and assurance—will be resolved in short order. Security on the Internet will quickly become as tight as security for telephones. The Internet will always confront the same types of insecurity issues as cordless phones, though, and the same problems of fraud and misrepresentation that are common with telephone communication will continue on the Internet.

Conclusion

In this chapter, we have explored the future of the Internet and how some of the coming changes will affect our global society. For all the exciting changes, improvements, and enhancements on the horizon, there are some things that will never disappear. Community and regional shopping malls will continue to flourish despite online shopping becoming a multi-billion-dollar industry. The popularity of e-mail will not unravel the telephone system, and fax machines will continue to be used by millions of people every day.

The Internet is not a substitute for interpersonal relationships, nor is it an excuse not to venture outside to meet your neighbors or pick up the phone to call someone you're thinking about. For all the convenience and cost-effectiveness of e-mail, there is still nothing quite like hearing the sound of a loved one's voice.

The Internet is not going to change who we are or the way we think; instead, the Internet is going to make it infinitely more convenient for people with common interests to find each other or for individuals to locate information about any topic at any time.

Sadly, the Internet is also providing an opportunity for those who take advantage of others in order to make a fast buck. It wasn't long after the birth of the World Wide Web that the first "How to Make Money on the Internet" e-mails began arriving. History is only repeating itself, of course. Rumor has it that within weeks of the Wright Brothers' first flight, some knicker-clad scammer was out Kitty-Hawking discounted airline tickets. The one thing we know as an absolute certainty about the future of the Internet is that the proliferation of Internet-based scams and get-rich-quick schemes will continue.

As interactive seniors, we must protect ourselves. And that can only happen if we accept the challenge of this technological era and educate ourselves. We must recognize the online flims from the flams, and that requires knowledge. Of course, good, old-fashioned common sense is never out of style. You have acquired a lifetime of experience, education, and common sense. Bring these unique skills with you when you go online and your Internet experience will be safe, happy, and very rewarding.

I began this chapter with some notable quotables that missed the mark. Fortunately, that wasn't always the case as we can see from the following remarkably insightful observation:

> The stage is being set for a communications revolution. Audio, video, facsimile and mainframe computers will provide newspapers, mail services, banking and shopping facilities, data from libraries and other storage centers, school curricula, and other forms of information too numerous to specify. In short, every home and office will contain a communications center of such breadth and flexibility as to influence every aspect of private and community life. Spreading quietly into every corner of the United States, slowly and unevenly and yet with its own air of inevitability, comes this new communications technology.

—*The Nation*, May 18, 1970, six months after the birth of the Internet.

Indeed, the best is yet to come.

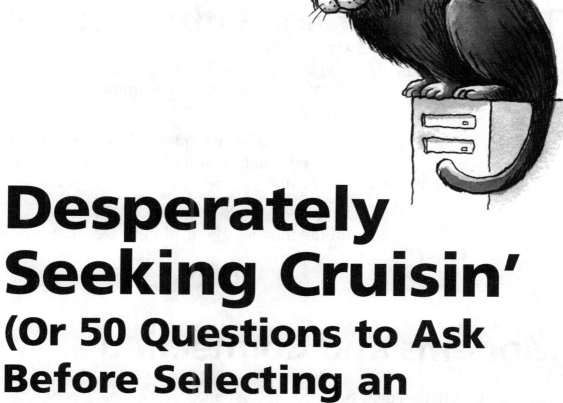

Desperately Seeking Cruisin'
(Or 50 Questions to Ask Before Selecting an Internet Service Provider)

S electing an Internet service provider can be intimidating or downright scary for those new to the Internet community. Mr. Modem believes you should ask lots of questions so your decision will be an informed one. What follows are 50 suggested questions to ask a prospective ISP before establishing your account.

The Internet and Other Services

1. What Internet services do you provide? (Should include at a minimum: e-mail, World Wide Web, newsgroups.)

2. Is there a limit on the size of e-mail messages that can be sent or received? (This is important if you plan to send or receive e-mail attachments or files.)

3. Is there a limit on the number of e-mail messages that can be transmitted each month?

Modems and Connecting

4. What modem types (protocols) and modem speed connections do you support? (Hint: Be sure the V.90 protocol is supported.)

5. Is high-speed (above 56Kbps) access available? (Examples: ISDN, DSL, Cable, Fractional T1.)

6. If high-speed access is available, what are its associated costs?

7. Do you provide toll-free number dial-in capability?

8. Is there a surcharge for connecting via your toll-free number?

9. How many local calling areas (telephone numbers) do you have throughout the country (or internationally)? (This is important if you travel or plan to connect to the Internet from different locations.)

10. Is there an additional fee for connecting to the Internet using any of your local calling areas other than the one I sign up with?

11. If so, what is that fee?

12. What is your user-to-modem ratio? (Hint: Ideally, it should be 12:1 or lower. Higher ratios—15:1 or 20:1—may result in a busy signal when attempting to establish your connection by dialing in.)

Automatic Disconnections

13. Do you have an automatic cut-off or disconnect feature? (Some ISPs will automatically drop your connection after a certain number of minutes with no keyboard or mouse input.)

14. If connections are terminated automatically, after how many minutes of inactivity?

15. Is there an option (fee or free?) to disable the automatic disconnect or extend the length of time permitted before the automatic disconnect is invoked?

Home Pages and Data Storage

16. Do you provide a home page with each account?

17. If I have a home page, can I edit or modify it at any time?

18. What, if any, fees are charged for maintaining or editing a home page?

19. How much space (in megabytes) do you provide for each home page?

20. If additional space is required, what is the cost?

21. What are your minimum, maximum or monthly flat fee data storage rates, if any?

Technical Support

22. Do you offer technical support?

23. Are there any fees associated with your technical support services?

24. What are the hours for your technical support or help desk?

25. Is there a toll-free number for technical support?

26. What is your average response time for technical support?

27. If I establish an account, will you send me an installation disk or CD-ROM containing the configured software I'll need?

28. What type of documentation or instruction manual will I receive with my account?

Account Cancellation and E-Mail Forwarding

29. How would I cancel my account?

30. Do you provide e-mail forwarding if I cancel my account?

31. Is there a fee associated with e-mail forwarding?

32. How long will you continue to forward my e-mail to a new e-mail address if I terminate my account?

33. Do you offer an e-mail forwarding service for a second or additional e-mail addresses?

34. If you do offer e-mail forwarding service for additional e-mail addresses, is there a fee?

Financial Matters

35. What types of accounts do you offer? (Examples: business, personal, family, multi-user.)

36. What are your rates for each type of account offered?

37. What is your installation or account setup fee, if any?

38. Are any fees waived or can I receive a reduced rate if I am switching from another ISP?

39. What is your monthly fee for Internet access?

40. Is it for unlimited connect time?

41. If you do not provide unlimited connect time, how many hours of connect time are included each month?

42. What is the cost per minute or cost per hour for connect time above the number of hours included with my account?

43. Do you send a monthly invoice or is your monthly charge automatically billed to my credit card?

44. Is there a free trial period?

45. If there is a free trial period, how long is it?

46. If I pay for a year in advance, can I pay for 11 months and receive the 12th month free?

47. If I refer a friend, will I receive a free month of service or other incentive?

48. How much does an additional e-mail address cost?

49. What browser is included: Netscape or Internet Explorer? What version?

50. Do you provide a method for keeping customers current with new versions of your software or updates?

FUIA: Frequently Used Internet Acronyms

Working in concert with emoticons (See Appendix C, "An Extravaganza of Emoticons"), are acronyms and abbreviations frequently used on message boards, in newsgroups and in chat rooms as a form of shorthand. Here is a collection of some of the most popular acronyms that have made their way into the Internet culture over the past few years.

Acronym	What It Means
AAMOF	As A Matter Of Fact
ADN	Any Day Now
AFAIK	As Far As I Know
AFK	Away From Keyboard
AOLer	America Online member
AWHK/AWSK	Ask, Wait; He'll Know or Ask, Wait; She'll Know
BAC	By Any Chance
BBL	Be Back Later
BBS	Bulletin Board System
BBFN	Bye Bye For Now
BCNU	Be Seeing You
BD	Big Deal
BFD	Big Freaking (or something else) Deal
B4N	Bye For Now
BFN	Bye For Now
BOBW	Best Of Both Worlds
BRB	Be Right Back
BTA	But Then Again
BTW	By The Way
BWG	Big Wide Grin
BYKT	But You Knew That
CMIIW	Correct Me If I'm Wrong
CU	See You

Acronym	What It Means
CUL	See You Later
CUL8TR	See You Later
CYA	See Ya
CYA	Cover Your ASCII
CYL	See You Later
DIIK	Damned If I Know
DILLIGAFF	Do I Look Like I Give A Flying Flip?
DL	Download
DOM	Dirty Old Man
DQOTD	Dumb Question Of The Day
DTP	Desktop Publishing
DTRT	Do The Right Thing
DYSWIM	Do You See What I Mean?
EMFBI	Excuse Me For Butting In
EOD	End Of Discussion
EOF	End Of File
EOL	End Of Lecture
EOT	End Of Thread
FAQ	Frequently Asked Question
FB	Furrows Brow
F2F	Face To Face
FDROTFL	Falling Down, Rolling On The Floor Laughing
FISH	First In, Still Here

Acronym	What It Means
FITB	Fill In The Blank
FOAD	Fall Over And Die
FOAF	Friend Of A Friend
FOTCL	Falling Off The Chair Laughing
FTL	Faster Than Light
FUBAR	F***** Up Beyond All Recognition (or "Repair")
FUBB	F***** Up Beyond Belief
FWIW	For What It's Worth
FYEO	For Your Eyes Only
FYI	For Your Information
GAFIA	Get Away From It All
GAL	Get A Life
GD&R	Grinning, Ducking and Running
GIGO	Garbage In, Garbage Out
GIWIST	Gee, I Wish I'd Said That
GOK	God Only Knows
GMTA	Great Minds Think Alike
GR8	Great
HHTYAY	Happy Holidays To You And Yours
HTH	Hope This Helps
IAC	In Any Case
IAE	In Any Event
IANAL	I Am Not A Lawyer

Acronym	What It Means
IC	I See
ICOCBW	I Could, Of Course, Be Wrong
ICTUBTIHTKU	I Could Tell You, But Then I'd Have To Kill You
IDKIDC	I Don't Know, I Don't Care
IDTT	I'll Drink To That
IKWUM	I Know What You Mean
IMCO	In My Considered Opinion
IME	In My Experience
IMHO	In My Humble Opinion
IMNSHO	In My Not So Humble Opinion
IMO	In My Opinion
IMWTK	Inquiring Minds Want To Know
INPO	In No Particular Order
IOW	In Other Words
IRL	In Real Life
ITSFWI	If The Shoe Fits, Wear It
IYKWIM	If You Know What I Mean
JIC	Just In Case
JTTOITSWPA	Just Threw This One In To See Who's Paying Attention
KISS	Keep It Simple, Stupid
L8R	Later
LA	Laughing Aloud
LLAP	Live Long And Prosper

Acronym	What It Means
LOL	Laughing Out Loud
LTMSH	Laughing 'Til My Sides Hurt
LTNS	Long Time No See
LTNT	Long Time No Type
MOFM	Male Or Female
MOTOS	Members Of The Opposite Sex
MOTSS	Members Of The Same Sex
MOTAS	Members Of The Appropriate Sex
NBALS	Not By A Long Shot
NRN	No Response Necessary or No Reply Necessary
NTYMI	Now That You Mention It
NW	No Way
OAS	On Another Subject
OIC	Oh, I See
OMG	Oh My Gosh!
OTF	On The Floor
OTOH	On The Other Hand
PBT	Pay Back Time
PITA	Pain In The Ass
PMBI	Pardon My Butting In
PMFBI	Pardon Me For Butting In
PMJI	Pardon My Jumping In
POODL	Passed Out On The Desk Laughing
POV	Point Of View

Acronym	What It Means
PTB	Powers That Be
PTMM	Please Tell Me More
ROFL	Rolling On The Floor Laughing
ROTB	Right On The Brink
ROTM	Right On The Money
RSN	Real Soon Now
RTFM	Read The Fabulous Manual (could be something other than *fabulous*)
SFLA	Stupid Four Letter Acronym
SIG	Special Interest Group
SITD	Still In The Dark
SNAFU	Situation Normal, All F***** Up
SO	Significant Other
SOB	(You're on your own with this one)
SOL	Sooner Or Later
SOP	Standard Operating Procedure
SOW	Speaking Of Which
SWAG	Scientific Wild Assed Guess
SYSOP	SYStem OPerator
SYT	Sweet Young Thing
10Q	Thank You
TAFN	That's All For Now
TANJ	There Ain't No Justice
TANSTAAFL	There Ain't No Such Thing As A Free Lunch

Acronym	What It Means
TDM	Too Damn Many
TGIF	Thank God It's Friday
TIA	Thanks In Advance
TIC	Tongue In Cheek
TINALO	This Is Not A Legal Opinion
TINAR	This Is Not A Recommendation
TJATAW	Truth Justice and the American Way
TLA	Three Letter Acronym
TOBAL	There Oughta Be A Law
TOBG	This Oughta Be Good
TPTB	The Powers That Be
TTBOMK	To The Best Of My Knowledge
TTFN	Ta-Ta For Now
TTKSF	Trying To Keep A Straight Face
TTMS	Talk To Me Soon
TTYL	Talk To You Later
TTYS	Talk To You Soon
TYVM	Thank You Very Much
WFM	Works For Me
WTGP	Want To Go Private? (Used in chat rooms)
WYGIWYPF	What You Get Is What You Pay For
WYSIWYG	What You See Is What You Get (pronounced Wizzy-Wig)

Acronym	What It Means
YAP	Yet Another Ploy
YAR	Yet Another Rumor
YASQ	Yet Another Stupid Question
YGLT	You're Gonna Love This
YIU	Yes, I Understand
YL	Young Lady
YM	Young Man
YMBK	You Must Be Kidding
YMMV	Your Mileage May Vary

An Extravaganza of Emoticons

In the world of e-mail and electronic messages, which are delivered without the benefit of body language, facial expression or vocal inflection, it's easy for any reader to misinterpret or question the spirit in which a message was written.

Emoticons (also called *smileys*) are a way to help readers understand what the writer had in mind when composing a message. Emoticons are simply variations of the ever-present, always annoying happy face. You create emoticons with keyboard characters, and you read them by tilting your head toward your left shoulder and looking at the characters sideways. In the wild and wacky world of online communication, a colon and a closing parenthesis spring to life as a sideways happy face. :) See? Suddenly the sun is shining, birds are singing, and the Internet is a warmer and fuzzier place. Well, that's the theory, anyway.

I would like to share with you a collection of smileys and emoticons that have been in my family for years and handed down from generation to generation. I've arranged the following emoticon extravaganza in alphabetical order for ease of reference, proving once and for all that I have no life and really need to get out more often.

Remember, tilt your head toward your left shoulder and look at each one sideways. Let the aerobics begin!

Emoticon	What It Means
:-(*)	About to be sick
':-)	Accidentally shaved one eyebrow
O:-)	Angel
(:-&	Angry
#-)	Another all-night party
=):0:=	Abe Lincoln
:-*	Ate a sour pickle
#:-)	Bad hair day
(:-)	Bald
d:-)	Baseball fan

Emoticon	What It Means
(:-)	Bicycle rider, wearing helmet
:>)	Big nose
:-D	Big smile
?-(	Black eye
:-)8	Bow tie
*:o)	Bozo
:-{#}	Braces
%-(	Broken eyeglasses
(:^(	Broken nose
}:-(	Bullheaded
----<;))><>	Caught fish
:-#	Censored
'@;;;;;;;;..	Centipede
C=:-)	Chef
:-8(	Condescending stare
%-}	Crossing eyes
:,-(	Crying
{O-)	Cyclops
*-(	Cyclops poked in the eye
:-e	Disappointed
===:-D	Don King
:-]	Dopey grin
:-)'	Drooling
<:-)	Dunce

Emoticon	What It Means
@;^[)	Elvis
X=	Fingers crossed
<:00><	Fish
:-!	Foot in mouth
}:>	Furrowed brow
[8-]	Frankenstein
*<(:')	Frosty the Snowman
:->	Goofy happy face
8:-)	Glasses on forehead
$-)	Greedy
<g>	Grin
/:-)	Gumby
\o/	Hallelujah
:-{	Handlebar moustache
:)	Happy face
:-)	Happy face with nasal option
<<<<(:-)	Hats for sale!
(:...	Heartbreaking
(:-[	Hulk Hogan
%-\	Hung over
[]	Hug
	Invisible man
X-)	I see nothing
:-X	I'll say nothing

Emoticon	What It Means
:-~)	I've got a cold
:-x	Kiss
:-?	Licking lips
@@@@@@@:)	Marge Simpson
:~)	Needs a nose job
:^-(	Nose is out of joint
(:-$	Not feeling well
:/)	Not particularly amusing
(:-<	Not a happy camper
:-X	Not saying a word
:-o	"Oh, nooooo!" (As in Mr. Bill)
.-)	One-eyed smiley
:-*	Oops! (Covering mouth with hand)
[name]	Personal hug
:-?	Pipe smoker
P-)	Pirate
+:-)	Priest
=:-)	Punk rocker
8-<:)>	Propeller head
@]'-,--	Rose
:-(	Sadness
:-@	Screaming
:-o	Shouting
:-O	Shouting loudly

Emoticon	What It Means
:-1	Smirk
:-Q	Smoker
:-'	Spitting
:-"	Spitting tobacco
:-b	Sticking tongue out
:-8	Talking out both sides of your mouth
2B|^2B	"To be or not to be"
:-J	Tongue-in-cheek
{(:-)	Toupee
}(:-)	Toupee in the wind
:-q	Trying to touch tongue to nose
<:>=	Turkey
(:|-K-<	Tuxedo
:-C	Unbelievable!
:-(	Unhappy
:-c	Very unhappy
\V/	Vulcan salute
{{name}}	Warm embrace
q:-)	Wearing hat backwards
8-)	Wearing eyeglasses
g-)	Wearing pince-nez glasses
(:)-)	Wearing scuba mask
@:-)	Wearing turban
;-)	Wink

Mr. Modem's All-Time Favorite Signature Tag Lines

Tag lines are one- or two-line philosophical statements—sometimes amusing, sometimes not—that people attach to e-mail they send. Some e-mail programs permit you to attach signature tag lines to every outgoing e-mail, which is a particularly nice touch if you're an outgoing person. (In the interests of time and to avoid disturbing other readers, kindly save your groans until the conclusion of the book. Thank you.)

Since 1988 (when I first ventured onto the Internet), I have collected some of the more interesting tag lines encountered and herewith present my all-time favorites:

A closed mouth gathers no foot.

All I ask is to prove that money cannot make me happy.

Anyone who makes an absolute statement is a fool.

Blessed are the censors for they shall inhibit the earth.

Can you think of another word for "synonym?"

Cole's Law: Thinly sliced cabbage.

Does the name "Pavlov" ring a bell?

Health is merely the slowest possible rate at which one can die.

HELP! MY TYPEWRITER IS BROKEN!—E.E. CUMMINGS

Honk if you love peace and quiet.

The precise duration of a minute depends which side of the bathroom door you are on.

I went to the 'Net and all I got was this stupid tag line.

Why is it that plumbers never bite their nails?

If it wasn't for muscle spasms, I wouldn't get any exercise at all.

If there is no God, who pops up the next Kleenex?

If your parents didn't have any children, neither will you.

If laws were outlawed, only outlaws would be lawyers.

Tired of being illiterate? Write for free information.

In English, any word can be verbed.

It's bad luck to be superstitious.

Know what I hate most? Rhetorical questions.

Many are cold, but few are frozen.

Multitasking allows you to screw up several things at once.

My Go , this keyboar oesn't have any 's.

Never, never, never moon a werewolf.

Quidquid latine dictum sit altum viditur. ("Anything in Latin sounds profound.")

The cynic says, "The pessimist is a realist who isn't afraid to admit it."

This is the sort of English up with which I will not put.

This sentence no verb.

Time flies like the wind, but fruit flies like bananas.

Toe: A part of the foot used to find furniture in the dark.

Vote anarchist.

When marriage is outlawed, only outlaws will have inlaws.

Why is "abbreviated" such a long word?

An idle mind is the Devil's Nintendo.

The Best of "Ask Mr. Modem!"

Every week I receive hundreds of e-mails from readers of my newspaper column "Ask Mr. Modem!™". The purpose of the column is to provide geekspeak-free answers to questions about the Internet, e-mail, computers, online communications, and other related topics of general interest. Here are some of the most frequently asked questions. As an added bonus, I'll even include some answers. (I can hear you now, "What a guy!")

E-Mail

Q. How do you change your e-mail address? My husband picked ours, but it's so ridiculous, whenever somebody asks me for it, I tell them I can't remember it. Help!

A. I notice you didn't include your e-mail address with your question submitted by fax, so now I'm really curious! It's actually just your username that you would like to change. Your username appears to the left of the @ sign in your e-mail addresses. You can do one of several things. First, contact your Internet service provider (ISP) or the organization that's providing the username you would like to replace. Tell them why you want to replace it. Depending on the provider, they may accommodate your request at no additional charge. Others may charge a fee to cancel your current e-mail account and provide you with a new one, so be sure to discuss this option with your husband, particularly if he's become attached to the address. The easiest solution is to let your husband keep the username he selected, but establish another e-mail account for yourself. Many households are now two-e-mail address households for precisely this reason.

Q. When I reply to an e-mail, should my reply appear before or after the quoted text of the e-mail I'm responding to?

A. For context purposes, most e-mail software programs automatically include the e-mail to which you are replying. This is called a *quote back*. Your response should appear before the quote back, not after. Responding before the quoted material is an online courtesy (called Netiquette) and will prevent the recipient of your response from having to wade through his or her own e-mail to get to your response.

Q. I received an e-mail from someone who seemed to know me, but the person didn't sign his name. How can I find out who the person is?

A. Here are two suggestions, the first is the easiest and most likely to result in a speedy response. If you believe the e-mail was sent by a friend or an acquaintance who simply forgot to sign it, try replying with a polite, "Thanks for your e-mail, but I don't recognize your e-mail address. At your convenience, please identify yourself." Most folks will quickly reply with an "Oops, sorry about that!" and provide a recognizable name.

If you would prefer a less personal approach, try one of the directory services located on the Web such as Yahoo!'s People Search at `http://people.yahoo.com`. Under E-mail Search, click on the Advanced link. In the Old E-mail Address field, type in the e-mail address you have. If it's in Yahoo!'s database, the person's name behind the e-mail address will be displayed.

Q. I know that you can send files as attachments to e-mail, but what does the recipient have to do to view an attachment?

A. The most important thing is to be sure the recipient has the same program that created the attachment. For example, if you send a WordPerfect document as an attachment, you need to be sure the recipient has WordPerfect. This holds true for spreadsheet files or any other program. The easiest way to be certain is to send an e-mail to the intended recipient first and inquire. Newer versions of a program provide the ability to save a file as an older version or even in the format of another program. Using Microsoft Word 97, for example, you can save a document in WordPerfect format. Most programs are *backward compatible*, which means that newer versions will read files from older versions, but not vice versa.

Q. When I send e-mail to several people, how can I prevent everybody who receives my e-mail from seeing everybody else on my mailing list?

A. There is a very easy way to avoid displaying your e-mail distribution list to every recipient on that list. Simply address the e-mail to yourself, and then include everybody that you're mailing to as a BCC (Blind *Carbon* or *Courtesy* or *Cyber* copy). In this way, recipients will see your name in the To and From fields and will not have access to the other recipients' e-mail addresses.

Browsers

Q. I use Netscape. If I delete the History file, is that going to cause any problems?

A. Not for me. Okay, okay, Mr. Modem is just yanking your cable. The history file is a text file that records the addresses of all Web sites previously visited. You determine how long you want Netscape to retain a log of your cyber travels by clicking on Edit ➤ Preferences ➤ Navigator. You will see a field where you can enter the number of days to retain that history, along with a Clear History button. Clearing your history in this manner is harmless and much easier than entering a witness relocation program as Mr. Modem (formerly known as *Big Tony, The Disconnector*) did many years ago. Come to think of it, I probably shouldn't have mentioned that.

Q. What's the difference between the Refresh and Reload buttons on my Web browser?

A. The Refresh button displays a copy of a Web page stored in your browser's cache or memory. The Reload button causes your browser to visit a Web site and retrieve or download a new copy of a specific page.

Q. Whenever I go onto the Web, the first page I see is the home page of my ISP. Is there some way I can change that to bring up something more interesting? It feels like a commercial every time I go online.

A. There sure is! You can change the default start page very easily and set it to any page your little modem desires. The process varies slightly depending if you're using Netscape Navigator or Internet Explorer as your Web browser.

If you're using Netscape, go to Edit ➤ Preferences. Then click on Navigator in the left directory tree. In the Location field to the right, under Home Page, type in the URL or Web address (`http://www...`, etc.) for the page you would like as your start page. Alternatively, you can navigate to the actual Web page first, then click on the Use Current Page button.

If you're using Internet Explorer 4, go to View ➤ Internet Options. Under the General tab, enter the address for the page you would like to be your start page. Alternatively, you can navigate to the actual Web page, then click on the Use Current Page button.

For Internet Explorer 5, navigate to Tools ➤ Internet Options. Under the General tab, enter the address for the page you would like to use as your start page. Alternatively, you can first go to the actual Web page, then click the Use Current button. You can also elect to Use Default (which is the Microsoft Network home page, `http://www.msn.com`) or Use Blank, if you prefer to start with a blank screen.

Life Online

Q. I've heard that whenever I visit a Web site, my address is recorded somewhere on the site. How much can somebody learn about me from this information?

A. When you visit any Web site, you are leaving a trail of cyber bread-crumbs behind you in the form of your IP (Internet Protocol) address, which is actually a string of numbers separated by periods, i.e. 298.35.26.14. How much information is obtainable depends where you get your IP address. Never get your IP address from a man selling them from the back of a '68 Chevy along with Elvis paintings on black velvet and unidentified seafood. However, if you dial into an ISP (Internet service provider) for access to the Internet, you are probably assigned a dynamic IP address that will only reveal the identity of your ISP. Permanent IP addresses are assigned by large companies to employees with full-time connections. These IP addresses can be used to identify both the company and the individual user, but not what you had for breakfast or the number of dust bunnies running around under your bed.

Q. When people talk about clicking on a link, what exactly is a link?

A. A hypertext link is actually a shortcut to another Web page. Links typically appear as blue, underlined text. When you encounter a link anywhere on the Web, your cursor will change from a pointer to a little hand with an extended finger, er—index finger, as it passes over the link. If you use your mouse to click on the link, you will be presented with another Web page containing related information.

Q. I hear the word *streaming* used in conjunction with files on the Internet, like a streaming audio or video file. What is streaming?

A. A *streaming* file is one that can start performing some action on your computer before it has finished downloading or transferring to your computer. In the days before streaming, you would have to wait until a large audio or video file completely downloaded before you could use it. Depending upon the size of the file and the speed of your connection to the Internet, that could take minutes or even hours. Streaming files are compressed files. Compressed files are smaller in size than uncompressed files and therefore download faster. The audio and video are sent as a continuous *stream* of individual sounds, pictures or animations and begin playing as soon as the downloading process begins, rather than after the downloading process concludes.

Q. Are there any programs that keep a record or log of what my children are doing on the Internet? I know programs exist to block their access to some adult-oriented sites, but I'd like to see for myself what they're looking at online.

A. A number of concerned parents have asked about this. A program called Win What Where for Families will keep an eye on your kids' computer usage by providing as many as 20 types of reports, including daily or weekly Internet use. The family version of this program costs $29 and is available from Win What Where Corp. (http://www.winwhatwhere.com).

Q. I keep getting stuck on Web pages that use frames. How can I get out of one of these sites? When I try to leave, the old frame continues to appear and the next site I visit appears inside the previous site's frame.

A. *Help! I'm framed, and I can't get out!* is rapidly becoming the mantra of Web surfers everywhere. It can be frustrating to get framed on the Web, but there is a way out. All you have to do is right-click within the frame or on a link and select Open in New Window. Voila! The old frame will disappear and you'll be face-to-face with a full-screen window once again.

Q. Sometimes when I visit a Web site, instead of seeing letters or characters, all I see are little squares. What's that all about?

A. I hate it when that happens! This phenomenon, known as *squarus characterus annoyinum* is due to the fact that your computer displays text using what's called the roman alphabet, and sometimes it roams off course. Badda-bing, badda-boom! But seriously, folks, the roman alphabet doesn't have the ability to display the text of other languages, such as Japanese, Chinese and other languages that use characters (rather than letters) to form words. So when you see the little squares, you're visiting a Web page displaying non-English text.

Q. If I want to print a Web page and I press the Print Scrn key on my keyboard, nothing happens. Why the (expletive deleted) won't it print?

A. Probably your attitude. Have you hugged your computer today? Go ahead, give it a little hug. Now, assuming a life-altering attitude adjustment has occurred, the reason Print Scrn or PrtSc won't work is because Print Scrn just copies the image to your Windows 95 or 98 clipboard. You would then have to jump-start your word processor, Paint or similar program and import the clipboard image, then print. However, there is a quickie way to print a screen that's active—meaning where your cursor is happily pulsating: Hold down the ALT key while pressing the Print Scrn button, and the window or frame where the cursor is positioned will print faster than you can say, "Holy (expletive deleted), the printer is jammed again!"

Computers

Q. When I start up my computer, I hear the 3.5-inch floppy drive making noises like it's trying to read a disk, but there's no disk there. Any idea what the problem is?

A. Fear not! What you are hearing is your computer going through what is known as POST or Power On Self Test. Don't you just LTA (Love These Acronyms)? The test is perfectly normal and is designed to check, among other things, your computer's memory, establish contact with your hard drive, your floppy drive and report any start-up problems to you.

Q. I'm using Windows 98, and my Desktop icons are scattered all over the place. Is there a way to automatically arrange the icons so it always looks organized?

A. Mr. Modem believes a tidy Desktop is a happy Desktop, so just place your cursor in any blank area of the Desktop and right-click. Place your cursor on Arrange Icons and a submenu will appear which will permit you to arrange your icons by Type, Size, Date, or Auto Arrange. Click on Auto Arrange and your icons will snap to a default grid configuration. To toggle Auto Arrange off, just repeat the above steps and click on Auto Arrange again to remove the check mark that appears to its left. This will work for Windows 95, also.

Q. The squeal of my modem is driving me crazy. Is there a way to silence the modem? I'm using Windows 95.

A. There sure is! Go to Start ➤ Settings ➤ Control Panel ➤ Modems ➤ Properties. Adjust the speaker volume control slider (also known as the little slidey thing) to the desired volume or lack thereof.

Q. The person helping me set up my computer kept referring to something that sounded like EX-ee—as in *EX-ee file*. I felt foolish asking because it sounded like something I should know. Can you explain what it is in terms that somebody like me can understand?

A. The EX-ee file you reference is actually spelled `.exe`, which is short for *executable*. An `.exe` file is a self-launching file that automatically runs—meaning that it does something—when you click on it. For example, `solitaire.exe` is the filename of the solitaire program that is included with every Windows program. Click on it and you can spend hours frittering away your precious time— which of course is the objective of all computing.

Q. I attended one of your seminars and noticed when you were at any location that required you to click OK before continuing, that your cursor was automatically positioned over the OK. In other words, you didn't have to move your cursor to that location. How did you do that?

A. Very observant! For years, I found moving my mouse cursor to be exhausting, so in an effort to prevent CMFS (Chronic Mouse Fatigue Syndrome), I purchased Microsoft's Intellimouse, available at finer mice supply houses everywhere. One of its most endearing qualities is its ability to *jump* to any selection box automatically. A related Mr. Modem tip: As an alternative to clicking the OK button, try pressing your Enter key instead. It won't matter where your cursor is located and the result is the same.

Q. I had been using Microsoft's Anti-Virus program, and it didn't detect any virus. Then you recommended McAfee, and it found *traces* of a virus, but no active ones. So I switched to McAfee figuring you knew what you were talking about, but now it detects nothing. So what gives, Mr. Modem?

A. Clearly, the first mistake you made was assuming that Mr. Modem knew what he was talking about. All kidding aside, my recommendation is to just use one virus-checking program. McAfee is excellent, as is MS Anti-Virus. What probably happened is that one virus-checking program detected the other one. In order for a virus-checking program to work, it has to have the virus patterns in its memory to match them and report them to you. If your virus-checking program doesn't know what it's looking for, it can't very well locate a virus. Sometimes when these virus patterns remain in memory or are left in a file, they can be detected by another program, but this does not indicate a virus infection.

One word of caution about virus-checking programs: They can only check for viruses they are programmed to check for so be sure to get the updates periodically for the virus-checking program you choose, and follow the vendor's instructions and recommendations.

Q. When I send a fax using a software program, is it necessary that the person I'm sending the fax to also have a fax modem or can she receive it through a standard fax machine? Also, when you send a fax to a location that has its machine or modem turned off, will it be received when it's turned back on?

A. You can use fax software to send something to a computer with a fax modem or to a regular fax machine. However, if you're sending to a computer, it has to be turned on, connected to a phone line, and properly loaded with fax software of its own. If the computer or fax machine at the other end is turned off, the transmission will fail. But don't take it personally. It can happen to the best of us.

For more fun-filled, informative Mr. Modem questions and answers, visit `http://www.mrmodem.net`!

Glossary:
Mr. Modem's Internet
Terms of Endearment

As you immerse yourself in the Internet culture, you will encounter certain cryptic terms often referred to as *geekspeak*. The following glossary is not intended to be all encompassing, but rather an attempt to present some of the terminology you are most likely to encounter along the Information Super—well, you know.

A

account   Access to the Internet through an Internet service provider. Uses a designated username and password for each individual subscriber.

active window   The window you are currently using; the window that contains your cursor.

ActiveX   A Microsoft application that allows a program to run within a Web page.

address book   A feature of e-mail programs that catalogs and retains e-mail addresses.

ADSL (Asynchronous Digital Subscriber Line)   A high-speed connection to the Internet using copper wire connections. Speeds range from 6Mbps downloading (from the Internet to your computer) to 640Kbps uploading (from your computer to the Internet).

alias   An abbreviation or shortened form of an e-mail address. Sometimes called a nickname, a user can enter an alias into an e-mail's address field instead of remembering an entire e-mail address. For example, MrM might be an alias for MrModem@home.com.

Alt key   Alt stands for *alternate*. This key is used in conjunction with other keys to perform certain functions. Within instructions or keystroke sequences, Alt + F means to press the Alt and the F keys simultaneously.

anonymous FTP   Accessing an FTP (File Transfer Protocol) site without the necessity of entering a username. Enter **anonymous** as the username and your e-mail address as your password.

Any key   A cyberspace version of an urban legend: The novice computer user who observes the instruction on screen to "Press any key," and cannot locate the *Any* key. Bulletin to all readers: There is no Any key; the instruction simply means to press any key on your keyboard. However, if you insist there is an Any key and this is simply a vast computer conspiracy, may I suggest you also consider obtaining the Sky Hook module to enhance your Internet experience.

AOL   America Online.

applet   A small application or software program that can be embedded in a Web page. Applets make Web pages more enjoyable or useful by providing animation, calculations and generally permitting interaction between you and a Web page.

application   A high-tech sounding term that means *program*. Apparently too many people became comfortable referring to software programs, so it must have been time to change the terminology. If you see *application*, think *program*. Technically, an application is a collection of commands and protocols that permits or commands a computer to perform certain tasks or functions. But who cares about technical definitions? Surely, not Mr. Modem.

Apply button   If you click this button when changing computer settings, your changes will be saved and implemented. You may have to restart (reboot) your computer for the changes to take effect and will be notified on-screen if this additional step is required.

article   A message posted to a newsgroup.

ASCII   Rhymes with *PASS-key* and should never be pronounced *ASK-2*. If you do pronounce it ASK-2 and we ever meet, let's pretend we don't know each other. ASCII stands for American Standard Code for Information Interchange. ASCII is the worldwide standard for the code numbers used by computers to represent all the upper and lower case Latin numbers, punctuation, etc. There are 128 standard ASCII codes, each of which can be represented by a seven-digit number, 0000000 through 1111111. (Insert yawn here.)

associate   No, not the newest member of a law firm, but rather it means to connect or relate files having a particular extension to a specific program. When you double-click on a file with a certain *extension*, the associated program is launched (started) and the file clicked on is opened. When you download (receive) files from the Internet and attempt to open them (after checking them for viruses, of course), the correct association of the downloaded file is necessary in order for the file to open. Associated files are often referred to as *registered* files.

attachment   A file or other document that is sent with an e-mail message. This file is said to be "attached" to the e-mail message.

B

backward compatible   Referring to a software program that will work with earlier versions of the same program. Example: Software written for Windows 98 will run under Windows 95.

bandwidth   The amount of data you can send through an Internet connection. Usually measured in bits-per-second. The greater the bandwidth of a connection, the greater your connection speed, assuming you're accessing via that connection.

baud   Often confused with how many bits-per-second a modem can transmit data. Technically, baud is the number of times per second that the carrier signal shifts value—whatever that means. For example, a 1200 bit-per-second modem actually runs at 300 baud, but it moves four bits per baud—and that ain't good. (4 × 300 = 1200 bits per second.)

BBS (Bulletin Board System)   A computer network to which members can connect via modem to read and post messages.

BCC   What was known as a Blind Carbon Copy in the era of typewriters, is also an available feature of e-mail. Other recipients of an e-mail will not see the name or names of individuals receiving BCC copies.

binary file   A non-ASCII file that contains special codes that can be destroyed or corrupted when traversing the Internet. For example, word-processing files, sound files, graphics, etc. *See also* **UUEncode**.

BIOS (Basic Input/Output System)   This is an information area inside your computer where software programs look to determine how your computer is configured so they can run properly.

bit   Short for Binary digIT, a bit is the smallest unit of data that a computer recognizes. There are eight bits in one byte and one byte equals one character, such as the letter *A* or a numeral. Bits are usually depicted with a lower case *b*: 40Mb, meaning 40 megabits.

bitmap   A graphical image composed of thousands of dots, which are saved as bitmap files. Bitmap files carry the extension .bmp. Graphical images that make noises during the evening hours are referred to as "things that go .bmp in the night."

bookmarks   A Netscape file used to store Web site addresses. Also called a Hotlist or Favorite Places list. *See* **Favorites**.

Boolean logic   Provides specific instructions to a search engine yielding more precise search results.

Boolean operators   Sometimes called Boolean expressions, these are specific terms that provide instructions to a search engine. Used with keywords they broaden or narrow a search. Major Boolean operators include **AND**, **OR**, **NOT**. Example: Searching for *tuna* **AND** *Charlie* narrows or refines a search. Searching for *tuna* **NOT** *Charlie*, broadens the search.

boot up   To start a computer. Also referred to as "power up."

'bot   A robotic program on the Internet that performs a function such as cataloging Web sites for search engines.

bounced mail   E-mail that's returned to sender. This could be due to an erroneous e-mail address, technical problems at the receiving end or an attached file that's too large for the recipient's mailbox.

bozo filter   An e-mail function that monitors e-mail received from certain less-than-welcome individuals and routes the e-mail to trash or deletes it upon receipt. *See also* **filter**.

bps   Bits per second. The quantification of speed at which data is transmitted between modems. Analogous to miles-per-hour (mph) in an automobile.

browse   To peruse information on the Internet. Often referred to as *surfing*.

browser   A software program used to view documents on the World Wide Web. The two most popular browsers are Microsoft's Internet Explorer and Netscape.

BUI (Bonus Useless Information)   A full page of English text is approximately 16,000 bits.

bus   The path or pipe through which data is transmitted between a computer's memory (RAM) and its microprocessing chip.

byte   A set of bits that represents a single character such as the letters *a* or *b*. Bytes are usually depicted with an upper case *B*: 40MB, meaning 40 megabytes. A kilobyte is one thousand bytes; a megabyte is one million bytes; a gigabyte is one billion bytes; an overbite is reason to see your orthodontist.

C

cache   Temporary storage space on a hard drive. Web browsers store copies of Web pages in cache for faster viewing on subsequent visits. Pronounced *cash*, not *ca-shay*.

cartridge   A plastic container in an ink-jet printer that holds black or colored ink.

case sensitive   Web site addresses (URLs) are case sensitive, meaning that you must pay attention to upper- and lower-case letters when entering a Web address within your browser to navigate to a particular Web page. For example, my Web site is `http://www.mrmodem.net`, which is not necessarily the same as `http://www.MrModem.net`. Accept no substitutes!

CD-ROM   Compact Disk-Read Only Memory. A multimedia device that installs software and plays music. Recordable disks are designated as CD-R disks, and rewriteable disks are CD-RW.

CGI (Common Gateway Interface)   A set of rules that describes how a Web server computer communicates with another piece of software on the same computer and how the other piece of software (the cgi program) talks to the Web server computer. Usually, a cgi program is a small program or script that takes data from a Web server and does something with it, like putting the contents of a form into an e-mail message.

channel   A Web site designed to deliver content from the Internet to your computer; an area on Internet Relay Chat (IRC) where users gather to discuss a topic of common interest. There are thousands of different channels in existence at any given time.

chat   Live, online conversation between two or more people. Typed comments appear instantly on each participant's computer screen.

click   To quickly press and release a mouse button to select something, such as a menu item.

click and drag   Besides being a great name for a law firm specializing in computer and software related matters, it also means to point to an object, press and hold down a mouse button, and move the object (said to be *clicked*) to a new location.

client   A computer that's part of a network that requests files or information from another computer called a server or host computer. Your home computer is a client in relationship to the Internet. A software program located on your computer within this context is referred to as client software.

clipboard   A temporary storage area for data that's been cut or copied before the information is pasted to a new location. Frequently used on the Internet to accurately preserve convoluted, case-sensitive Web site addresses and other information gleaned from Web pages for personal use.

Close button   An X in the upper right-hand corner of a Web page viewed within Windows. When you click the Close button, the window or Web page closes.

.com   An Internet domain extension that stands for *commercial*.

COM port   Communications port. A place typically on the back or side of a computer where you can plug in a modem or other peripheral device. Also called a serial port.

compress   The process of compacting a file to make it smaller so it will transmit faster over the Internet.

connect speed   The rate at which your modem receives data from another server's modem. When you type in a URL and press Enter, the connect speed regulates how fast the site can transmit its information back to your modem. V.34, V.42 and V.90 are terms used to describe modems capable of a particular connect speed. V.34 modems can download up to 33.6K; V.90 describes 56K-capable modems.

cookie   A very small piece of information sent by a Web server to a Web browser (software program) that the browser saves and then sends back to the server whenever the browser makes additional requests from the server. Most frequently used to customize or personalize and thus enhance a user's visit to a Web site. Note: Cookies do not read your hard drive or send your life story to the CIA.

CPU (Central Processing Unit)   Specifically, the microchip "brains" of a computer. Generically, CPU is used to refer to a computer "box" or tower case. Also refers to the intake facility for inmates at federal and state prisons. When it comes to worthless information, think "Mr. Modem."

cracker   Criminal hacker; an individual who breaks into computers. *See* **hacker**.

crash   When a computer or software program bytes the dust. Could be a temporary meltdown or the destruction of a hard drive, in which case all data will be lost. Truism: If you use a computer, at some point you will experience a crash.

cross-post   Posting the same article (message) to multiple newsgroups. Don't do it.

Ctrl key   The Control key, which is used in conjunction with other keys to perform certain functions. Within instructions or keystroke sequences, Ctrl + C means to press the Ctrl and the C keys simultaneously.

cursor   The little blinking line on your computer screen that you can move with your mouse. It indicates where information you type on your keyboard will appear on screen.

cyberspace   A term originated by author William Gibson in his 1982 novel *Neuromancer.* The word *cyberspace* is currently used to describe all the informational resources available through computer networks.

D

daemon   Originating with the Unix operating system, a program that is continually operational and awaiting input to which one or more predetermined responses will be made.

data sponge   Slang for a handheld scanner.

default   The *normal* setting; a configuration created and installed by a computer manufacturer or software publisher.

defrag   Short for defragment. The process of organizing file fragments on your hard drive to improve access speed. Windows 98 has a built-in disk defragmenter. Click Start ➢ Programs ➢ Accessories ➢ System Tools ➢ Disk Defragmenter.

Desktop   The main screen of Windows 95/98 that contains icons representing shortcuts to files located on your hard drive. When downloading files from the Internet, I recommend downloading to the Desktop.

dialog box   A window that appears presenting questions that force you to make crucial-yet-uninformed decisions at inopportune moments, thus elevating your anxiety. Dialog boxes were designed to keep us all humble in the face of technology that nobody really understands, but that is continually updated. When installing programs downloaded from the Internet, dialog boxes will frequently appear requesting additional information or personal preferences, which can usually be changed at a later time.

dial-up connection   The way most of us connect to the Internet using a modem and a telephone line. Internet service providers (ISPs) offer dial-up service. *See also* **direct connection**.

digest   A grouping of mailing list postings distributed via e-mail as a single message. Rather than subscribing to a mailing list and receiving multiple e-mail messages, some individuals prefer to subscribe to mailing list digests.

digital signature   Encrypted data attached to a message or e-mail used to identify the sender.

digitari   The digital version of *literati*. A reference to a nonspecific group of people believed to be knowledgeable or otherwise in-the-know in regard to the digital revolution at hand.

direct connection   A full-time, high-speed connection to the Internet such as that provided by cable access. Direct connections are generally more expensive than dial-up connections, but they're also a lot more fun.

DLL (Dynamic Link Library)   Usually seen as a filename extension, .dll files contain information needed by specific software programs. Unless you've got a yearning for computer problems, don't delete .dll files. You life will never be the same if you do.

domain extension   The three characters appearing to the right of the final dot in a Web address. These three characters, sometimes referred to as Moe, Larry and Curly, display the type of organization that owns a particular domain name. For example, the extension .com denotes a commercial organization, .edu, an educational institution, .org, a nonprofit organization, .gov, a branch of the government, .mil, a part of the military.

domain name   The unique name that identifies an Internet Web site. Domain names have two or more parts—the host name and name extension—separated by periods, or "dots." In the Web site address for this book, `http://www.mrmodem.net`, the domain name is *mrmodem.net*.

DNS (Domain Name Server or Domain Name System)   Computers which translate Internet Protocol (IP) addresses into user-friendly domain names for ease of reference. For example, without a domain name, instead of typing in *website.com*, we would have to type in the numerical IP address which would be something like 123.456.78.9.

DOS (Disk Operating System)   An older operating system for running software programs. I just included it in this glossary for old-time's sake. Gone, but not forgotten.

double-click   Pressing and releasing the left mouse button twice in rapid succession. Generally, you will double-click to launch or open a program by clicking on a small, graphical image or *icon*.

download   To retrieve data (files) from the Internet to your computer.

DPI   Dots per inch. A unit of measurement that represents the sharpness or clarity (resolution) of printed materials or the image on a computer monitor.

drag   Make up your own jokes if you must, but within the context of computers, it's a mouse movement that transports an object (such as a file or icon) to a new location. This is accomplished by holding down a mouse button while simultaneously moving the selected object.

driver   A small program that serves as a translator of commands or instructions between a piece of hardware (such as a printer) and the software that uses that printer. A small driver is sometimes referred to as a Minnie Driver. Sometimes not.

drop   The last step in the dragging sequence. An object is dropped when the mouse button is released.

DVD   No, not a brand of underwear, but rather Digital Versatile Disc or Digital Video Disc, depending who you talk to. Think of DVD disks as very high-capacity CD-ROMs. A CD-ROM has a capacity of approximately 650MB (megabytes or million bytes). A DVD disk has the capacity to hold 4.7GB to 17GB (gigabytes or billion bytes) of data. One DVD disk can hold nine hours of studio-quality video or 30 hours of CD-quality audio, or 47 years of scratchy, static-laden radio.

E

.edu   An Internet domain extension that stands for educational, as in educational institution.

EFF (Electronic Frontier Foundation)   A lobbying group with a focus of protecting and preserving freedom in cyberspace.

e-mail   Electronic mail; private communication between the sender and recipient. (Is this easy or what?)

e-mail address   A unique Internet address to which your e-mail is sent. Always appears in the format *username@host.domain*. Example: MrModem@home.com.

e-mail filters   Rules that you define for your e-mail program to forward, redirect or block incoming messages. Your e-mail program will "look" at a sender's e-mail address, the subject line or any other data contained in an incoming e-mail and perform a particular action.

emoticon   The use of punctuation marks and other symbols or characters to convey moods in online communication. Turn your head sideways to view. An example is a wink ;). See Appendix C, "An Extravaganza of Emoticons."

encode   To convert by any method a document or data file into a format in order to attach it to an e-mail message.

encrypt   To jumble the contents of an e-mail message or file so that it cannot be read by individuals who do not have the appropriate encryption code or key.

Ethernet   A very common method of networking computers in a local area network (LAN). Ethernet can transmit approximately 10 million bits-per-second and can be used with almost any kind of computer.

Eudora   A very popular e-mail software program.

executable file   A file that automatically runs when you click it. It usually has an .exe extension.

extension   The three digits that appear after the period or *dot* in a filename. For example, `Windows.exe` or `Readme.txt`. Extensions tell us mortals what kind of file we're looking at. Extensions also permit computers to recognize files as particular types so they can *associate*.

F

FAQ (Frequently Asked Questions)   Documents located on most Web sites that list and answer the most common questions about a particular subject relating to the site.

Favorites   An Internet Explorer file used to store Web site addresses. Also called a Hotlist or Favorite Places list. *See* **bookmarks**.

56K line   A digital phone line connection (sometimes also called a leased line), capable of carrying 56,000 bits-per-second. At this speed, it would take about three minutes to download a one-megabyte file.

file   Anything stored in electronic format on a computer. Examples: software, graphics, spreadsheets, documents.

filter   A personal mail sorter that monitors incoming e-mail and performs certain designated functions such as moving e-mail received from a particular sender into a designated e-mail box, opening it, playing a sound, or in the case of a bozo filter, routing it directly to the trash. Also used with newsgroups to avoid viewing articles posted by certain individuals.

firewall   For security purposes, a combination of hardware and software that protects computer networks against unauthorized entry by Internet users.

flame   A hostile or negative response to an e-mail message or newsgroup posting. Most flames are intended to be provocative and cause the recipient(s) to respond. Don't take the bait. The person sending such a message is referred to as a *flamer*. A series of flames and counterflames is referred to as a *flame war*.

folder   A means of organizing files. Folders are what we used to know as *directories*, but since many of us knew, understood and felt comfortable with the term *directory*, it was obviously time to change the terminology.

follow-up   A reply to a newsgroup message.

FQA   Frequently Questioned Acronyms.

free-mail   A Web-based e-mail service that allows you to send and receive e-mail from a Web page rather than an e-mail software program. Free e-mail programs typically contain one or more advertising messages that appear with each e-mail transmitted.

Freenet   Free public access to the Internet, typically sponsored by a municipality.

freeware   Free software available for downloading from the Internet. *See* **shareware**.

FTP (File Transfer Protocol)   A common method of moving files between two computers. The same as uploading and downloading. Visit `http://www.mrmodem.net` for more information about FTP.

FUQ   Frequently Unanswered Questions.

G

garbage   Computeresque characters that telephone line noise or static may cause on computer screens.

Gates, Bill   Is it possible that anybody doesn't know who Mr. Gates is? On a personal note, Mr. Gates and I enjoy a wonderfully harmonious professional relationship: He doesn't know I exist; I refer to him as Mr. Gates. It works like a charm.

gateway   A threshold to the Internet. For example, America Online and CompuServe both serve as a gateway to the Internet for their respective members.

geekosphere   The area in and around a computer user's desk and workspace.

generation lap   The phenomenon of seniors becoming *more* technologically savvy than their children and *as* technologically savvy as their grandchildren.

GIF   Stands for Graphic Image File or Graphics Interchange Format, depending on who you're talking to. Regardless, it's a format used frequently on the Internet. Files in this format have a .gif extension. Pronounced "gif," as in Gifford, not "jiff," as in jiffy.

gigabyte   1,000 megabytes. Abbreviated GB. If you're trying to sound ultra cool and computer savvy, you might refer to it as a "gig." But hopefully, not often.

.gov   An Internet domain extension used by any nonmilitary branch of the government.

GUI (Graphic User Interface)   A method of utilizing software through the use of windows, pictures, icons, avatars, buttons, etc. Pronounced "GOO-ey."

guru   Highly regarded spiritual advisor or computer nerd. Mr. Modem is often referred to as a guru, though guru of what has yet to be determined.

H

hacker   Cyberspace scoundrels who break into computers and computer networks.

hit   As used in reference to the World Wide Web, a hit means a single request from a Web browser for a single item from a Web server or Web site. In order for the Web browser to display a page that contains three graphics, four hits would occur on the server: One for the HTML page and one for each of the three graphics.

home page   The first screen of a Web site that contains pointers (links) to resources located within the Web site.

host   A computer that provides services or information to other computers connected to it or having access to it. Connected computers are called *clients*.

Hotlist   A bookmark or favorite places list of Web site addresses. *See* **Bookmarks** or **Favorites**.

HTML (Hypertext Markup Language)   The coding language used to create Web pages.

HTTP (Hypertext Transfer Protocol)   The protocol for transmitting hypertext files across the Internet.

hyperlink   No, not an over-stimulated link, but rather a navigational element within hypertext that allows users to navigate the World Wide Web. A hyperlink can be text, a graphic, or multiple links within a single graphic.

hypermedia   A combination of hypertext and multimedia. Of course, it could have been called textmedia, but that wouldn't be nearly as impressive.

hypertext   Any text that contains 'links' to other documents. Words or phrases in a document can be selected by mouse-click, which causes another document to be retrieved and displayed.

I

icon   A technologically motivating chant or mantra recommended by Mr. Modem. When confronted with computer or Internet difficulties, keep repeating, "Icon if I think icon." An icon is a little picture that represents an object, program, file, or command.

.ini   Short for initialization and pronounced "inny." An .ini file extension appears on files that contain special programs or system settings. Despite rumors to the contrary, there is no .oute extension.

ink jet   A type of printer that employs small nozzles to spray ink onto paper. Ink jets can print in black or color and are usually less expensive than laser printers.

instant messages   Private exchanges or communications between two participants in a chat room. Instant messages are not seen by any other participants in the chat room.

Internet   The vast collection of interconnected networks that all use the TCP/IP protocols that evolved from the ARPANet of the late 1960s and early 1970s.

internet   Any time you connect two or more networks together, you have an internet. The *inter* prefix has the same meaning as in international or interstate.

Internet Explorer   Microsoft's Web browser software. Biggest rival: Netscape.

Internet Phone   A protocol that permits individuals with a microphone, sound card, and speakers to speak with other similarly equipped individuals via their computer. Sure, it's easier to pick up the phone, but that's not the right attitude.

InterNIC   Internet Network Information Center. The organization responsible for registering Web site domain names. Go to `http://www.networksolutions.com`.

intranet   A private network inside a firm or company that uses the same types of software that you would find on the public Internet. However, an intranet is for internal use only.

IP (Internet Protocol)   The basis for the Internet, defines how packets of data are transmitted from point of origin to destination.

IP address   The numerical address (Internet Protocol address) assigned to computers on the Internet. In the Address field of any Web browser, you can type in a domain name or numerical IP address and navigate to the same location. *See also* **domain name**.

IRC (Internet Relay Chat)   An Internet protocol or system through which you can talk in realtime with other chat participants utilizing the same system.

ISDN (Integrated Services Digital Network)   A standard for digital communications using telephone lines. Data is transmitted at 64 or 128Kbps.

ISP (Internet Service Provider)   An organization or business that provides access to the Internet, typically for profit.

issue   A euphemism for a bug or problem. Some companies will alert users to "issues" with their software. Mr. Modem's interpretation: "Run for your life!"

J

Java   A programming language invented by Sun Microsystems that is designed for writing programs that can be safely downloaded to your computer through the Internet and run immediately, without fear of viruses.

JavaScript   A scripting language developed by Netscape that is embedded into the HTML code of a Web page. JavaScripting, confusingly enough, has nothing to do with the Java programming language.

JPEG   A preferred graphic file format popular on the Internet, as opposed to GIF. A file in this format will have a .jpg extension. Pronounced "JAY-peg."

K

Kbps   Kilobits per second. The speed at which data is transmitted online. Newer modems transfer data at 56Kbps. Not to be confused with kilobyte. Bits, bytes, it's enough to drive anybody crazy.

key   In encryption, the code that permits you to unscramble a message or document.

kill file   A newsgroup newsreader software file that acts as a filter. Enter keywords and e-mail addresses to prevent receiving articles from those individuals or sources.

kilobyte   A thousand bytes. Technically, it's 1024 bytes, but what's a few bytes between friends? Abbreviated K or KB.

L

LAN (Local Area Network)   Two or more computers connected together within a relatively small area such as a home or office setting. *See also* **WAN**.

landscape   A printer setting in which words and graphics are printed sideways along the 11″ length of an 8.5″ × 11″ sheet of paper. *See also* **portrait**.

lapjack   The practice of stealing unattended computers, usually in airports.

LCD (Liquid Crystal Display)   The type of screen found in most notebook computers.

link   In a Web page, a link is a connection to another Web page. When you click a link, that document will be displayed through your Web browser software.

Linux   A freeware operating system that is thought by many to be an up-and-coming challenger to Windows. Created in 1991 by Linus Torvalds. Pronounced "LYNN-ex."

Listserv   A type of mailing list.

lockware   Software programs that you can download but not use until you purchase a password or key that will allow you to unlock and run the program.

login (noun)   The account name or username used to gain access to a computer system. Not private, such as a password.

log in (verb)   The act of entering into a computer system: e.g., to log in to CompuServe or America Online or the Internet.

log out *or* log off   To terminate an Internet session; go offline.

lurking   Nonactive participation on the part of an individual in a newsgroup or other online discussion group. To be a *lurker* means that you're generally just reading what others are saying without participating yourself. Lurking is acceptable and recommended when you first join any online community in order to get a feel for it; however, the success of any discussion group depends on everybody's participation.

M

mailing list   An automated system that allows people to send e-mail to one address, whereupon their message is copied and sent to all of the other subscribers to the list. Sometimes referred to as a *mail list*.

Majordomo   A type of mailing list software.

MAPI (Messaging Application Programming Interface)   An e-mail standard that allows different kinds of Windows-based e-mail programs to exchange e-mail messages with each other.

megabyte   One million bytes or one thousand kilobytes. Technically, it's 1,024 kilobytes, but who's counting? Abbreviated MB.

memory   "Light the corners of my mind, misty water color memory…" An area computers use to store frequently accessed data.

Metoobies   Chat participants who contribute little more than "Me, too!" or "Ditto" sentiments.

MHz   Megahertz. A measure of the speed of your computer's processor referred to as clock speed. Example: 400 or 450MHz.

microprocessor   Often referred to as a computer's brain, it's really a small silicon chip located inside your computer that determines, among other things, how fast your computer can process information.

MIDI (Musical Instrument Digital Interface)   A standard adopted by the electronic music industry governing soundcards and synthesizers.

.mil   An Internet domain extension used by branches of the military.

MIME (Multipurpose Internet Mail Extensions)   The standard for attaching nontext files to standard Internet e-mail messages. Nontext files include graphics, spreadsheets, formatted word-processor documents, sound files, etc.

mirror   Generally speaking, to maintain an exact copy of something. The most common use of the term on the Internet refers to *mirror sites* which are Web sites or FTP sites that maintain exact copies of material available at other locations. FTP sites, for example, that receive a great number of visitors are typically *mirrored* to provide additional download locations in order to minimize accessing delays. If hamburger stands were FTP sites, McDonald's would represent the McMirrored site model.

modem   An acronym for MOdulate/DEModulate. A device connected to a computer and phone line that allows your computer to talk to other computers through the telephone system.

moderated   Messages submitted for posting to moderated mailing lists and newsgroups are first screened for acceptability by a moderator, usually a volunteer.

Mosaic   The first Web browser developed by NCSA, the National Center for Supercomputing.

motherboard   The main circuit board inside your computer on which chips, dips, and other gismos are attached.

mouse   A hand-held pointing device used to select and move objects displayed on a computer monitor.

MP3   A file format which stores compressed audio files, but without distorting the sound. MP3 files have an .mp3 file extension. A player is required to listen to MP3 files. For more information visit `http://www.mp3.com`.

MPEG   A compressed video file format. Files in this format are named `filename.mpg`.

MSN   Microsoft Network.

MUD   MultiUser Domain, sometimes referred to as a dungeon. A fantasy, role-playing arena.

Multimedia   A combination of graphics, text, video, sound, animation, and photographs integrated within a software program, Web page, CD-ROM, or other device.

N

nag screens   Messages incorporated within shareware programs that remind you that you need to register the software. In 30-day trial periods, every time you launch a program it will count down, "25 days remaining, register now! 24 days remaining, register now!" Nag, nag, nag.

Net, the   Shorthand for the Internet. Used by those who want to sound like they're cool, groovy, and in the know. Also used in Sandra Bullock movies.

Netiquette   Etiquette for using the Internet. For example, rules of courtesy regarding use of e-mail, posting forum messages, etc.

Netizen   Derived from the term *citizen*. Referring to a citizen of the Internet. The term connotes civic responsibility and participation.

Netscape   Netscape Communication's Web browser software. Biggest rival: Microsoft's Internet Explorer.

network   A group of computers connected together that share information, hardware, software, etc.

newbie   A newcomer to the Internet; recent arrival. Not a disparaging term.

newsgroups   Also called Usenet; ongoing public discussion groups devoted to particular topics of interest.

newsreader   A program used to read Usenet newsgroup messages.

NNTP (Network News Transfer Protocol)   The standard for sending and receiving Usenet newsgroup articles across the Internet.

O

OCR (Optical Character Recognition)   Refers to converting data from a scanned image into text.

offline   Not connected to the Internet.

offline mail reader   An e-mail program that connects to the Internet, retrieves e-mail, then disconnects. You can then read and compose replies to e-mail offline, before going back online and sending or uploading responses.

offline news reader   Similar to an offline mail reader except it connects to Usenet newsgroups, retrieves unread articles, then disconnects. Articles can then be read and responses or replies composed offline.

online   Connected to the Internet.

online trading   The ability to buy and sell stocks via the Internet.

.org   An Internet domain extension for nonprofit organizations.

OS   Operating System. The software that allows your computer to run. Examples: DOS, Linux, Unix, Windows.

P

packet   A standard unit of data sent across the Internet. Packets usually contain identification and address information regarding the destination location.

packet loss   Speaking for myself, not nearly as troubling as hair loss, but rather the failure of data to transfer successfully between two or more points on the Internet.

packet switching   The protocol used to transmit data over the Internet. It's the Popeil DataMatic approach to data transmission. Data is sliced and diced into small units, called packets. Each packet is assigned an address. The data is then routed through the Internet, taking the most expeditious route possible, and using the assigned addresses, reassembled at its final destination.

parallel port   The larger connection thingy (term of art) on the back of your computer, usually used to attach a printer.

parental filters   Browser and other software settings that can be configured by parents to restrict access to certain Web sites and Web activities inappropriate for children.

password   A textual key, usually a word or a combination of words and numbers, without which access to a specific area, program or feature is prohibited.

patch   A temporary fix to resolve a software problem.

PC   Personal computer.

peripheral device   A geekspeak way of saying "piece of hardware." Modems, printers, monitors are all peripheral devices.

phreaker   A person who hacks or breaks into telephone systems.

Ping   Not referring to golf clubs, but rather an Internet-based program that sends a signal to a host computer to see if it's available or functioning. Derived from a sonar *ping* sound.

pixel   One of hundreds of thousands of tiny dots or points of light that compose any image you see displayed on your computer monitor. If you put your nose right up against your monitor, you can see the pixels.

platform   A computer operating system like Windows 98, or more generically, any computer-based environment such as a chat platform, newsgroup platform, etc.

Plug and Play   A technological miracle for all novice computer users. Technology that identifies the existence of a new device—such as a printer— once it's been attached to the computer, and then configures itself.

plug-in   A small piece of software that adds features to a larger piece of software. Common examples of plug-ins are used for the Netscape and Internet Explorer browsers or some chat software. Plug-ins are sometimes referred to as *helper applications*. See "Plugging Along with Plug-Ins" in Chapter 9.

POP   Two commonly used meanings: Point of Presence and Post Office Protocol. A Point of Presence usually means a city or location where a user can connect to a network. Post Office Protocol refers to the way e-mail software, such as Eudora, retrieves mail from a mail server computer.

port   A connector, usually located on the back or side of your computer, into which you plug a printer, modem, scanner, etc.

portal   A point-of-entry to the Web that offers a wide selection of services such as access to search engines, free e-mail, and access to other sites.

portfolio tracking   The ability to monitor the performance of your financial portfolio via Web page. A free service offered by many financial Web sites.

portrait   The usual way a page of text is printed, with lines of text running across the 8.5″ width of an 8.5″ × 11″ sheet of paper. *See also* **landscape**.

port speed   The rate at which data is transferred between your modem and your hard drive. Speed is measured in kilobits per second or Kbps. Typical port speeds are 33,600, 57,600, 115,200.

post   A message contributed (by uploading) into an online discussion group is said to be *posted* by the writer of the message.

PostScript   A computer language that controls the positioning of text and graphics on a page. More popular with graphics professionals, print shops, and Macintosh users than personal computer users.

PPM   Pages per minute. Refers to the output speed of a printer.

PPP (Point-to-Point Protocol)   The most popular protocol that allows a computer to use a regular telephone line and modem to make an Internet connection.

propagation   The process of distributing and disseminating information throughout the Internet, as it passes from computer to computer.

protocol   An agreed-upon method or standard by which computers "talk" to each other, transmit data, files, graphics, etc.

proxy server   A computer located between a client, such as your Web browser software, and the host server. Generally used to improve performance by delivering frequently requested Web pages. Rather than a request going out from your browser to the Internet and retrieving a popular Web page, the request will only need to go as far as the proxy server which will then return the requested page to you faster. At least that's the theory.

push technology   Technology that delivers customized news and information to your computer as contrasted with the "get" model of information retrieval that requires you to go to an Internet source for information.

Q

query   A search request, typically a keyword, submitted to a search engine database.

queue   Pronounced "Q"; refers to the printing order of documents.

QuickTime   A free plug-in player that enables short audio-visual movies, but not full screen, motion pictures to be played over the Web. For more information or to download the latest version, visit `http://www.apple.com/quicktime`.

R

RAM   An acronym for Random Access Memory. RAM is the area of memory accessed by your computer to perform the tasks you see taking place on your computer screen.

RealAudio   A standard for transmitting or *streaming* compressed audio over the Internet. Supported by Web browsers Internet Explorer and Netscape. A player device is required which can be downloaded for free from `http://www.real.com`.

realtime   Without any delay. For example, when talking in a chat room, participants communicate in realtime, one person types words and all other participants see those words on their computers. Contrasted with a newsgroup posting where the words are posted and a response may appear sometime later.

refresh   A command issued to update the information displayed on the computer screen. Sometimes referred to as Reload in the case of retrieving a current and up-to-date copy of a specific Web page or Web site.

register   *See* **associate**.

Registry   The command center for Windows 95 and 98 that houses system and program configuration settings.

removable storage   Floppy disks, backup tapes, Zip disks, portable hard drives.

resolution   The number of horizontal and vertical rows of pixels that comprise an image displayed on a computer monitor. 800 × 600 is a frequently used resolution. *See also* **pixel**.

right-click   Clicking and releasing the right mouse button to display a shortcut menu of commands related to the object you clicked.

robot   A program that automatically performs certain functions on the Internet. One example is a program that prowls the Internet cataloging newly arrived Web sites. Sometimes referred to as a *'bot*, for short.

S

scanner   A hardware device that plugs into your computer and converts documents and photographs into electronic format or files. This data can then be imported into documents, attached to e-mail messages, or saved. The objective is to save as many things as you can until you reach the point where you can't remember what you've previously saved, so you can start saving things again.

search engine   A program that will allow you to enter keywords and launch a search for Internet resources containing those keywords. Yahoo! and WebCrawler are two examples of Web search engines. See Chapter 10, "Internet Search Engines."

serial port   A place typically on the back or side of a computer where you can plug in a modem or other peripheral device. Also called a COM or communications port.

server   A computer that provides or serves data and information upon request to software residing on other computers called *clients*.

shareware   Downloadable software that you can try before you buy. If you use shareware software, you are on your honor to register it if you decide to keep it. The good folks who write this software depend on our honesty, so please register any shareware you intend to use.

shelfware   Software programs that are purchased but never used. The ultimate objective of computing is to see how much shelfware one can collect.

Shockwave   A plug-in that enables interactive multimedia to display over the Web. Download the latest version at `http://www.macromedia.com/shockwave`.

signature   An ASCII text file that can be automatically attached to the bottom of e-mail that identifies the sender. See Appendix D, "Mr. Modem's All-Time Favorite Signature Tag Lines."

SLIP (Serial Line Internet Protocol)   A standard for using a regular telephone line (a serial line), and a modem to connect a computer to the Internet. SLIP is being replaced by PPP.

SMTP (Simple Mail Transfer Protocol)   A popular protocol for transmitting outgoing e-mail. SMTP stores e-mail messages on your computer, not on a remote server.

space hogs   A term of endearment that refers to extremely large software programs, graphics files, sound files, and video sequence files. Making snorting sounds can often alleviate the anxiety one feels when installing programs that are known to be space hogs.

spam   An inappropriate attempt to use a mailing list, newsgroup, or other net-worked communications capability as a broadcast medium—which it is not—by sending the same message to a large number of people who didn't ask for it. The term is believed to have originated from a Monty Python skit which featured the word *spam* being repeated over and over. Another school of thought believes that the term may have originated from someone's low opinion of the food product, which is perceived by some as a generic, content-free waste of resources. (Spam is a registered trademark of Hormel Corporation.) In its simplest form, spam is junk e-mail.

spamouflage   Bulk e-mail messages delivered from generic e-mail addresses with innocuous subject headers in order to confound filtering pro-grams and spam-intolerant readers.

SSL (Secure Socket Layer)   A means of providing a secure environment for transmitting data (such as credit card information) via the Internet.

start page   The first Web page that appears on your monitor when you launch your browser. This can be any Web page you want it to be or the default page, typically the Netscape or Internet Explorer home page.

stopword   A word that a search engine ignores when doing a search. These words occur so commonly in language that they do nothing to narrow a search. An example would be the word *the*.

streaming   Around the holidays, Internet users are usually streaming of a white Christmas. Sorry. Streaming refers to the process of retrieving data (audio or video) in realtime as opposed to downloading and then executing or launching a program. A good example of streaming is RealAudio, which per-mits audio to begin playing via your computer's speakers without having to wait to download large audio files. *See also* **RealAudio**.

Stuffit   You should pardon the expression. Nothing personal intended, I assure you. Stuffit is a Macintosh file compression program and Stuffit

Expander is the Windows version. For additional information visit `http://www.aladdinsys.com/products/index.html`.

subdomain   A portion of an Internet domain, typically a network host such as an Internet service provider. In my e-mail address MrModem@home.com, *home* is the subdomain, also referred to as the host.

subscribe   To join a mailing list or begin to receive or participate in a newsgroup. There is typically no charge for subscribing. *See also* **unsubscribe**.

surf   Arguably the most overused term associated with the Internet, though *Information Superhighway* can't be far behind. Surfing refers to moving from Web site to Web site following hyperlinks.

SVGA (Super Video Graphics Array)   A video standard that provides more colors and higher clarity than its predecessor, VGA standard.

T

T-1   A leased-line connection to the Internet capable of carrying data at a blistering 1.54 million bits-per-second rate.

T-3   A very expensive leased-line connection to the Internet capable of carrying data at 45 million bits-per-second. Not practical for home or office access.

tabs   A dialog box feature in many Windows-based programs that permits a single dialog box to contain several layers. You can navigate among the layers by clicking on what appear as file folder tabs to reveal a different set of formatting or set-up configuration options.

TCP/IP (Transmission Control Protocol/Internet Protocol)   A collection of rules that defines how data is transmitted on the Internet.

telephony   Never talk to phonies, so I wouldn't recommend telling them anything. Nobody likes a groaner, so let's move on. *Telephony* refers to the technology that lets us use our personal computers to make and receive telephone calls without incurring long-distance charges. Ma Bell has her cables in a knot over this issue.

Telnet   Also called *remote login*. Telnetting to a site is very similar to logging onto America Online or CompuServe. Using your modem, you connect to a host computer, where you are then presented with a menu. You can use this menu to navigate the Internet, explore remote computer sites and execute programs as well as rodents or other annoying household pests.

terabyte   One thousand gigabytes.

terminal   A device that allows you to send commands to a computer located elsewhere—said to be in a *remote* location.

thread   An online conversation consisting of messages and responses.

time out   To fail to connect to a Web site, usually because the remote host—the computer you're attempting to connect with—fails to respond in a timely manner. When this happens, just try again later. It's often the online equivalent of getting a busy signal on the telephone.

TLA   Three-letter acronym.

toolbar   One or more rows of icons and buttons used as shortcuts for a program's frequently used commands.

tooltips   Short, descriptive words and phrases that appear when you place your mouse cursor on a toolbar or other navigational button.

Trojan horse   A type of computer virus that masquerades as normal software, but instead contains harmful or destructive programming code. *See also* **virus**.

Trumpet Winsock   A Windows-based program that provides dial-up SLIP or PPP access to the Internet. The predecessor to Windows 95/98 Dial-Up Networking.

U

Unix   An operating system upon which the Internet was constructed. Used mostly by Internet service providers. Avoided like the plague by most Internet users.

unsubscribe   To remove yourself from a mailing list or newsgroup. *See also* **subscribe**.

upload   The opposite of download. Duh! To send data (files) from your computer to the Internet.

URL (Uniform Resource Locator)   A Web page address, typically beginning with `http://www`.

USB (Universal Serial Bus)   A standard that has been touted as the successor to the serial, parallel, mouse, and keyboard connectors. A one-size-fits-all port into which you can plug a printer, monitor, scanner, digital camera, Zip and Jaz drive, and other devices. *See also* **bus**.

Usenet   Users Network. Topical discussion groups referred to as newsgroups. *See also* **newsgroups**.

username   The name you log in or connect to the Internet or a Web site with. Typically used in conjunction with a password. It's also the part to the left of the @ sign in your e-mail address. For example, in my e-mail address `MrModem@home.com`, *MrModem* is my username.

utilities   Software tools that perform specific functions, typically maintenance related.

UUEncode (Unix-to-Unix Encoding)   A popular method of converting files from binary to ASCII format so they can be transmitted on the Internet. *See also* **binary file.**

V

vaporware   Nonexistent software. Vaporware often makes a nonappearance when a company announces a new product that never materializes.

virtual   Used to describe computer simulations. For example, virtual tours, virtual buildings, virtual cities. In the world of computer simulation, it can be virtually anything.

virus   A program created by cyberhooligans and often spread through attachments to e-mail, that intentionally causes harm to infected computers.

voice recognition   The ability to enter computer commands or text in word processing software by speaking as opposed to using a keyboard or mouse.

W

WAN (Wide Area Network)   Unlike a LAN (Local Area Network), a WAN spans large distances and usually connects LANs in multiple locations. *See also* **LAN.**

Web authoring   Creating Web pages using HTML.

Webmaster   The person responsible for keeping a Web site up, running, and available to the public by maintaining the Web server that hosts the Web site.

Web page   A document written in HTML that you can view using your Web browser software. Every Web page has its own unique URL or Web page address.

Web ring   A collection of Web pages, typically individual home pages, all linked together, all with the same theme or special interest.

Web site   A collection of Web pages usually sharing a common focus. A Web site is typically owned or managed by a single entity, company, organization, corporation, association, club, or individual. *See also* **home page**.

WinZip   A compression program for Windows. *See also* **Zip**.

World Wide Web (WWW)   The fastest-growing portion of the Internet in which Web pages containing text, graphics, audio and video are linked together and easily searchable with browser software.

worm   Not technically a virus, but close enough. A worm is a bit of computer nastiness that replicates itself and can gobble its way through a computer network.

WYSIWYG   What You See Is What You Get. What you type on your keyboard and what appears on your monitor is the way it will appear in printed or other format. Pronounced "Wizzy-Wig."

Z

Zip   A file compression format for personal computers using PKZip or WinZip software. Zipped files display a .zip file extension. It's the approximate equivalent of Stuffit or Zipit for Macintosh users. For more information visit http://www.winzip.com.

Index

Note to the Reader: Throughout this index **boldfaced** page numbers indicate primary discussions of a topic. *Italicized* page numbers indicate illustrations.

...arn ...ing you ...t started on the Internet, without all the confusing computer jargon.

Mr. Modem's Internet Guide for Seniors...

...is perfect for people who are curious about the Internet, but feel overwhelmed by the technology.

In *Mr. Modem's Guide to the Internet*, you'll learn:

- What equipment you need to get online
- What the Internet is all about
- Tips for making the most of the World Wide Web
- How to use e-mail effectively
- How to send photographs via e-mail
- The latest browser software and how it works
- How to use search engines to find <u>anything</u> on the Internet
- How to start surfing right away with hundreds of recommended Web sites
- The do's and don'ts of online communication
- What WebTV is all about
- What the future of the Internet holds for seniors and for everyone
- The POE (plain old English) meanings of important Internet terms